AF400860

Phil and Me

By AMANDA TETRAULT

TROLLEY BOOKS

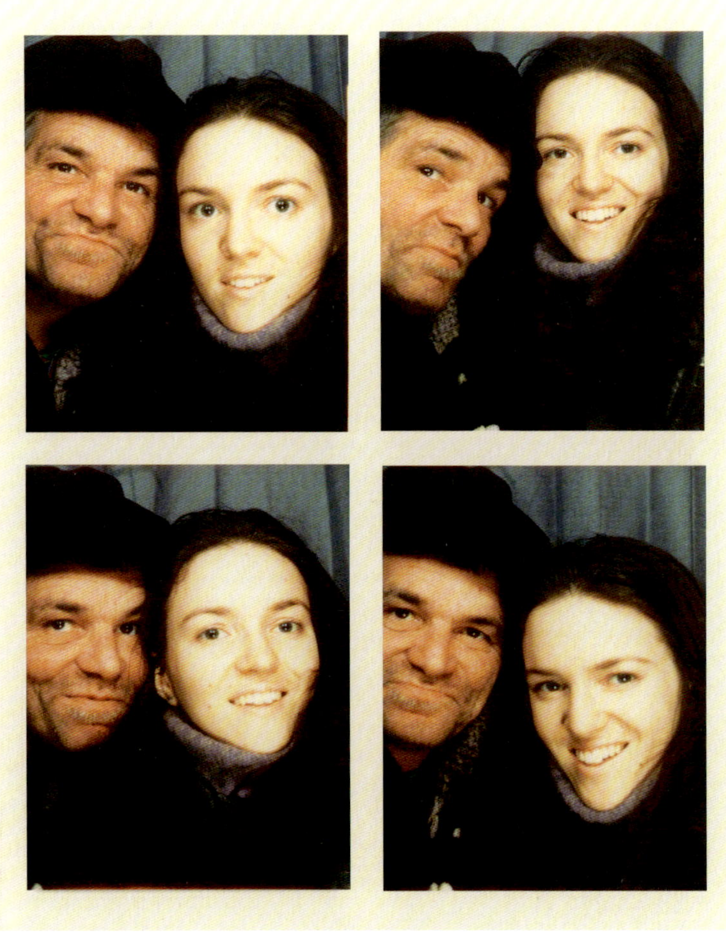
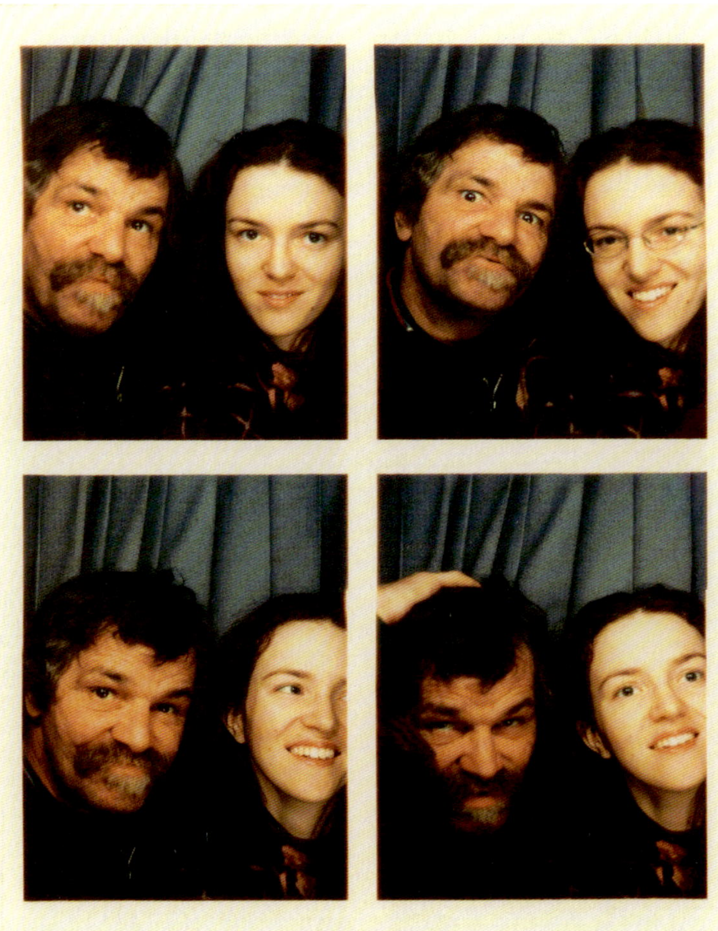

The ethereal
smooth
of a soft
dive into sleep;
the ephemeral
touch that
governs the
harsh, sadness of
brutal fact;
oppressive reality;
and then there
is blue sky;
the astral
munificence,
that the blue
will touch everything
and soothe
the suffering
of our daily
burden,
the why, and, the wherefore

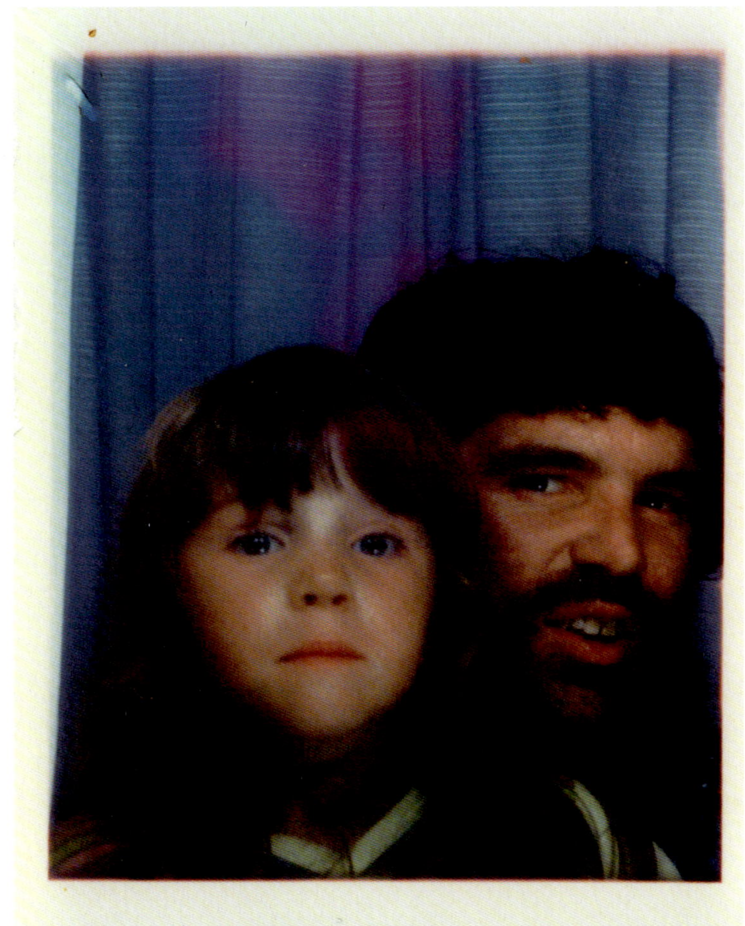

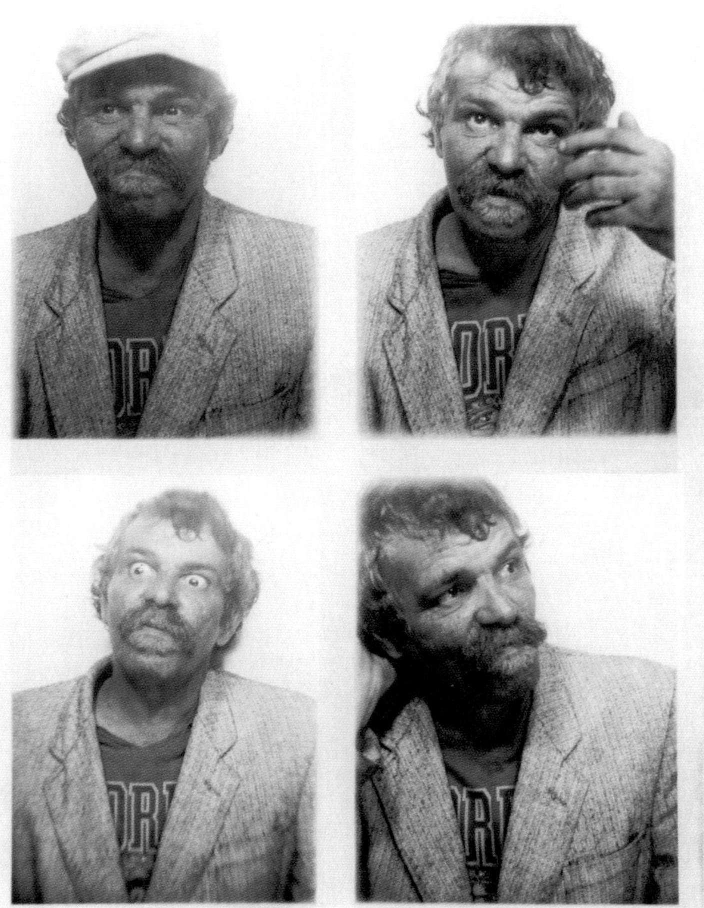
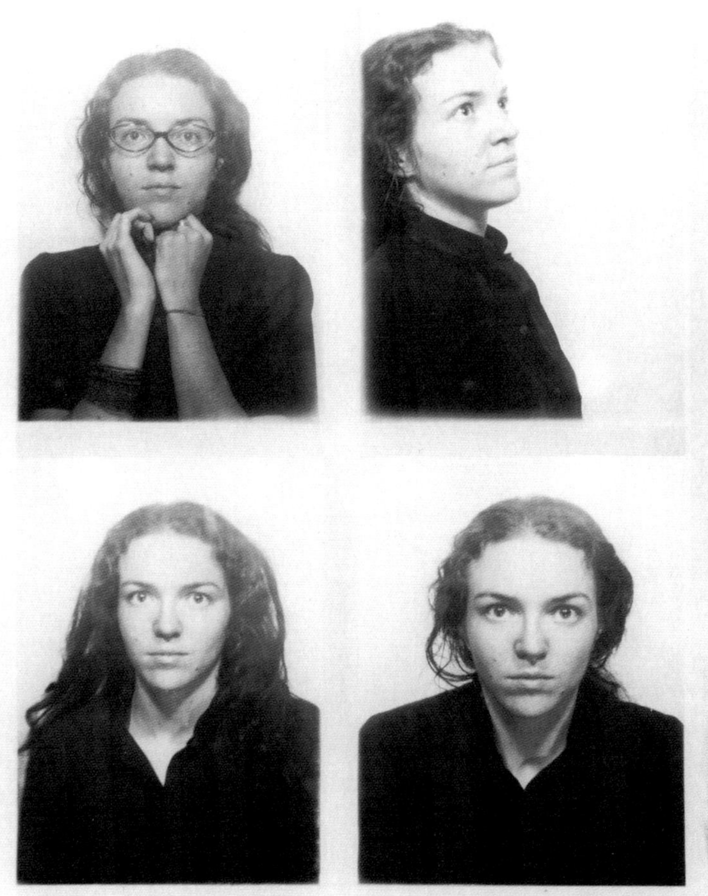

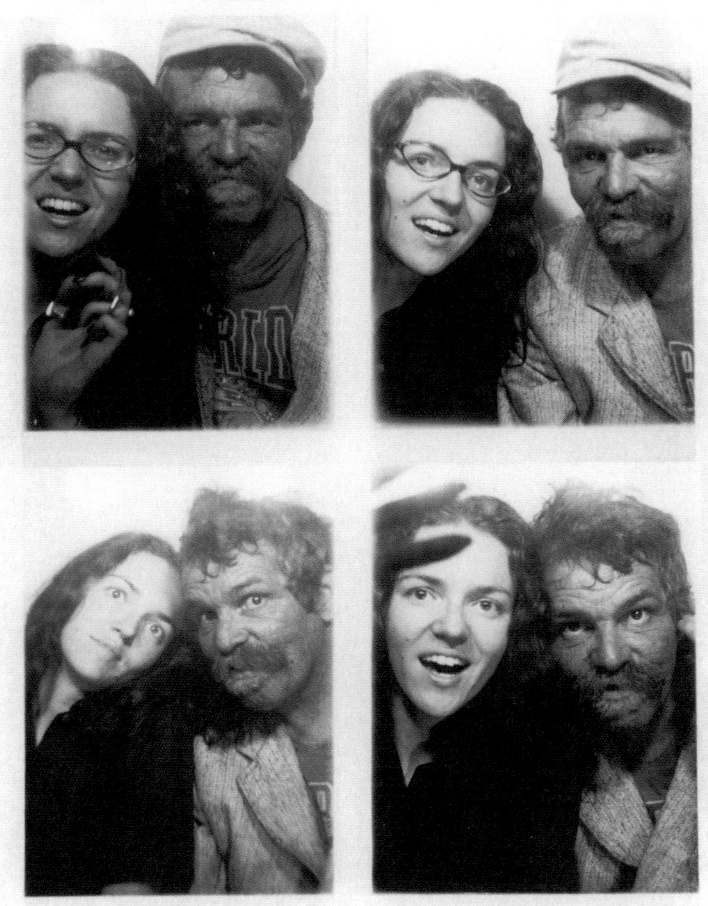

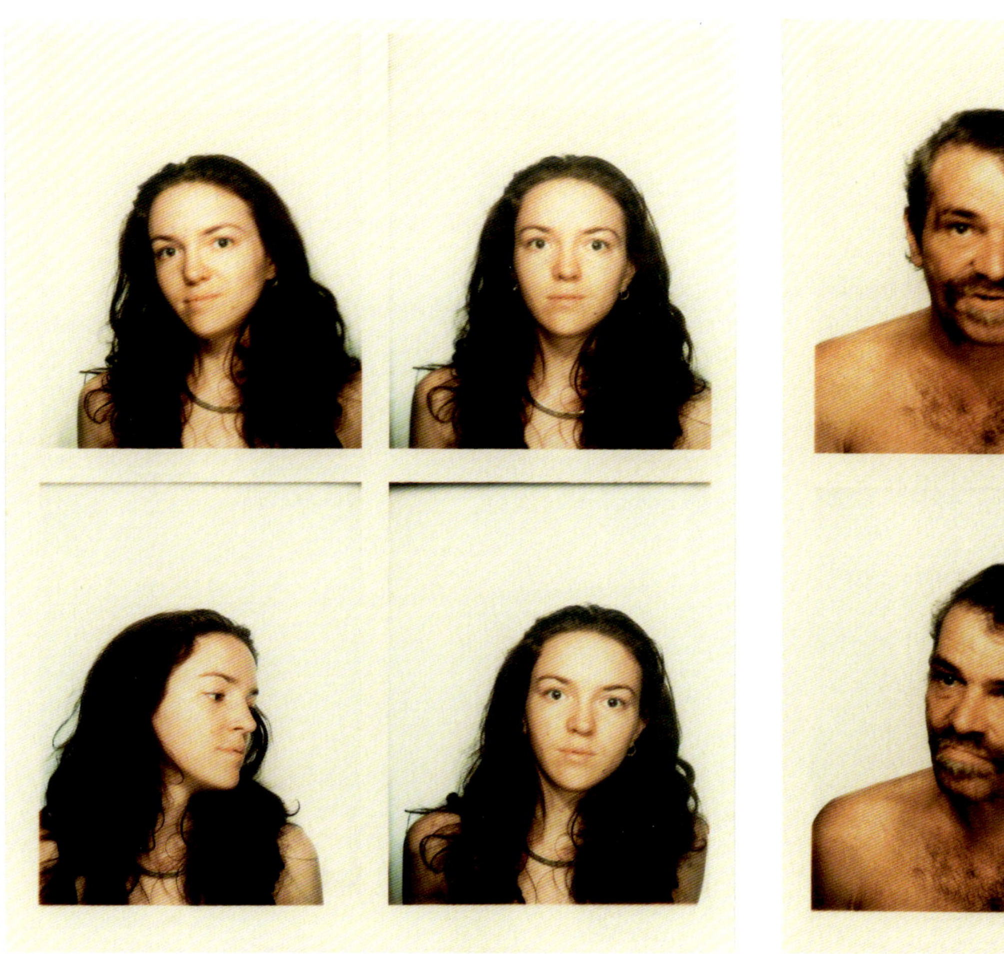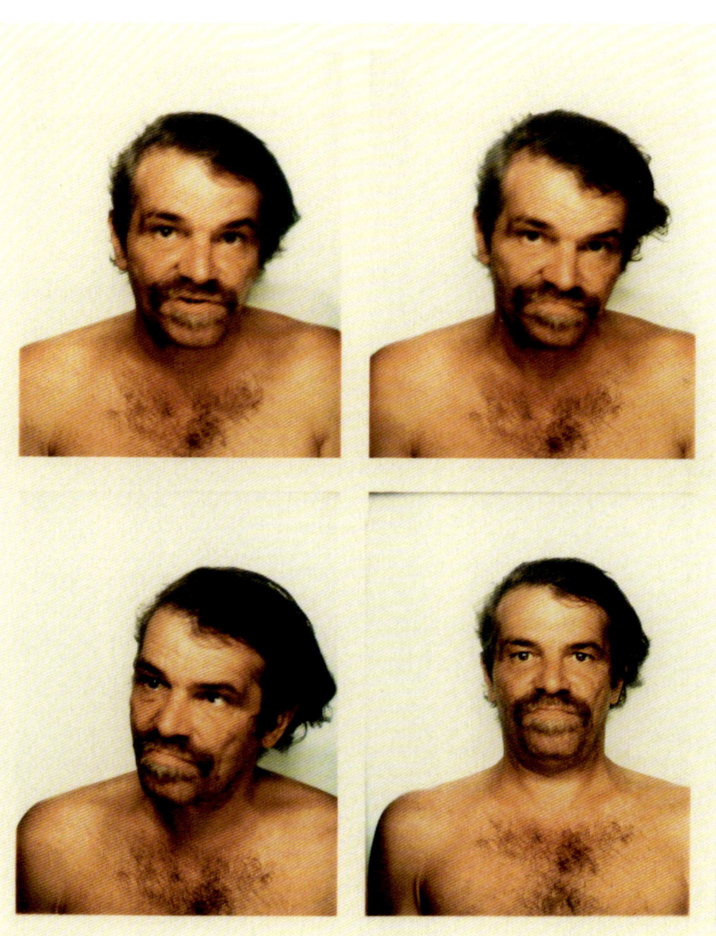

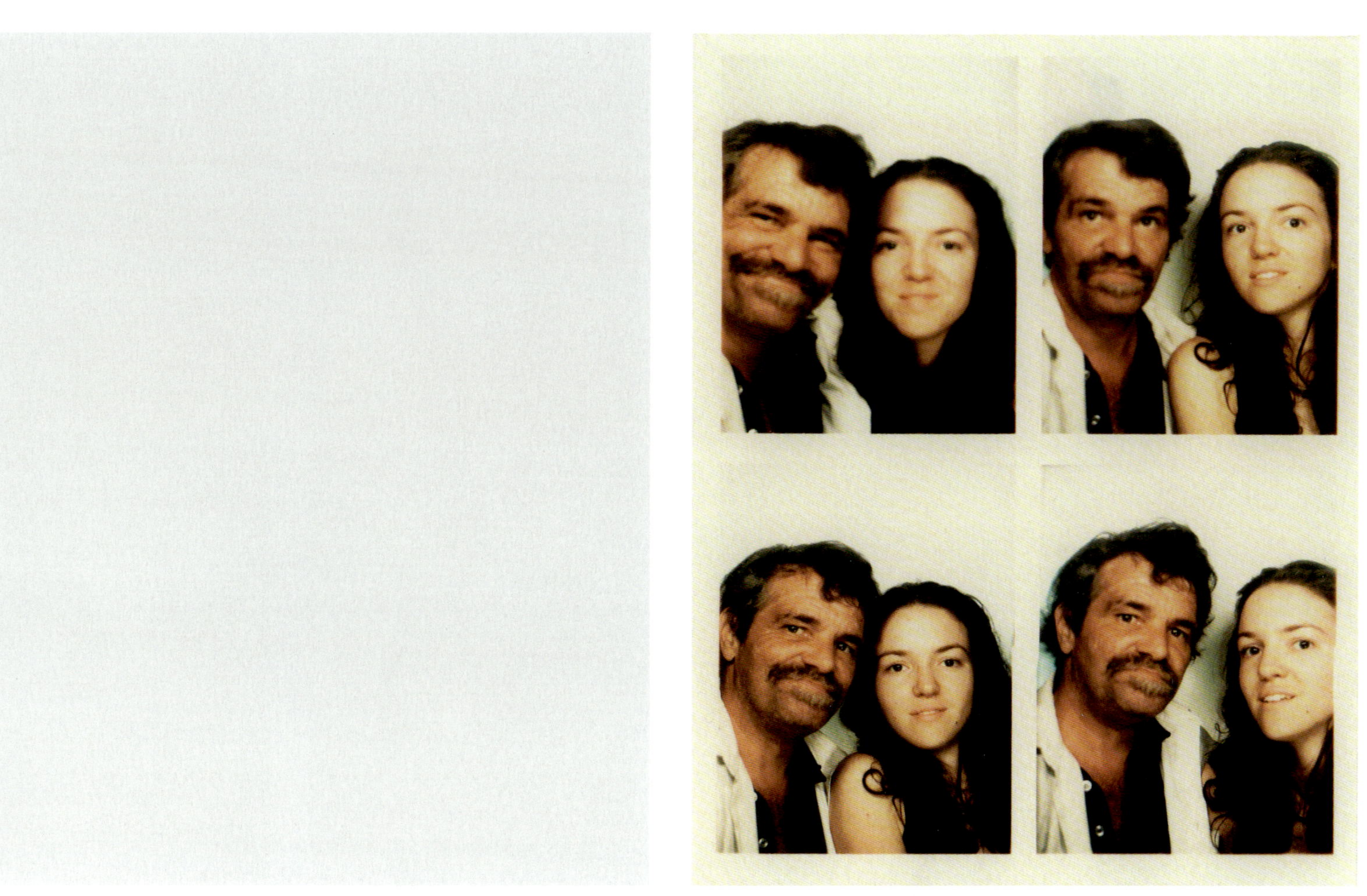

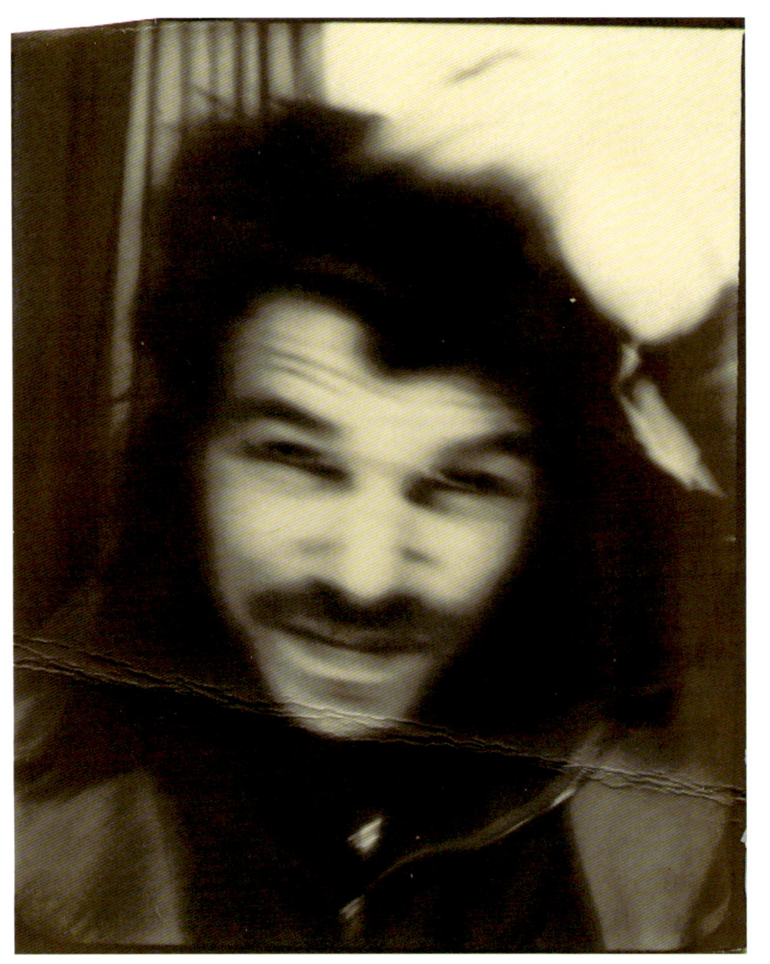
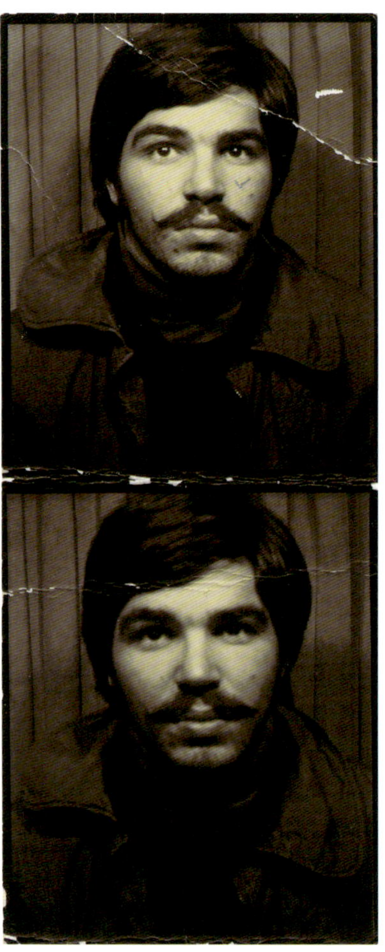
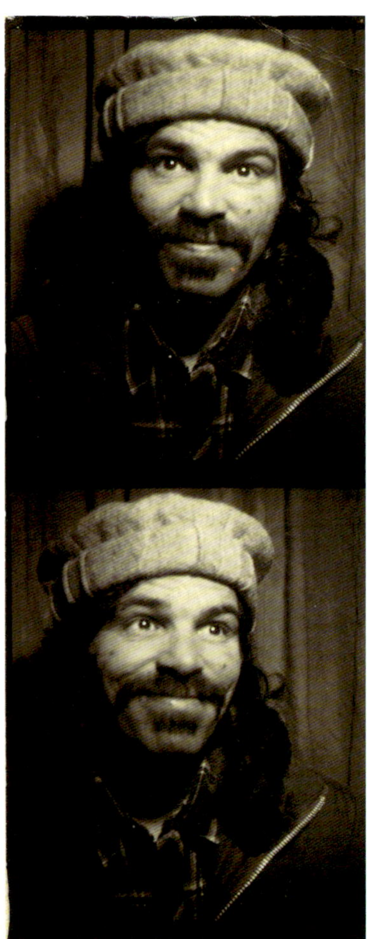

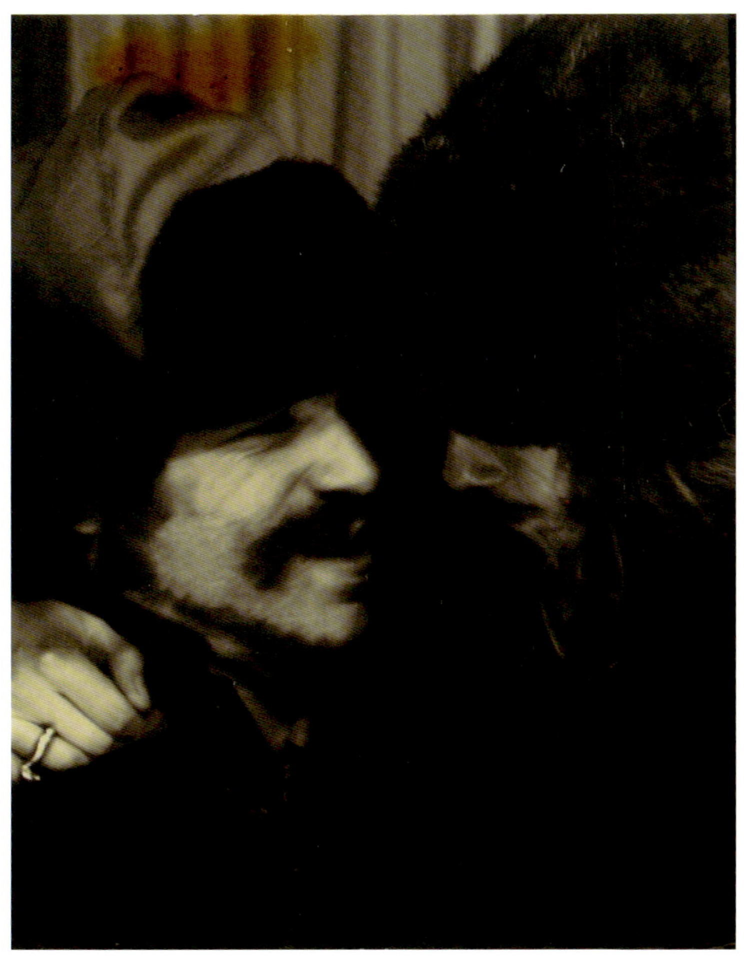
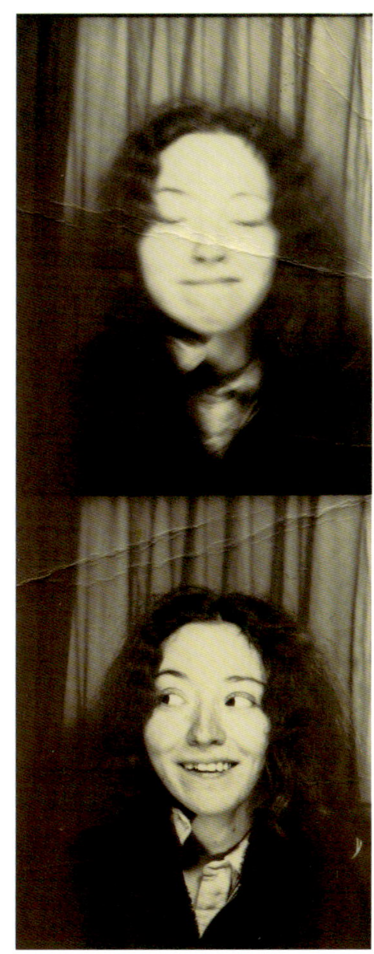
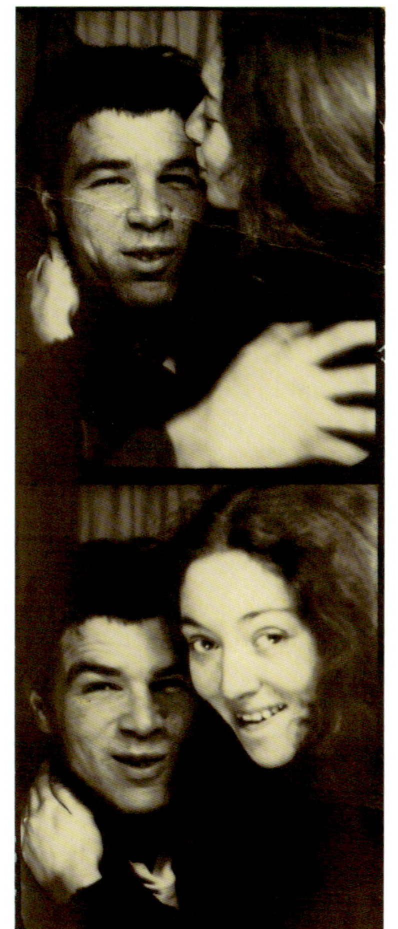

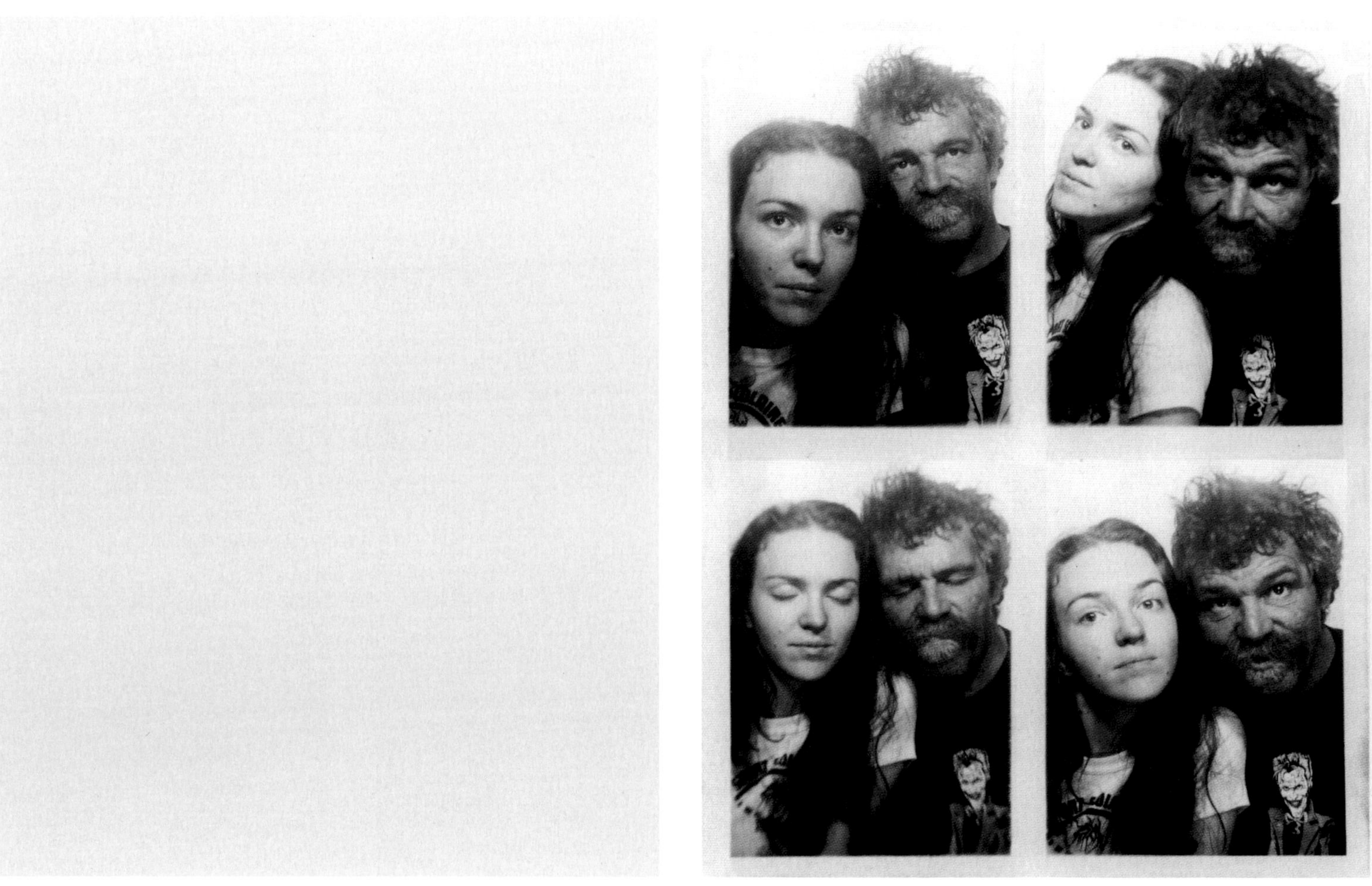

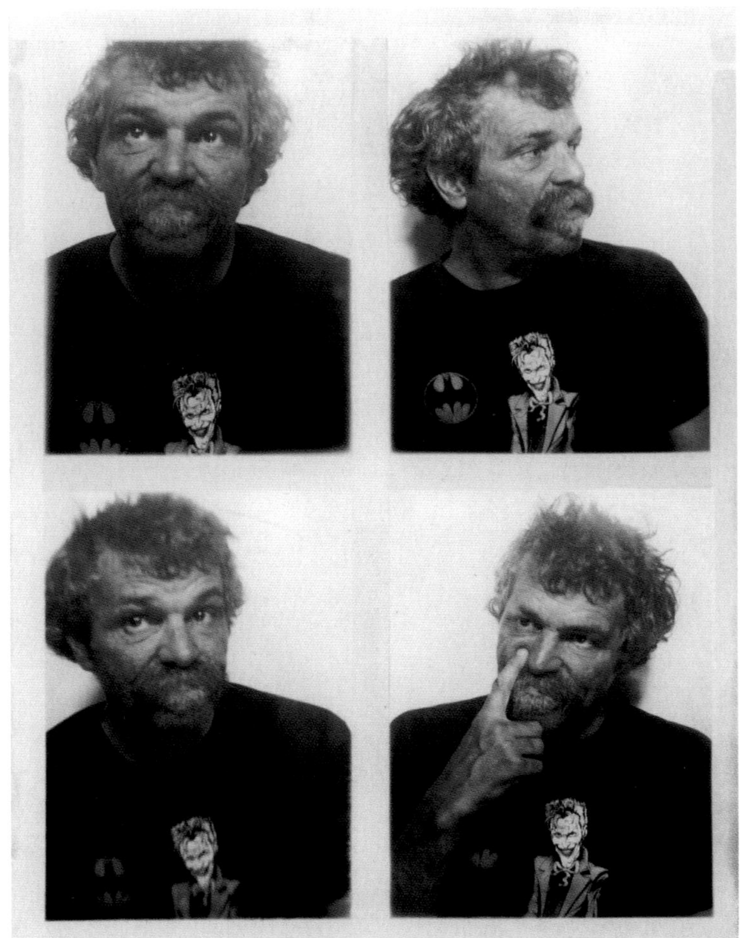
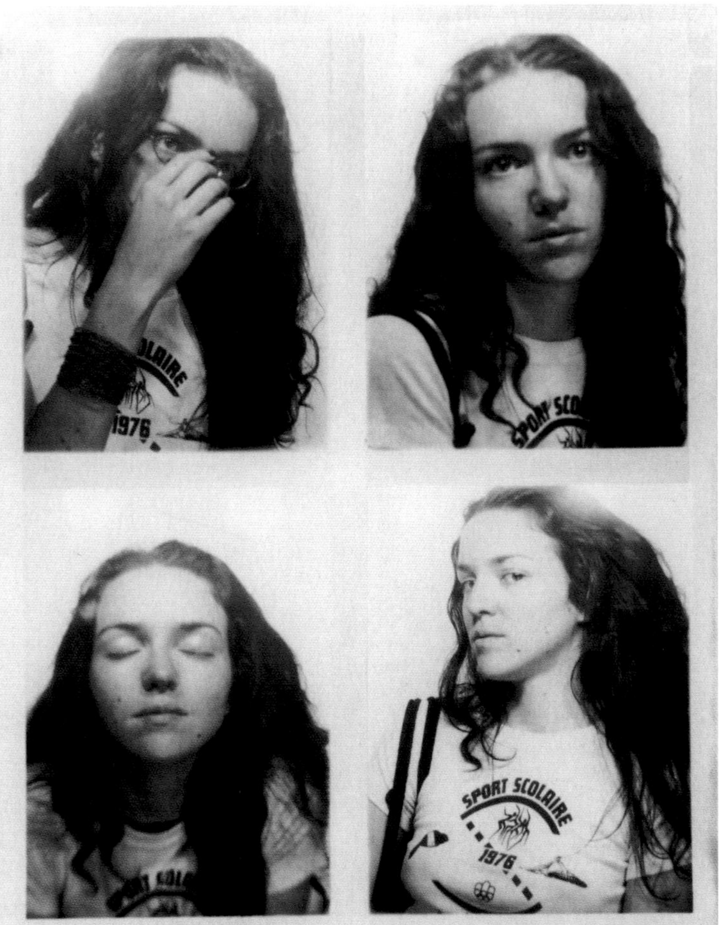

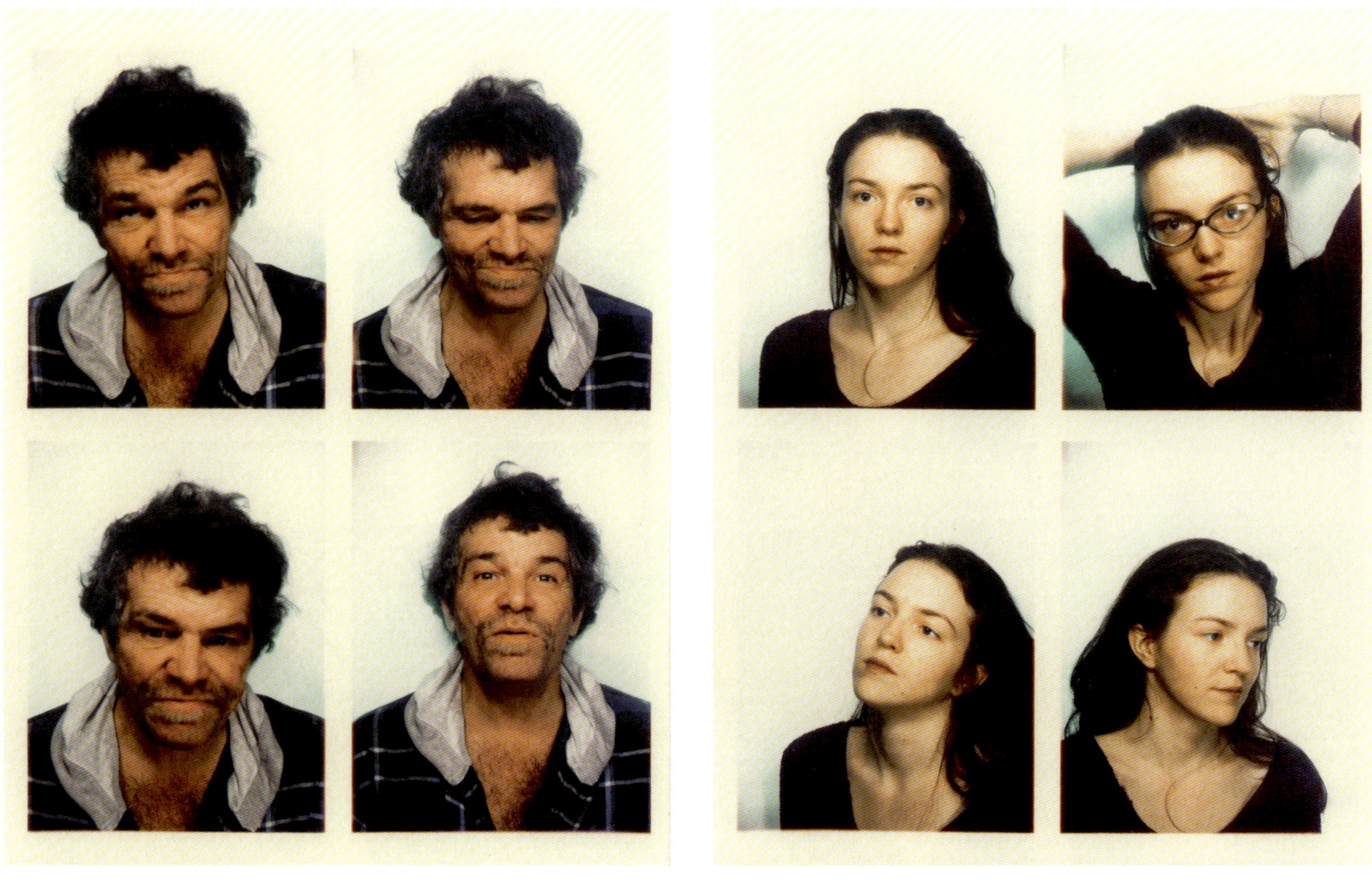

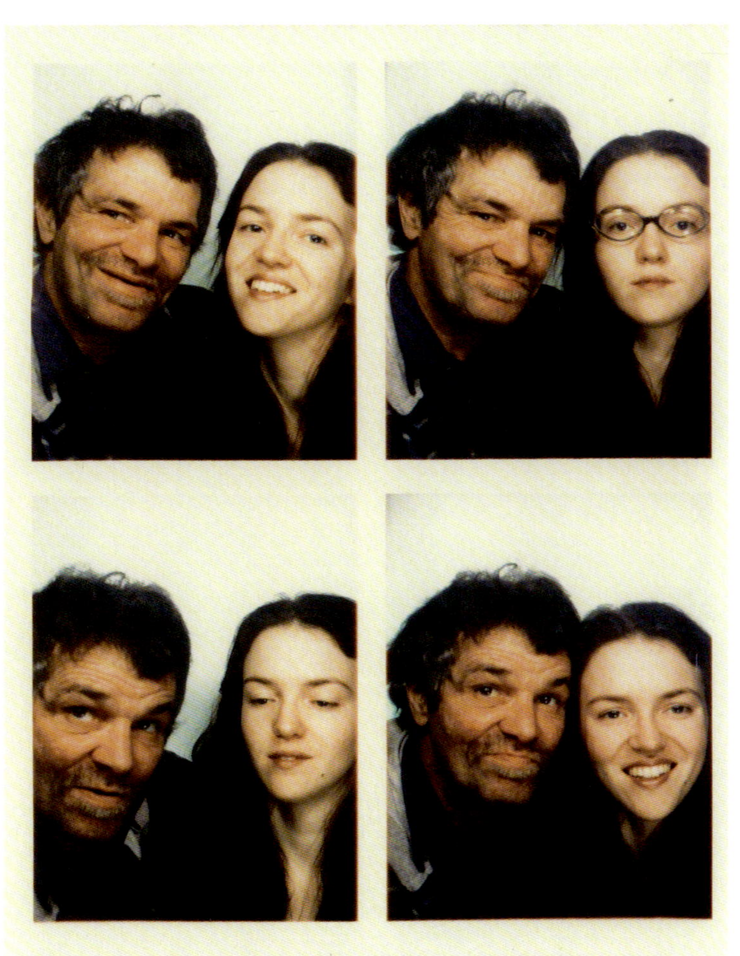

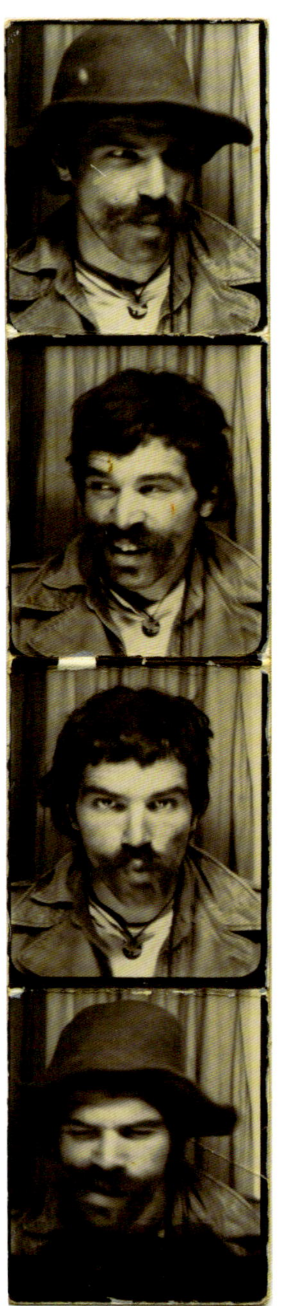
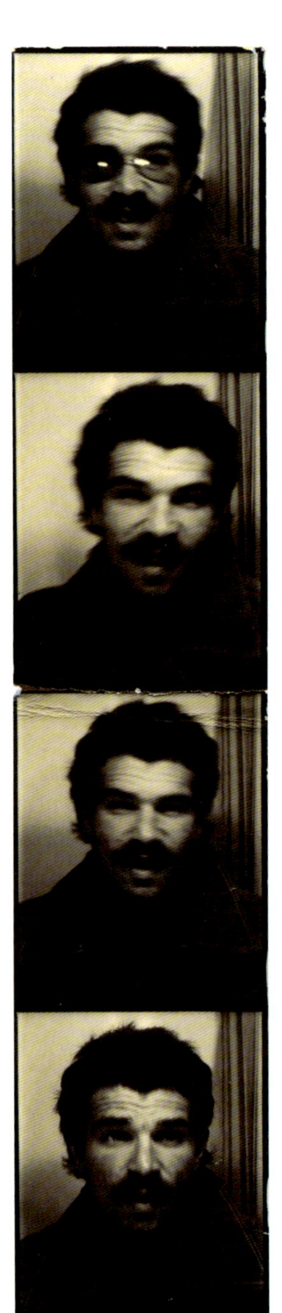
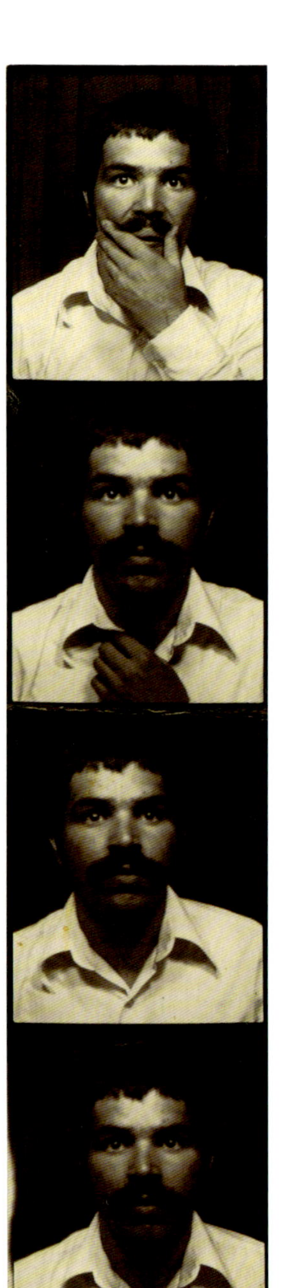

THERE ARE FIELDS FOREVER,
THE UNIVERSAL FIELDS OF
THE GREEN EARTH;
STRETCHED OUT ON THE
FRINGES OF THE CIVILISED
WORLD
CONTAIN WHAT IS BEST AND
BEAUTIFUL FOR THE animal
WORLD;
THERE I HAVE passed as a
pilgrim; as between
earth and sky;
one perfectly solitary
motion of ~~earth and~~ man
BENEATH THE sky.
And said, and swore
THAT THESE places so
easily ignored
Helped me more to travel
than EVERYTHING ELSE
I KNOW....

⊢————⟨⟩————⊣

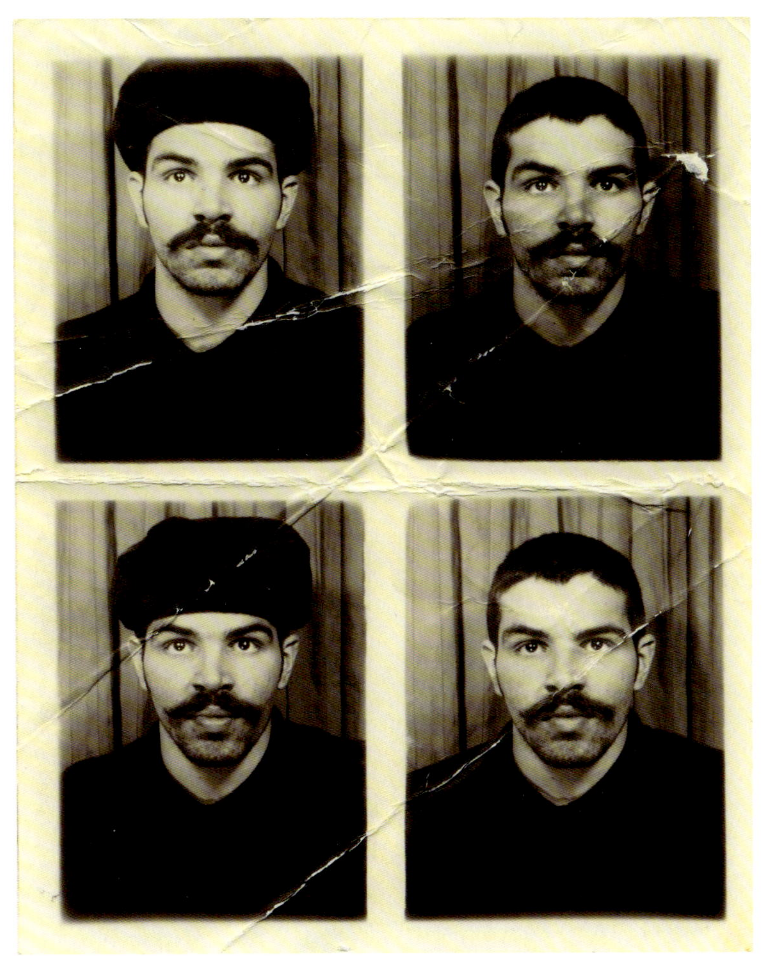
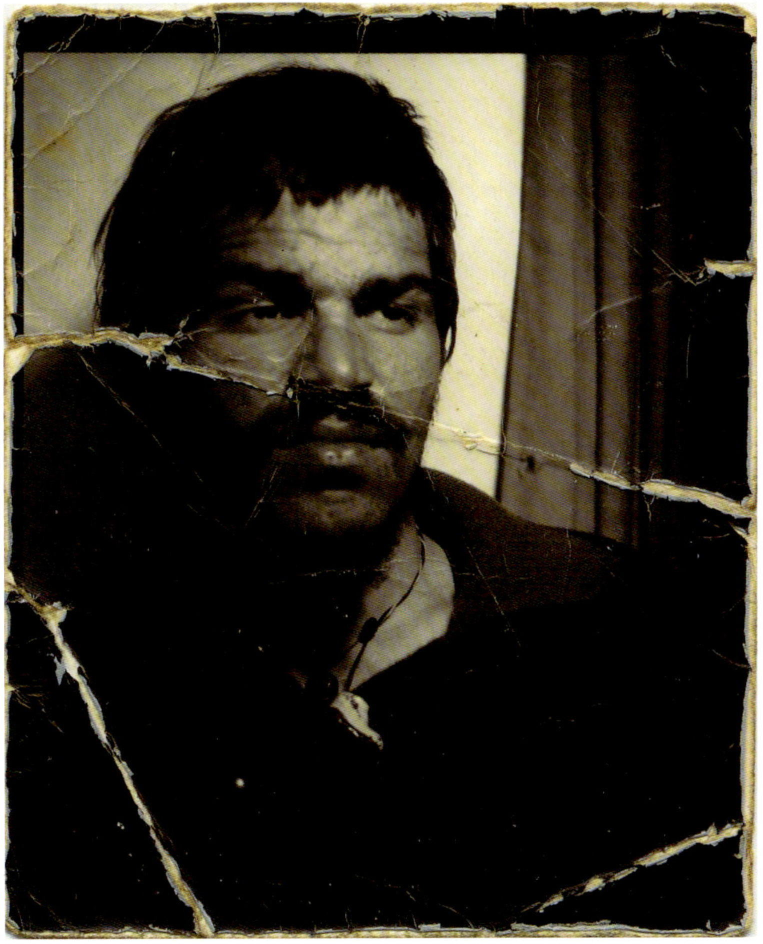

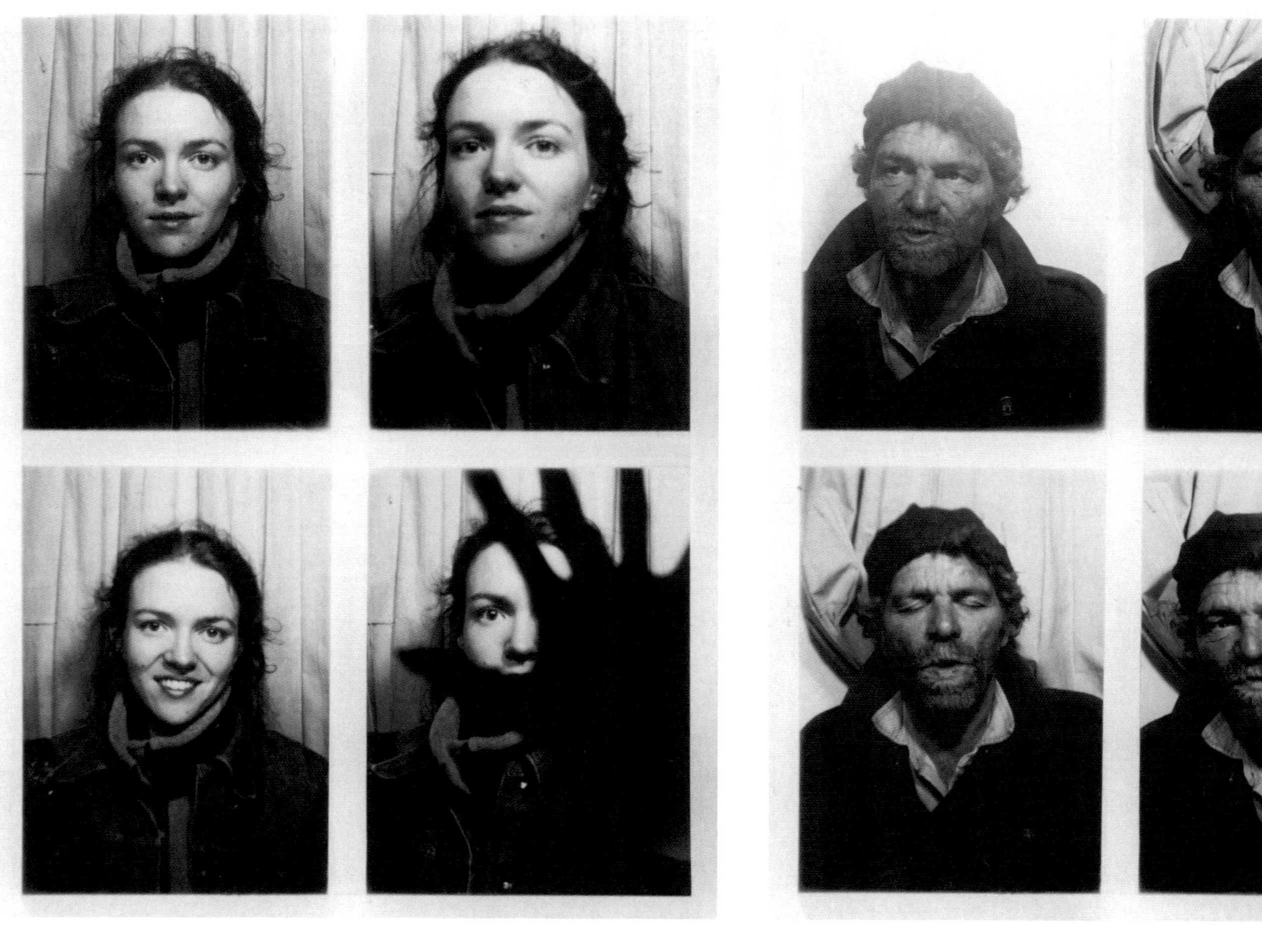

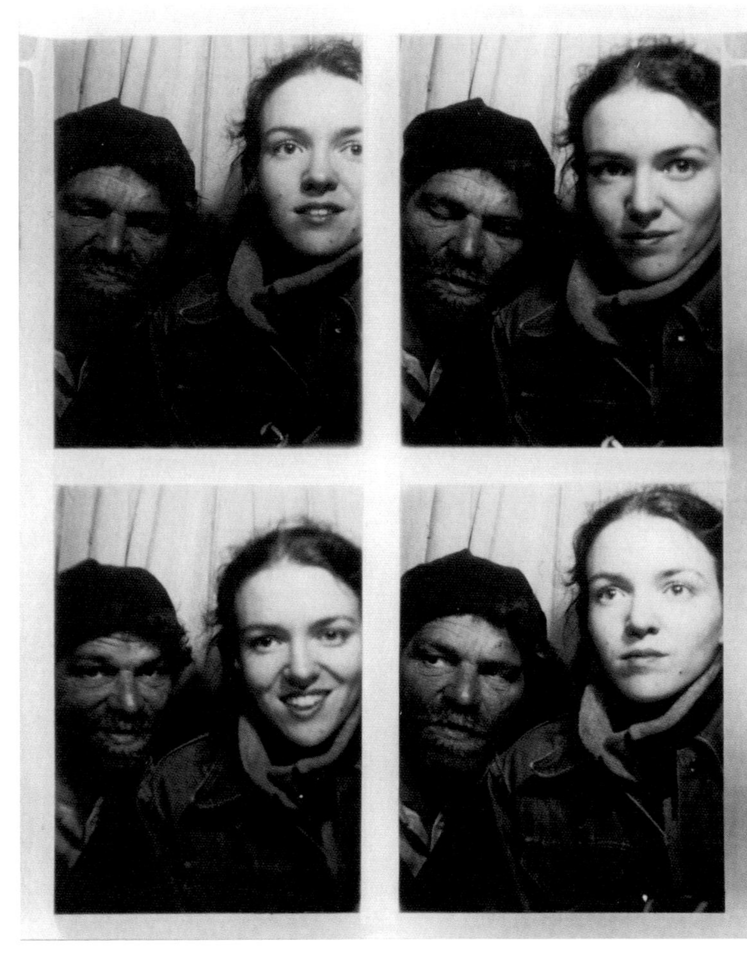

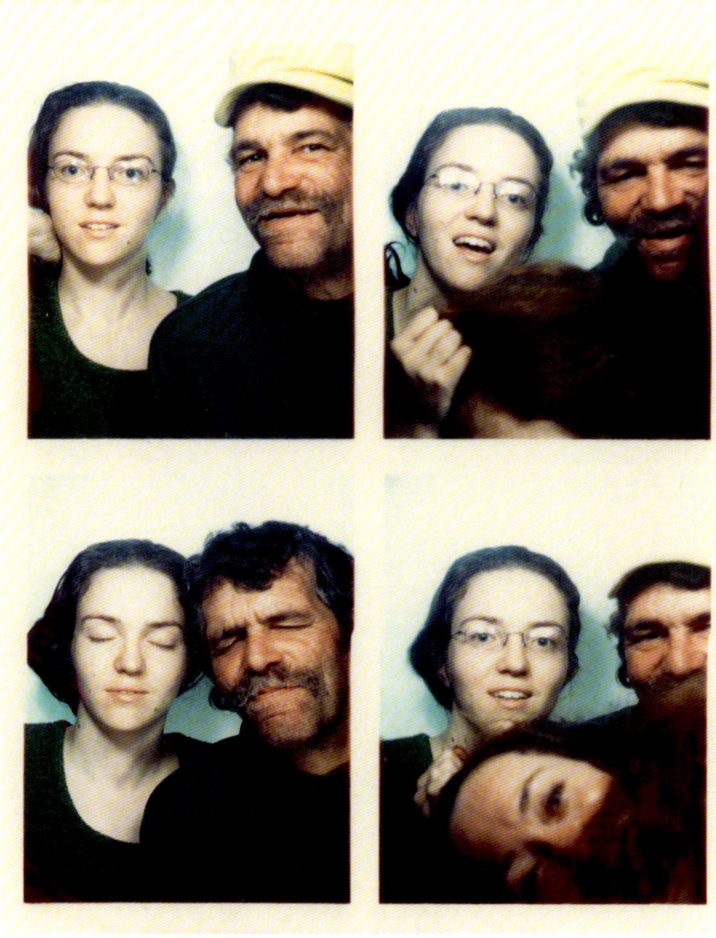

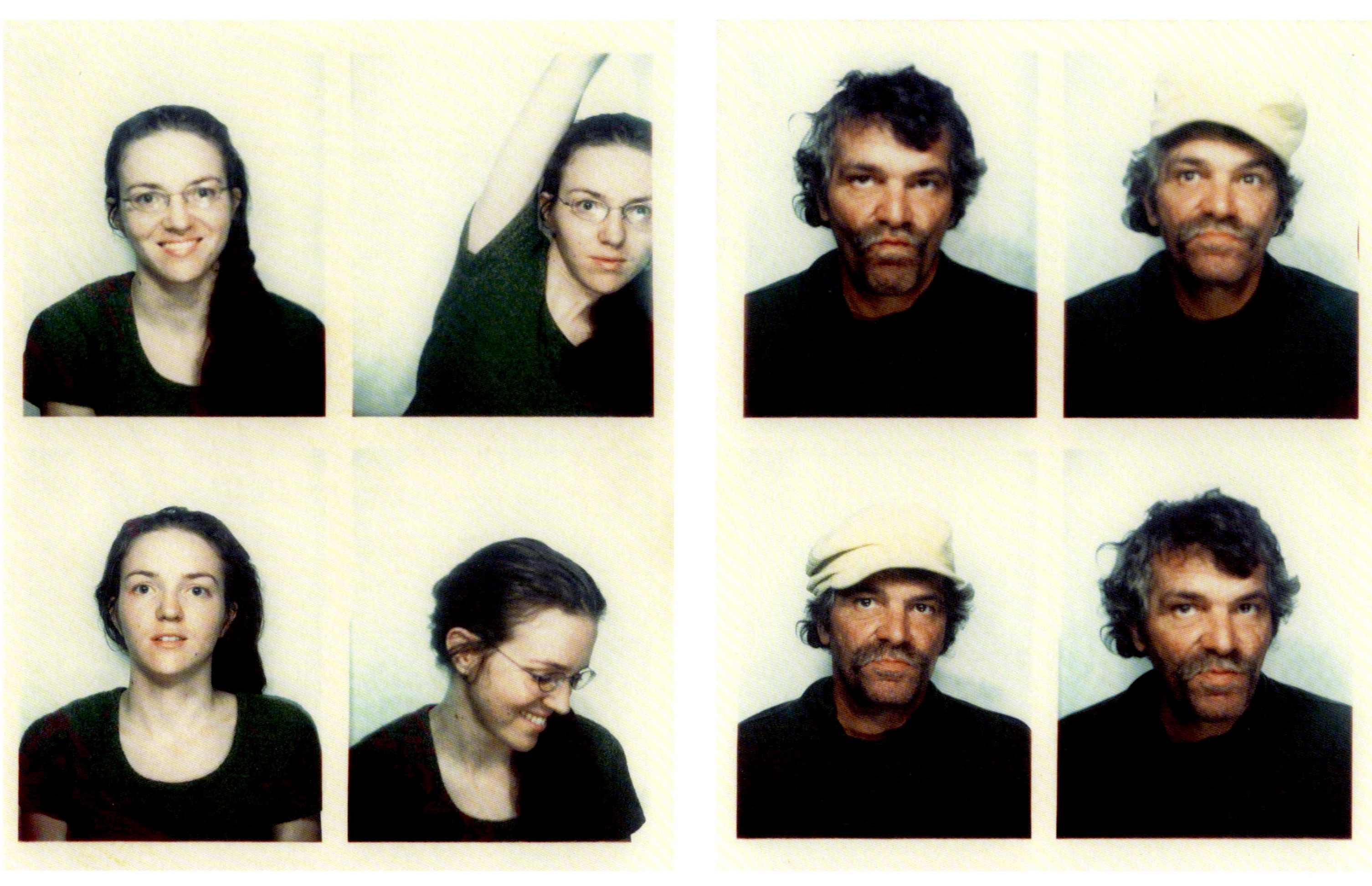

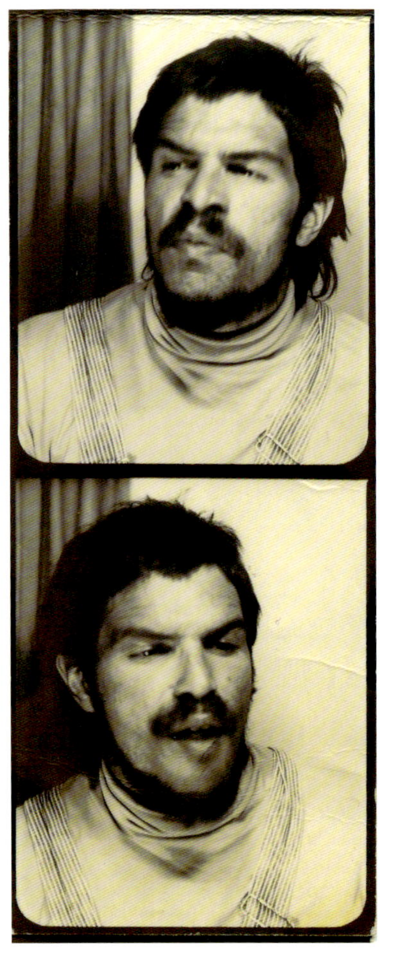
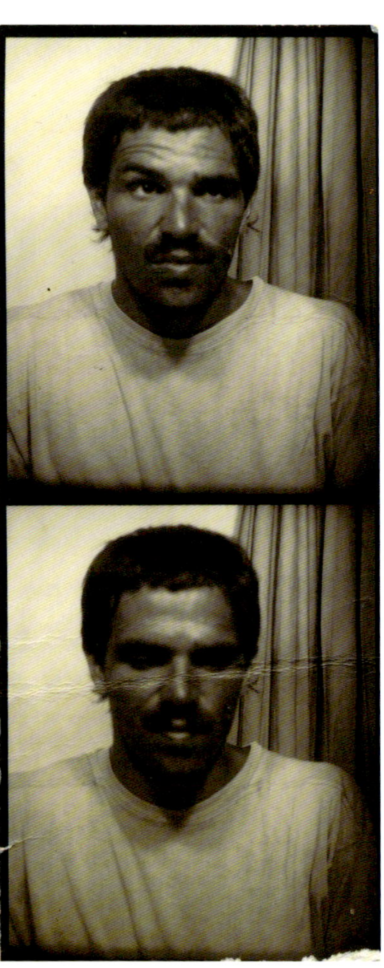
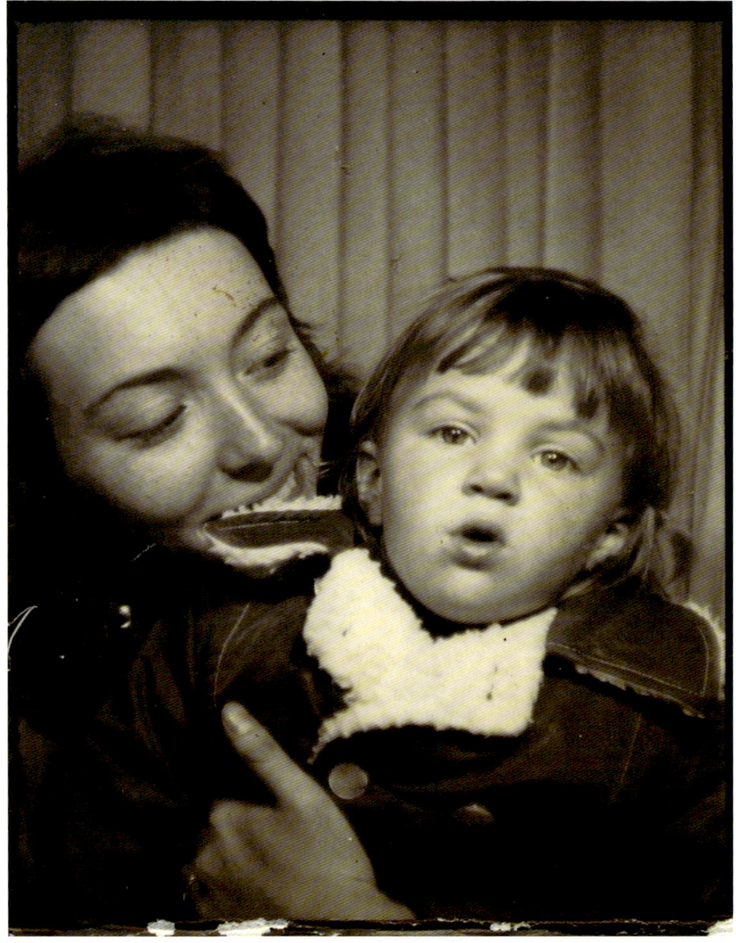

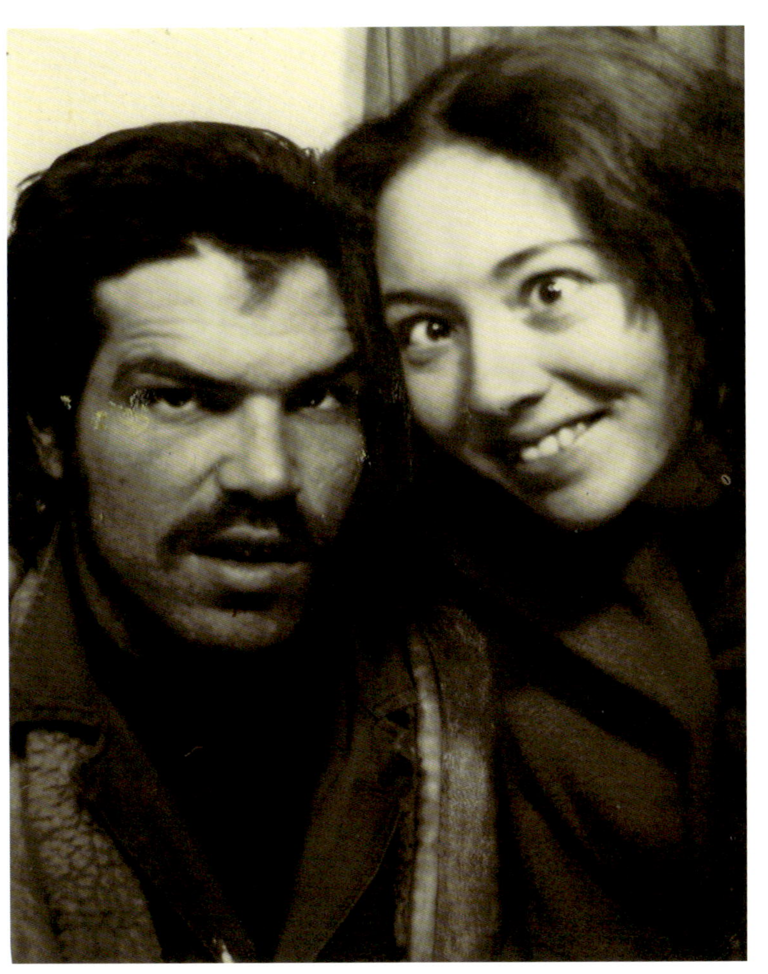
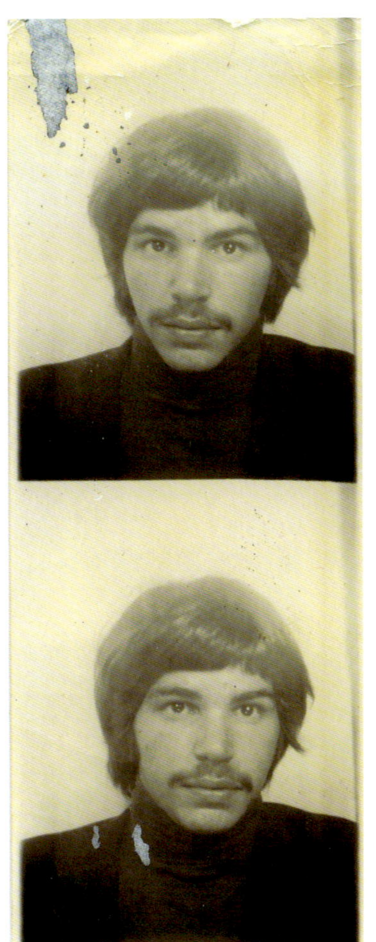
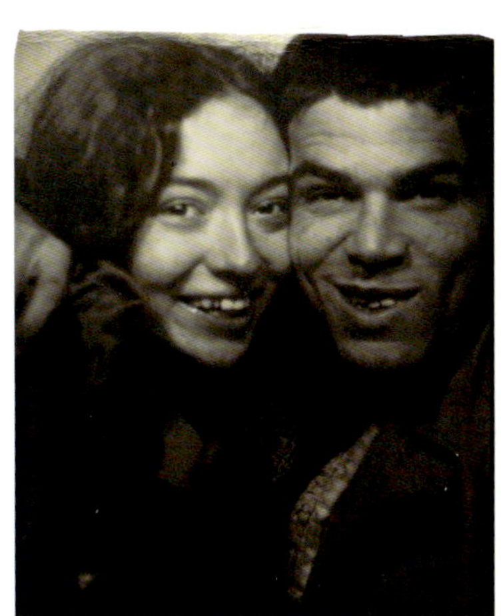
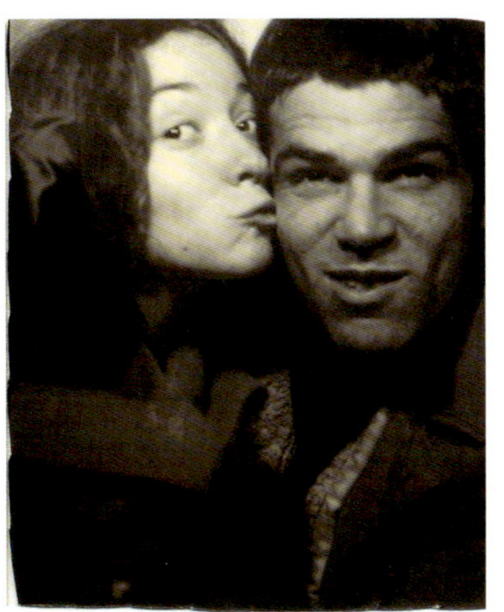

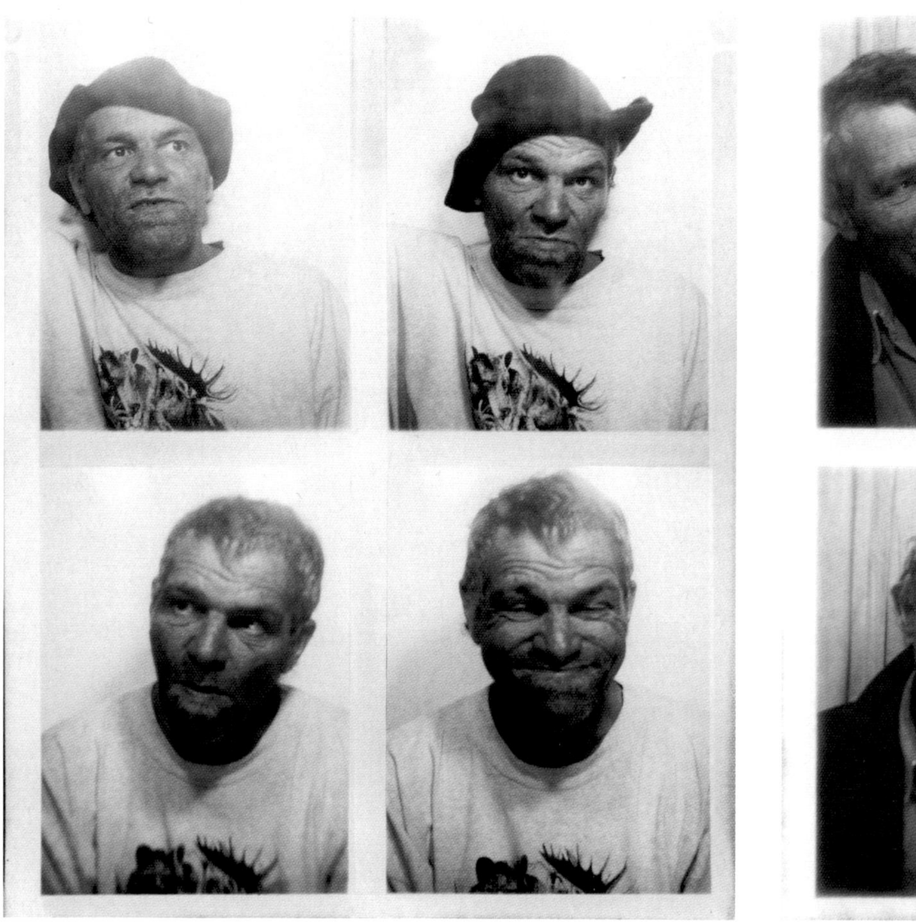
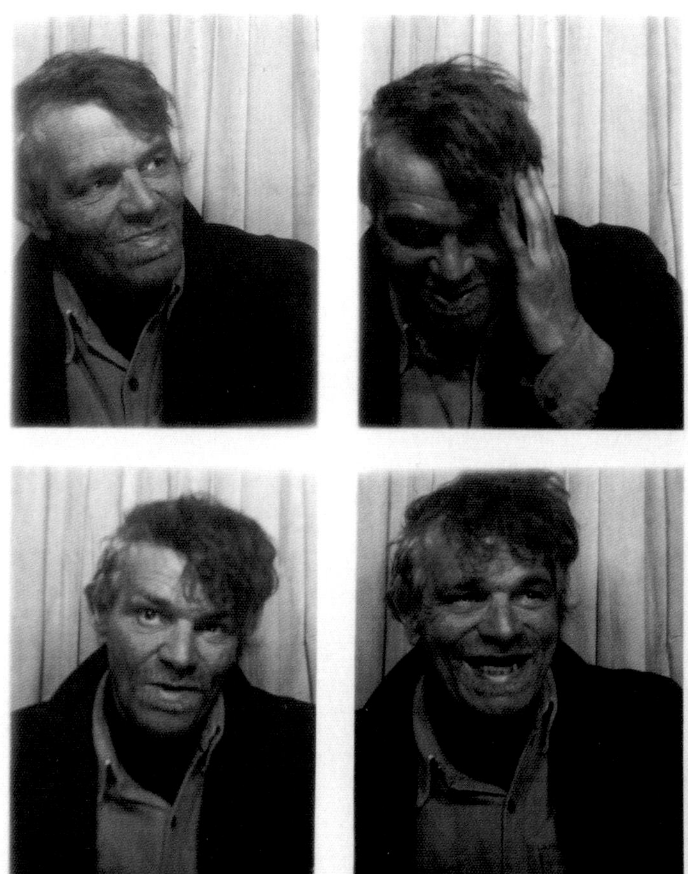

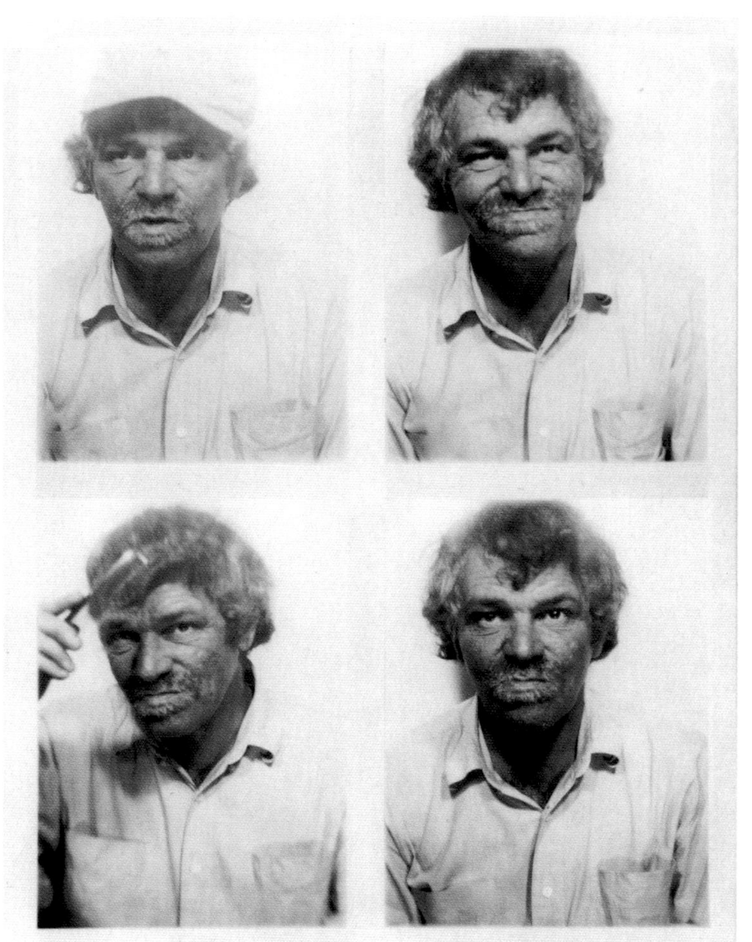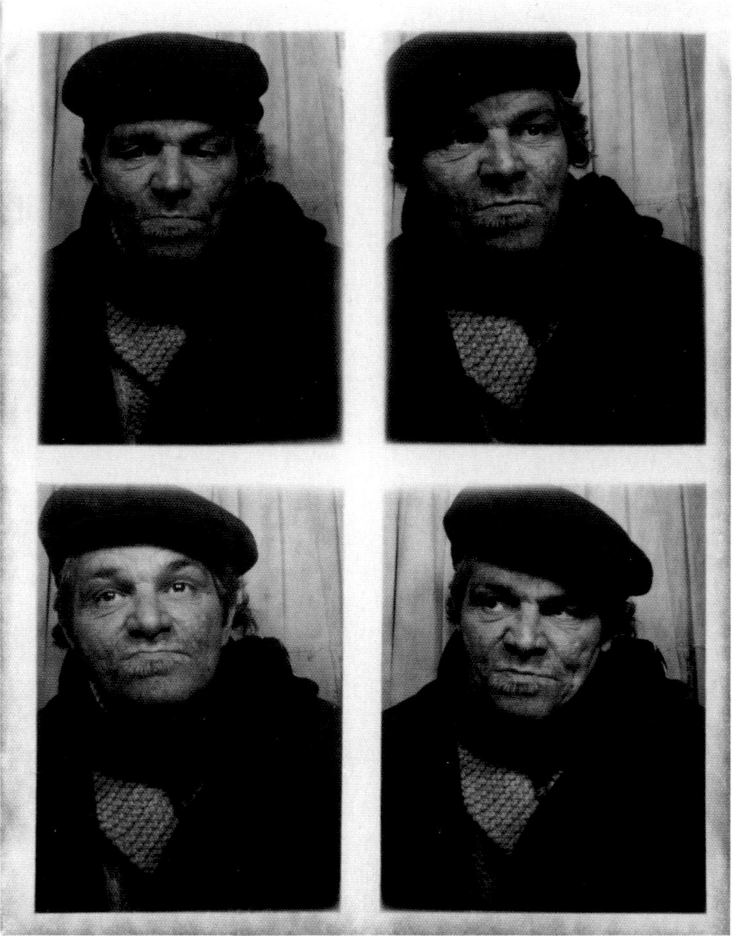

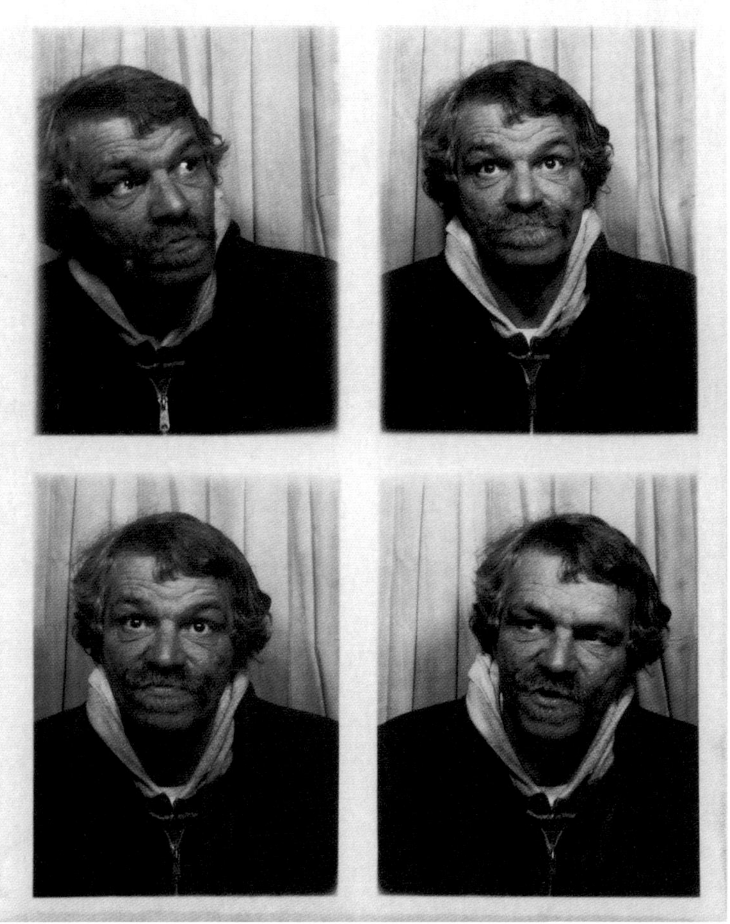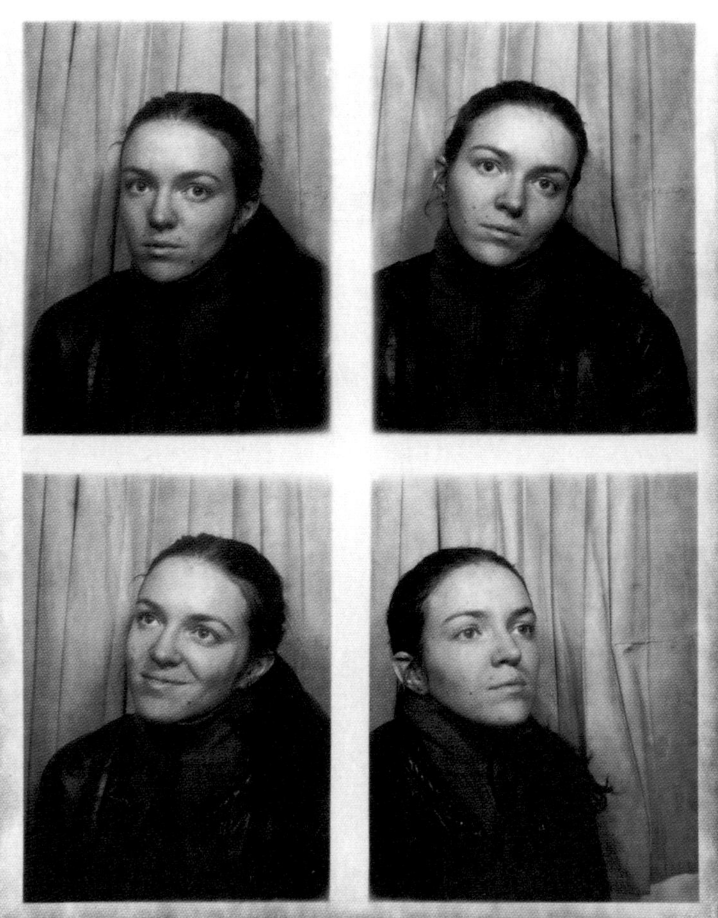

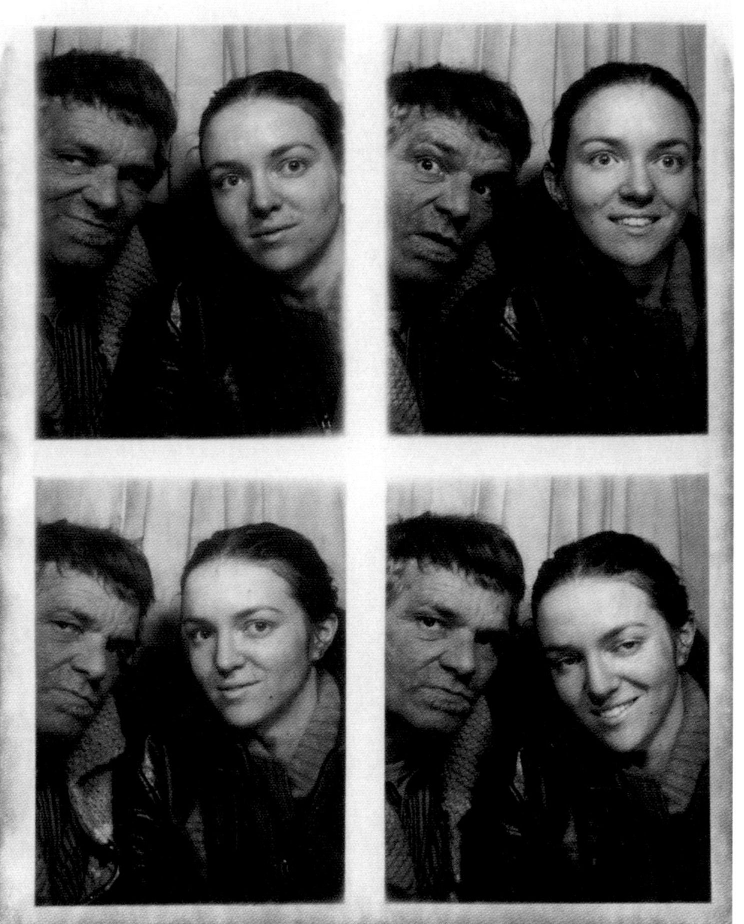

Dear Phil, Philop, Flip Flop, Daddy,

I started taking photographs of you, and me with you around eight years ago. I was 19 and had come back from a summer working in Maine, you probably don't remember this, but that fall you were really ill. Crazier than I had seen you in years. You were drinking hard, smelling, wearing underwear on your head and spewing all kinds of nonsense. You didn't believe you were ill, you weren't taking your medication and there were very few lucid days.

Taking photographs of us was, and continued to be, the only way for me to stay sane or meet you at all when you were sick and drunk.

One morning that fall we had set up a meeting outside of Accueuil Bono when you were supposed to pick up your cash, it was raining and as I walked up past the church I saw you. You were half dressed, bashing on the windows, screaming for Mr Dubuc and your money. That was the only day I remember that my camera couldn't help me. You saw me, came up to me cursing and asking for money and I turned around and left.

I think you need to understand the fear, the shame and then of course the guilt, the huge guilt after the shame that your schizophrenia unleashed in me.

I must have been around 8 years old, I was crossing the street with friends in front of my school and I saw you on the other side talking to yourself and waiting for me. I was in shock.

I put my head down and started to run. I ran right by you, screamed at my friend that a monster was following us and didn't stop until I reached the afterschool program that was a mile away.

When I was around 14 with friends walking near the Faubourg I saw you sitting on the corner filthy and mumbling to yourself. I froze, turned around and walked away. My friends didn't understand until years later what happened to me.

There was another time I remember clearly I was older, it was the end of winter on one of those Sundays when you, me and Nat met at the diner on the corner of Mackay and De Maisonneuve. That weekend Nat was sick and couldn't come, but I decided to meet you anyway so it was the first time that we were meeting for breakfast alone. I got off the bus to walk down the hill and saw you picking something out of the garbage half a block away. I didn't call your name or wave or anything, that gut-wrenching fear and embarrassment took over and propelled me down the hill to the diner. I couldn,t see you like that on the street. As I ran I was so terribly ashamed of myself for running away from you but I still ran and then I fell and slid in the dirt and slush down

Guy Avenue. I remember thinking it was instant karma and then limping up to the diner and explaining to you that I had fallen.

When I was a girl and you became sick you were a monster to me. When I was a teenager and at my most self-conscious, you and schizophrenia were my biggest secrets. I hated the madness, hated the drinking and hated that you made us so different and alone.

I'm so sorry for those times I ran away from you, for not calling out your name, for caring what other people might think.

Phil, I forgive you for being such an asshole and scaring me so many times over the years, for not ever being there, for not taking your pills and for drinking way too damn much.

And I thank you for trying hard anyway, loving me like you do, wanting to give me whatever you have left and for being such a decent, intelligent and funny guy. Thank you for showing me the street, the squirrels and the crows and for making me see so many other sides.

This is for you and for me and for every mother, father, daughter, son, brother, sister, husband, wife that has ever had to live with or alongside mental illness.

I love you.

Mandy xo

Bangalore, India 10/07/04

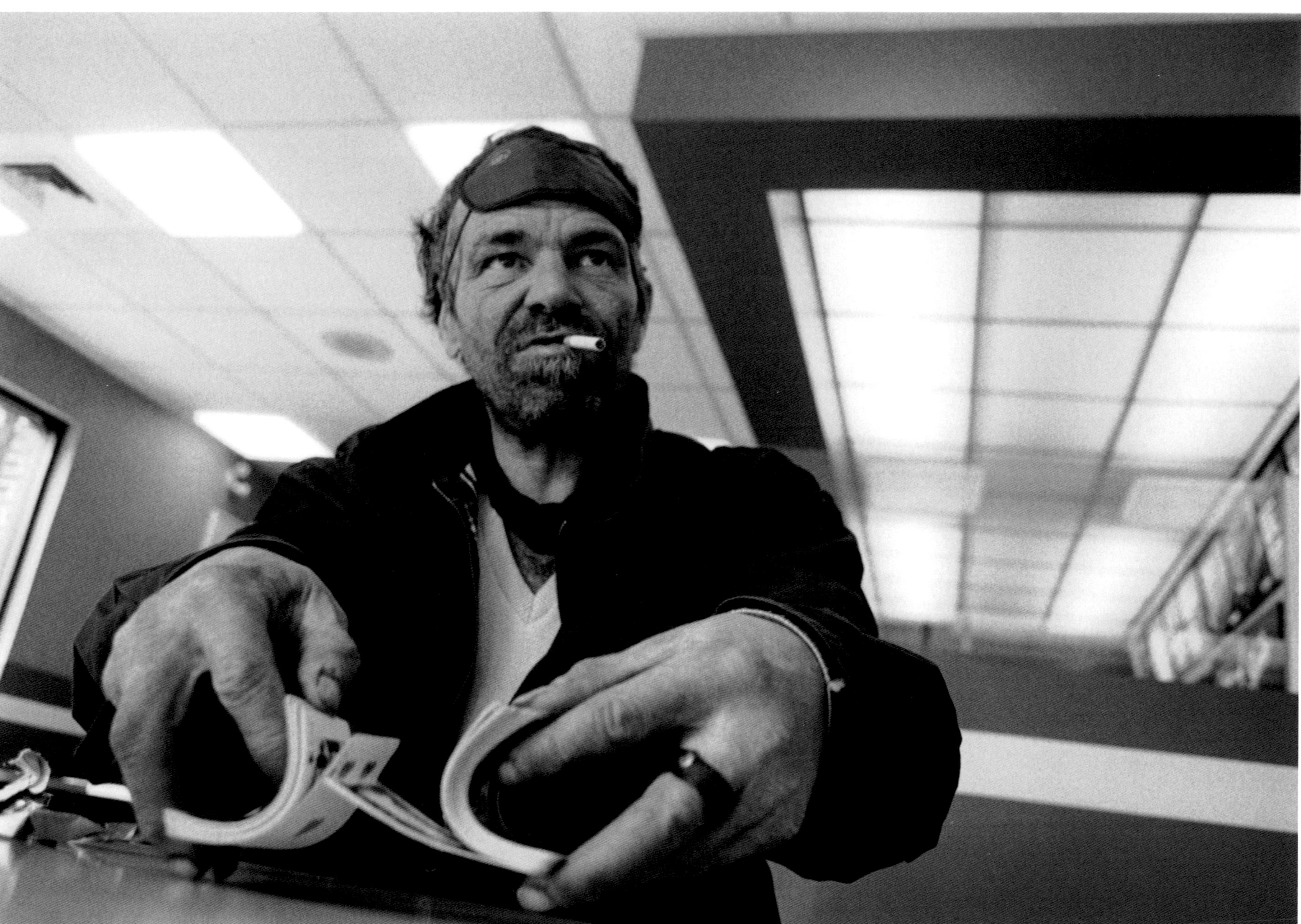

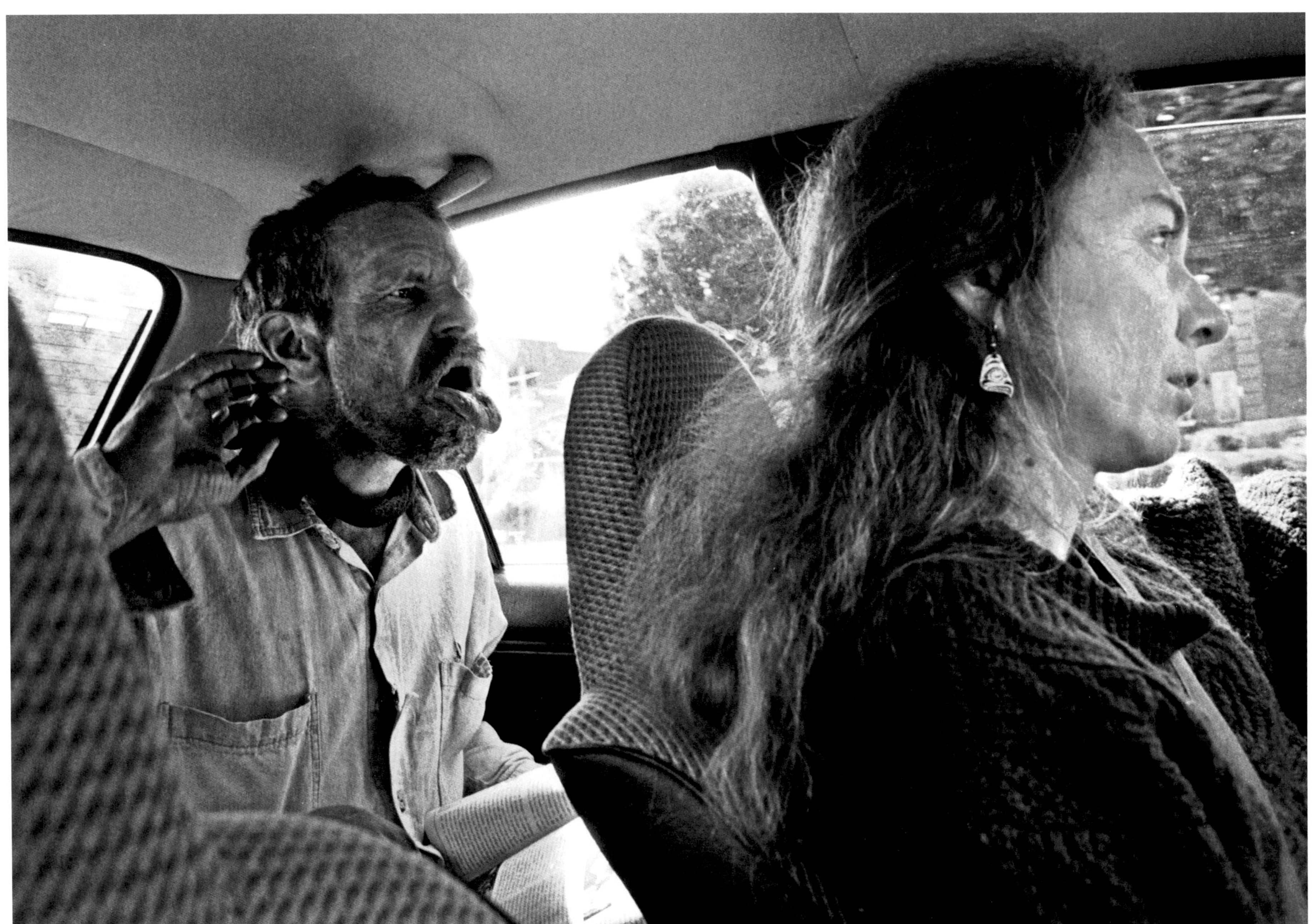

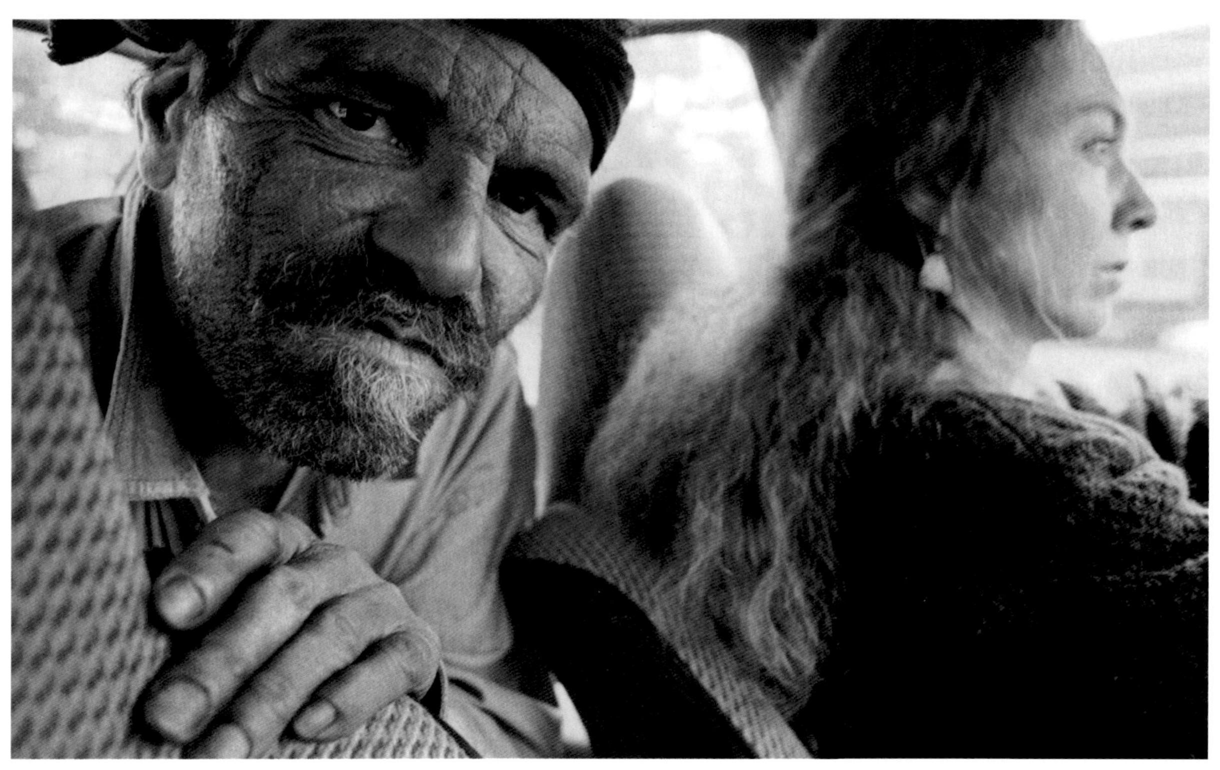

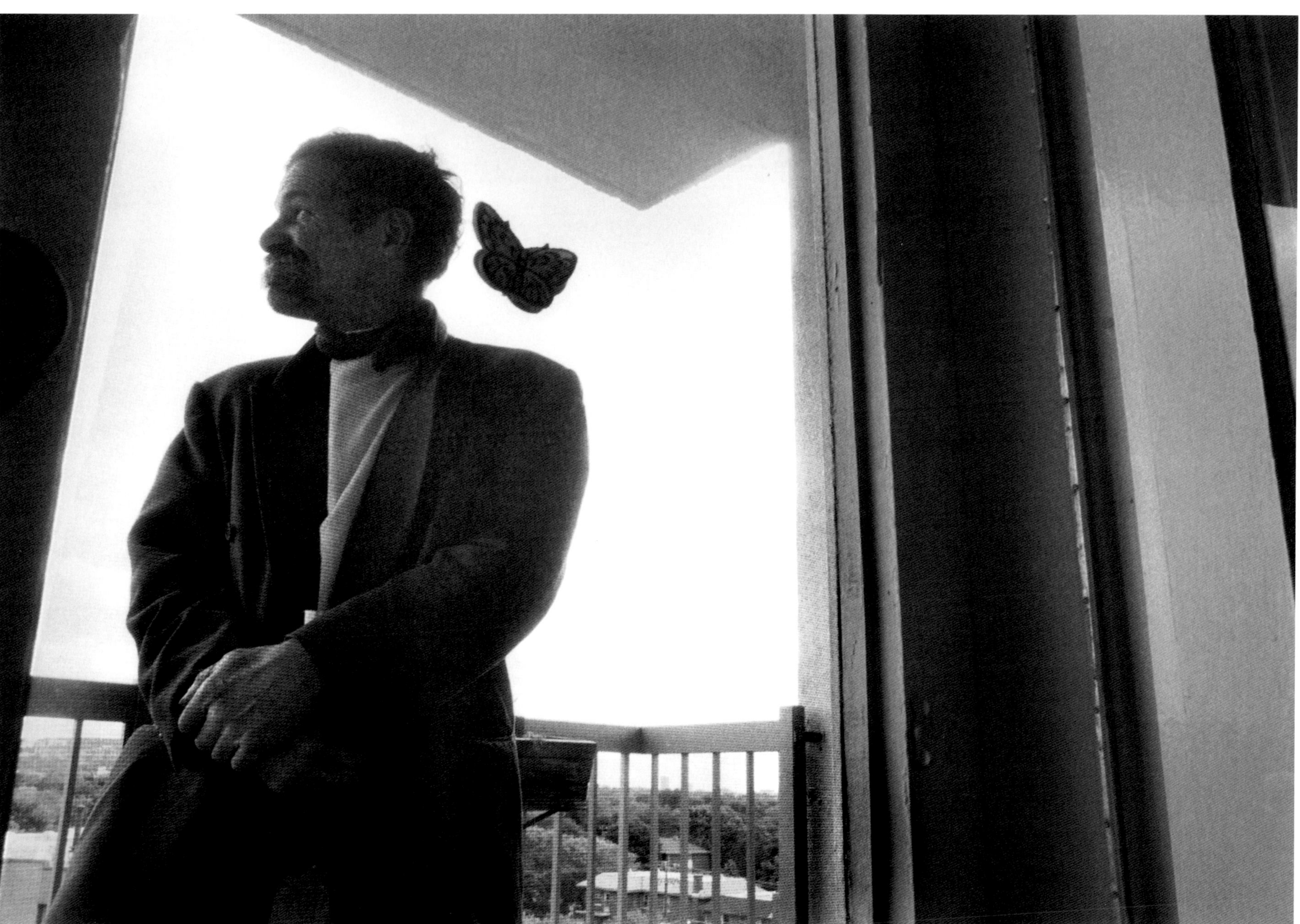

Lindsay of the Linsey Fields;

There is Kierkegaard
walks the morning;
Told me, sun-Light
and the source
            thereof;
I walk the right-
      time, yes
      with a little patience
my eyes grow dark
and I covet this,
because if I cannot
be accepted,
then right-time is
      not right;
      and how long my Lord
      must I walk.
For my eyes are black
      Holes, I pass by, I am
and a black crow.
that most try to ignore
This happens, all by the Linsey
            fields.

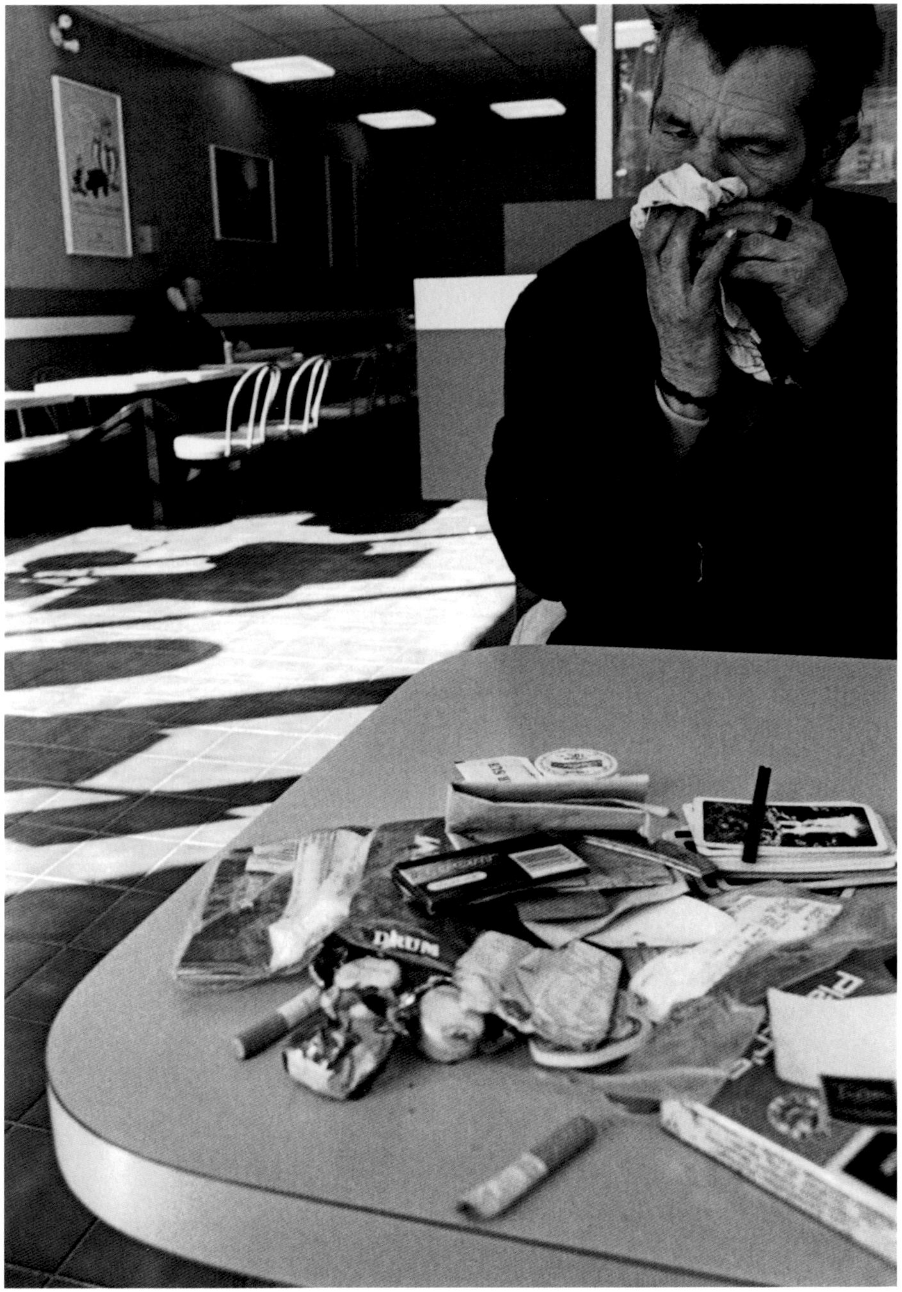

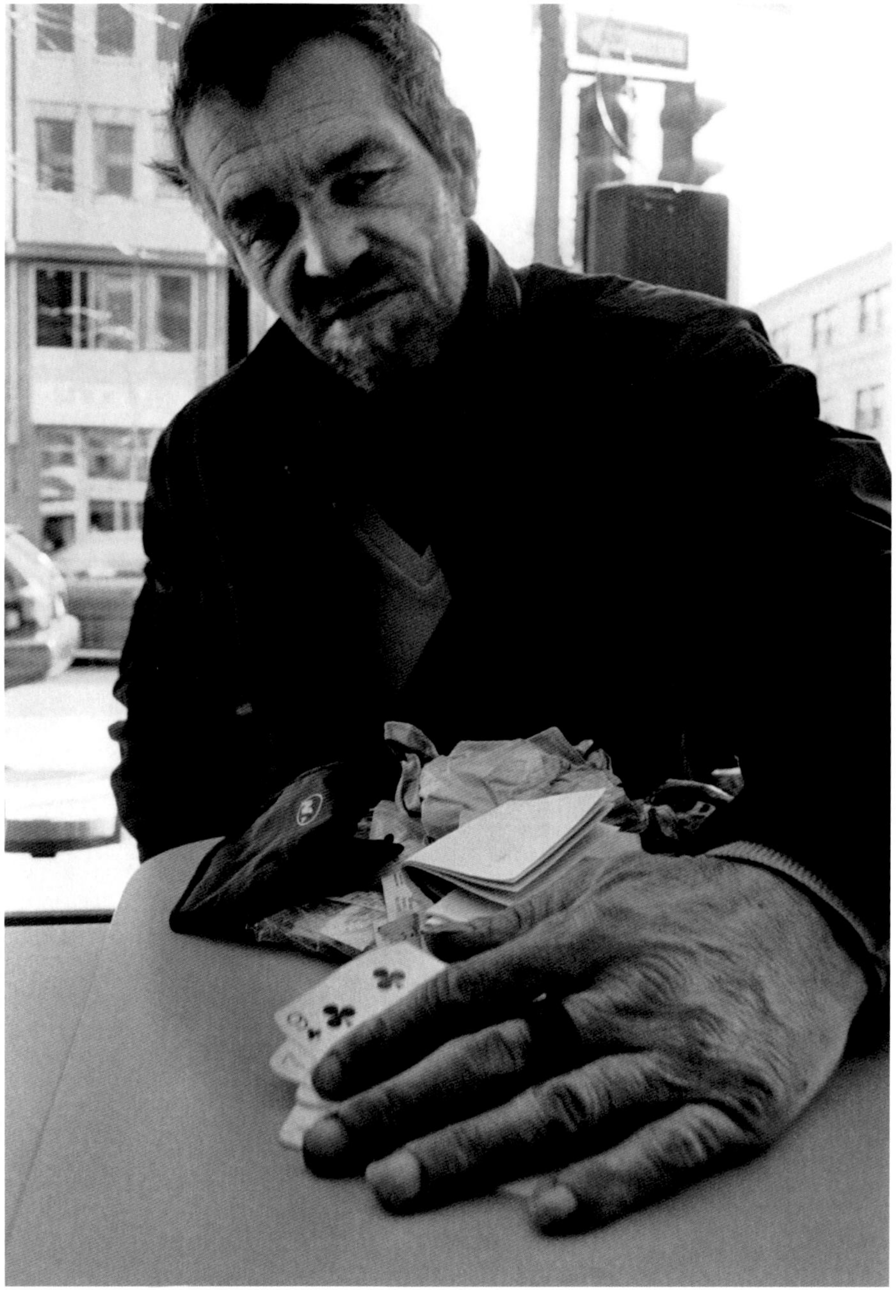

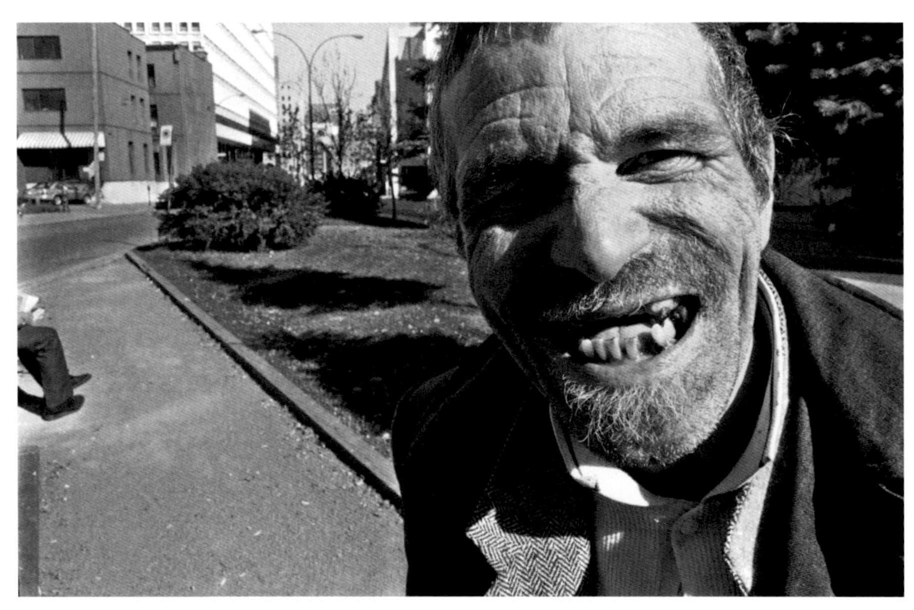

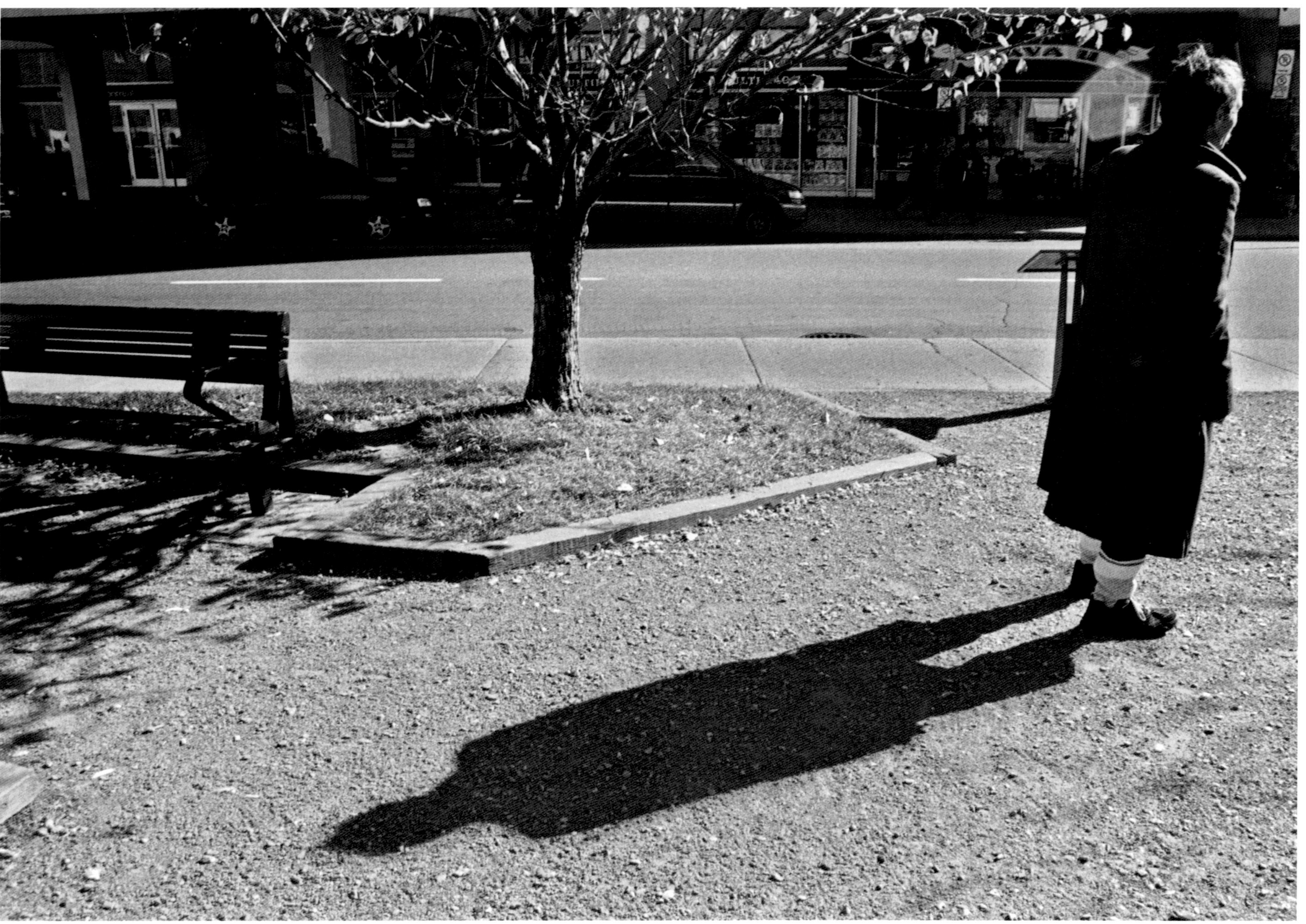

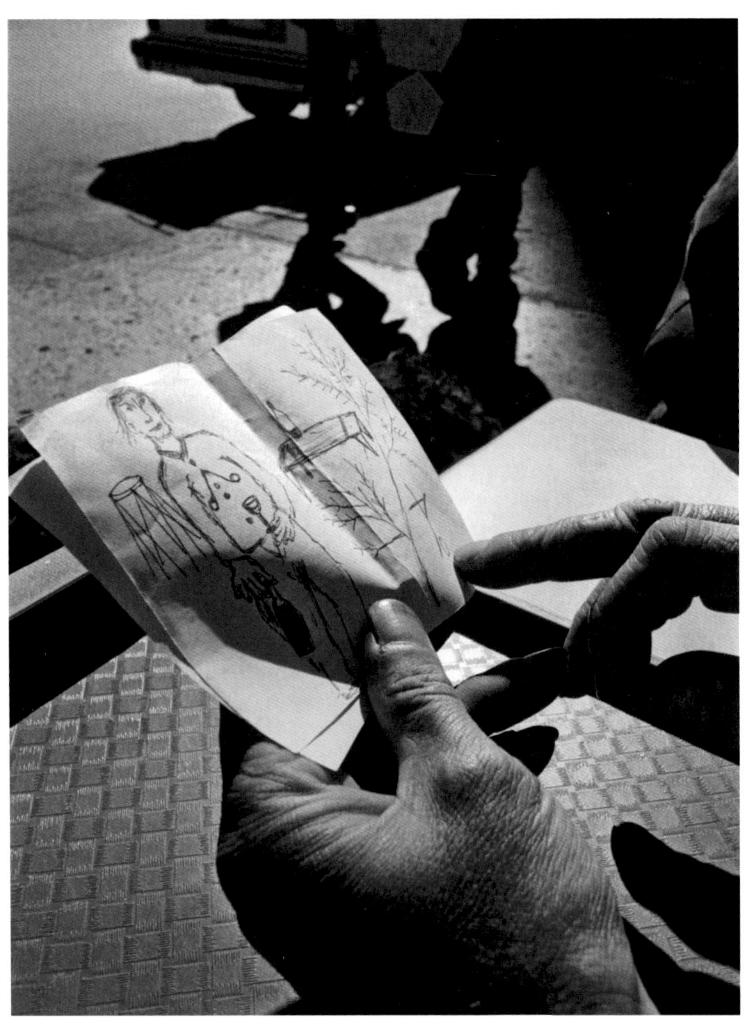

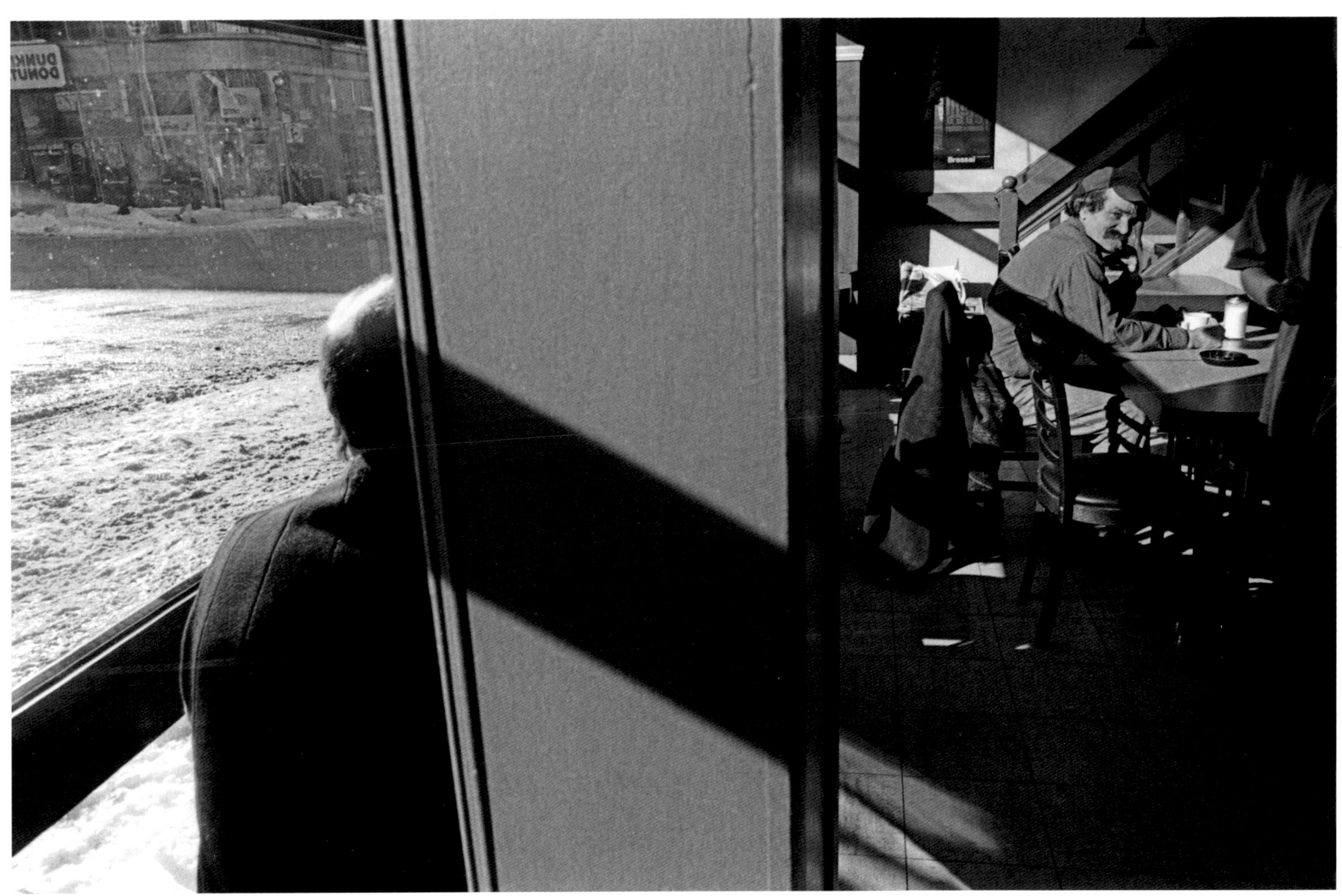

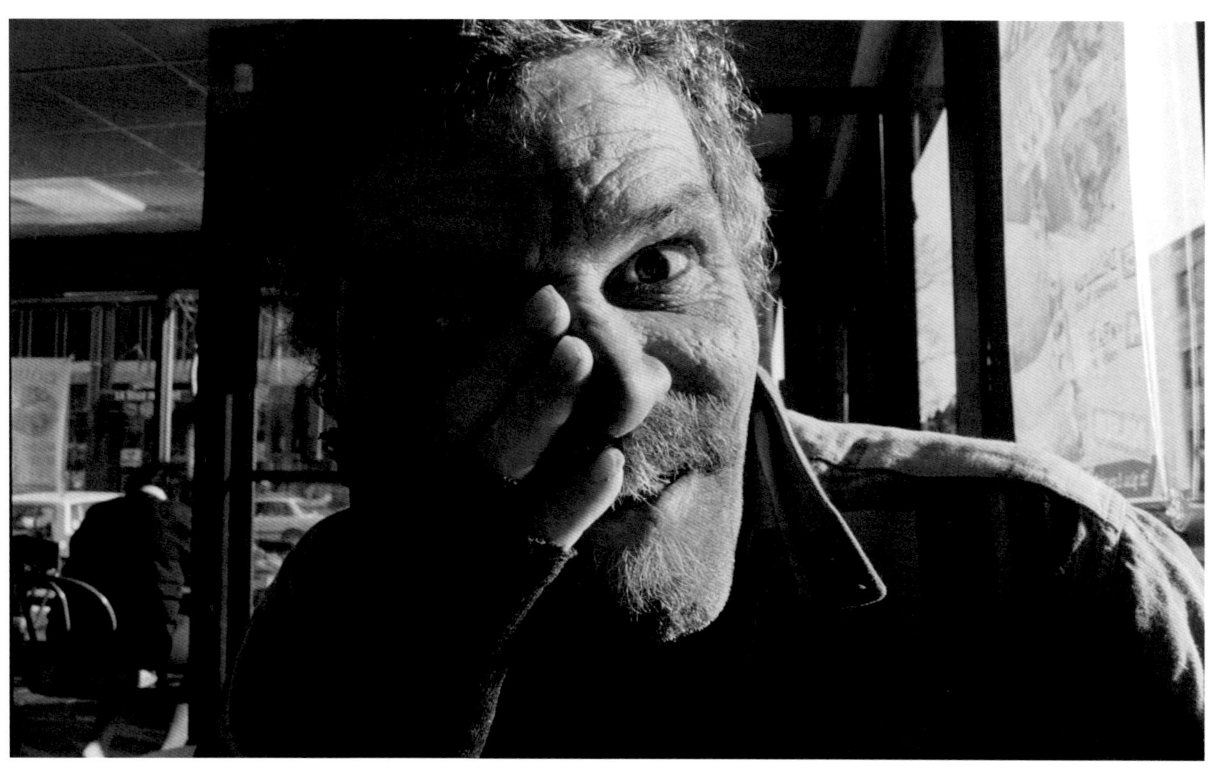

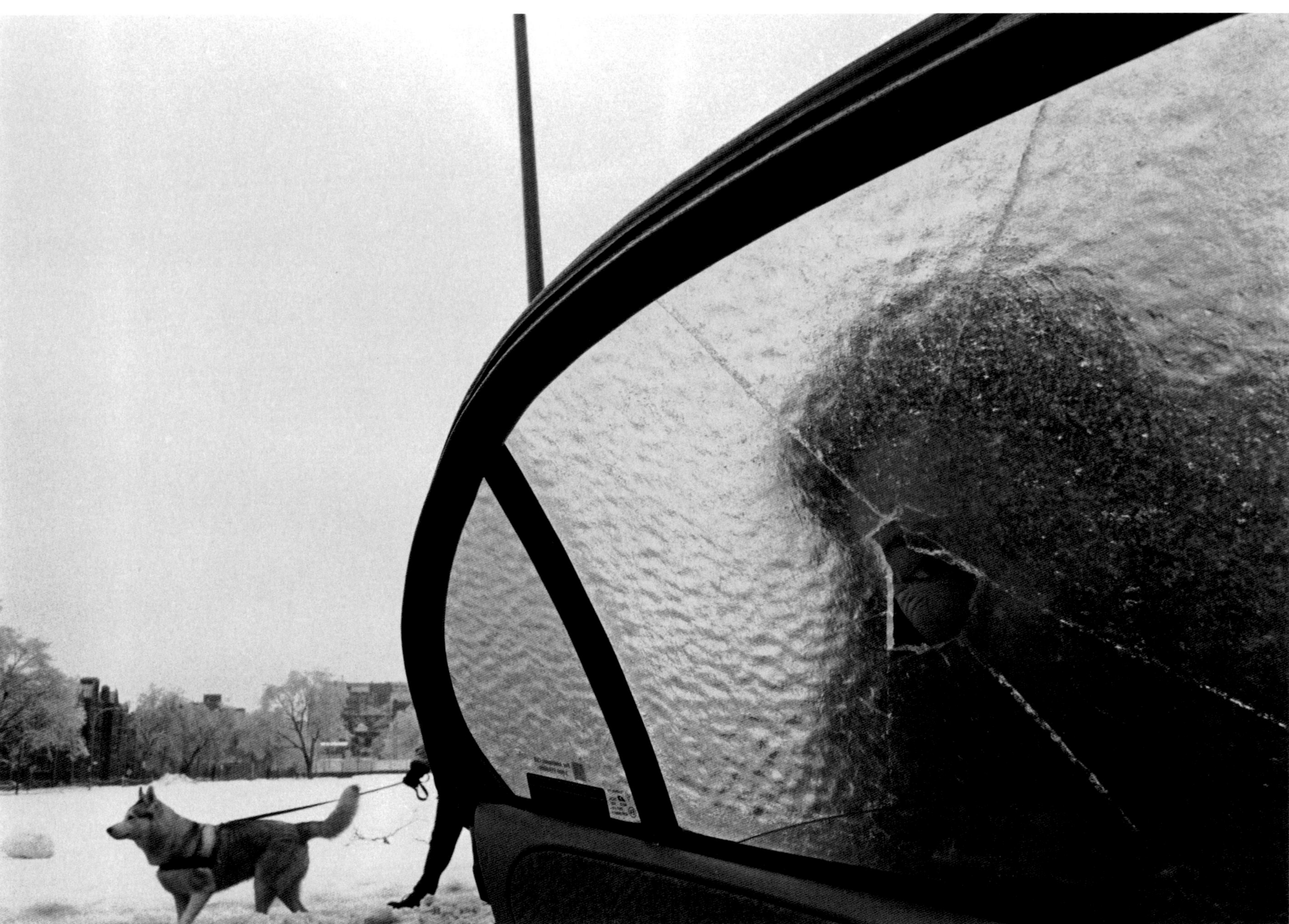

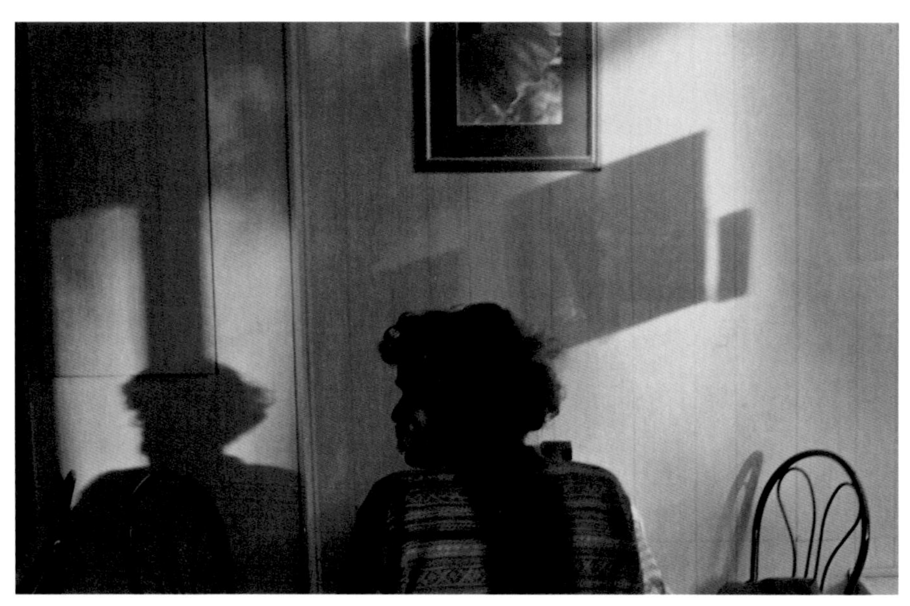

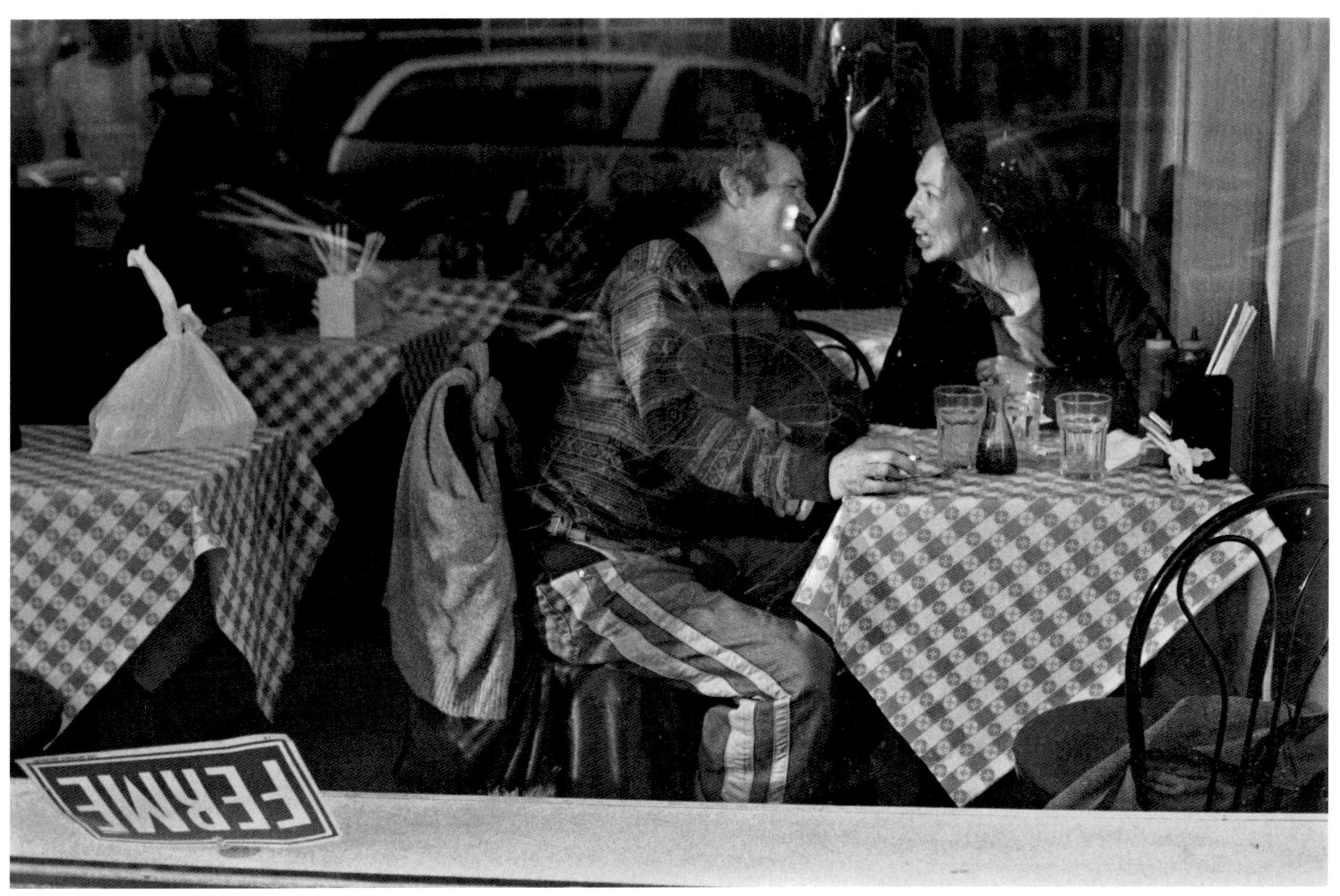
FERMÉ

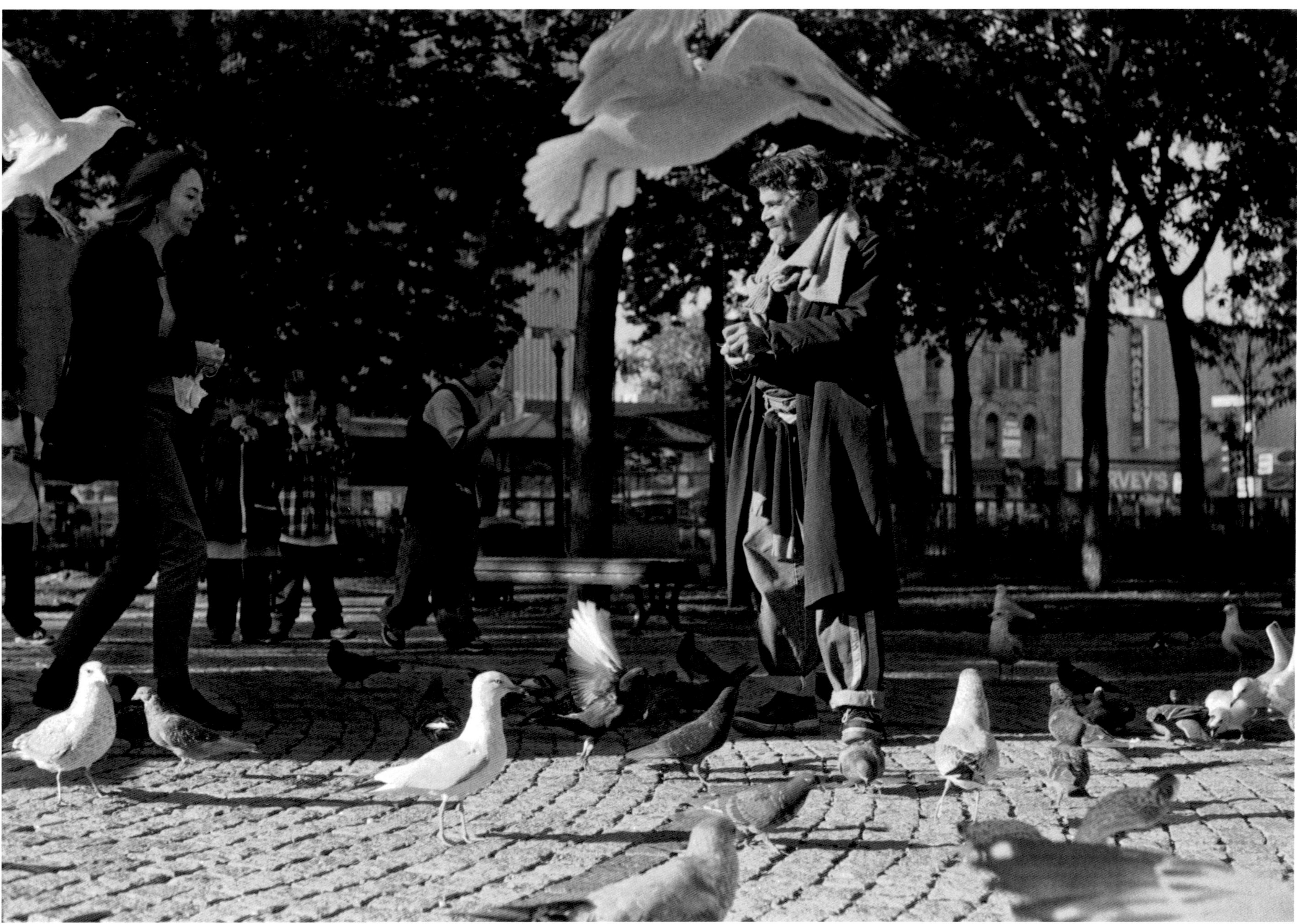

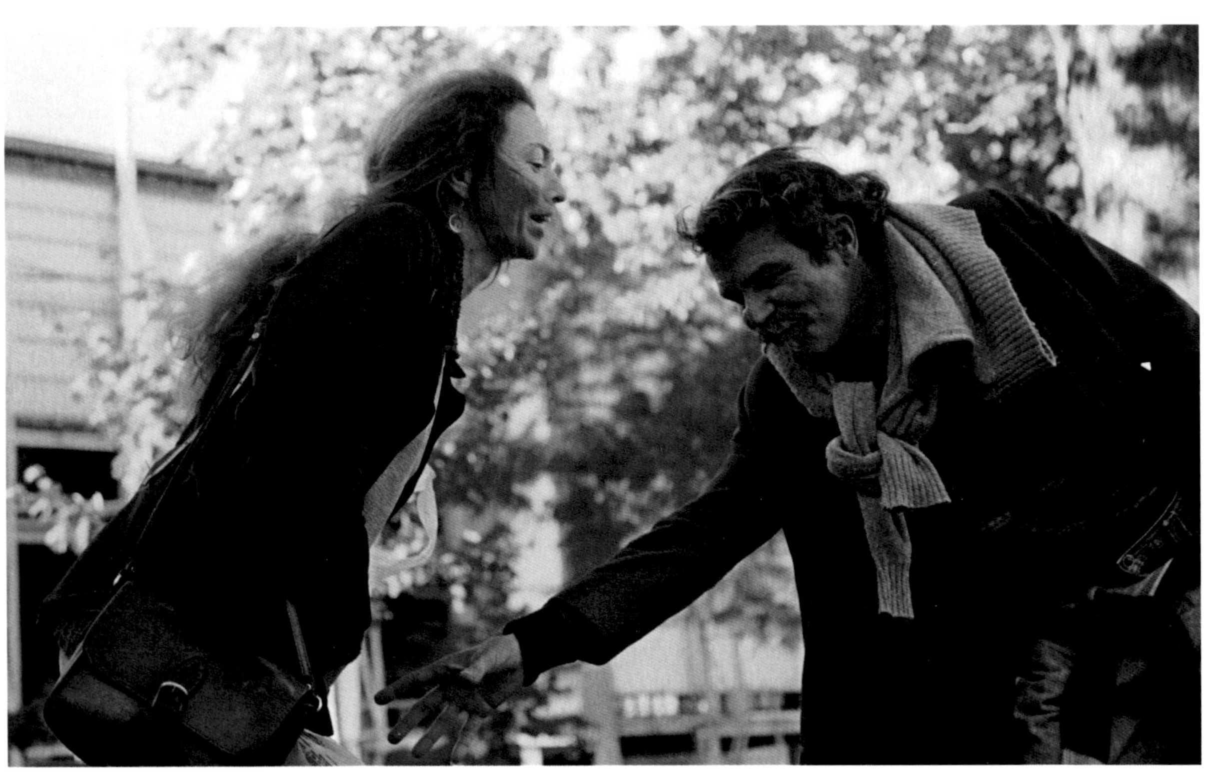

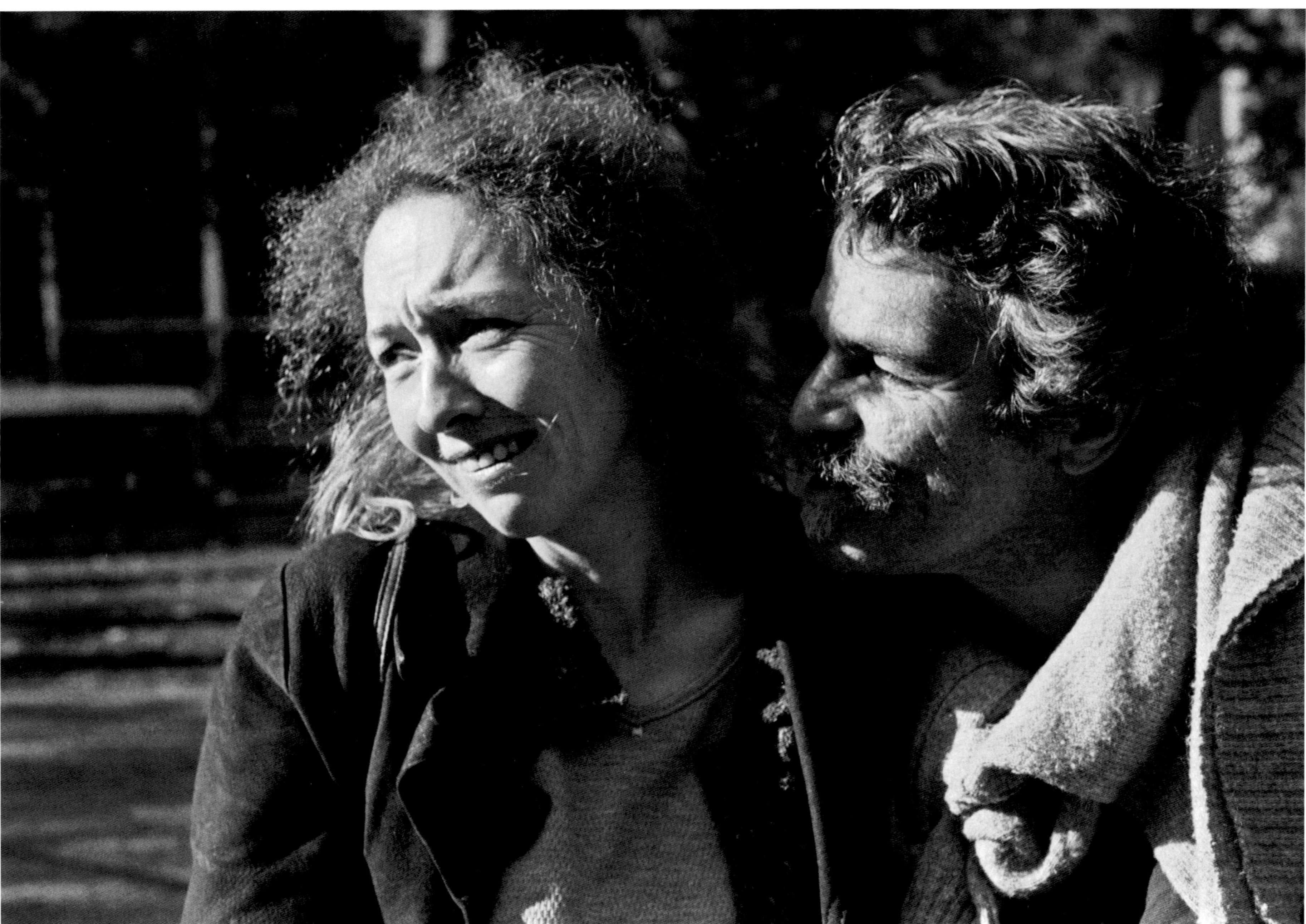

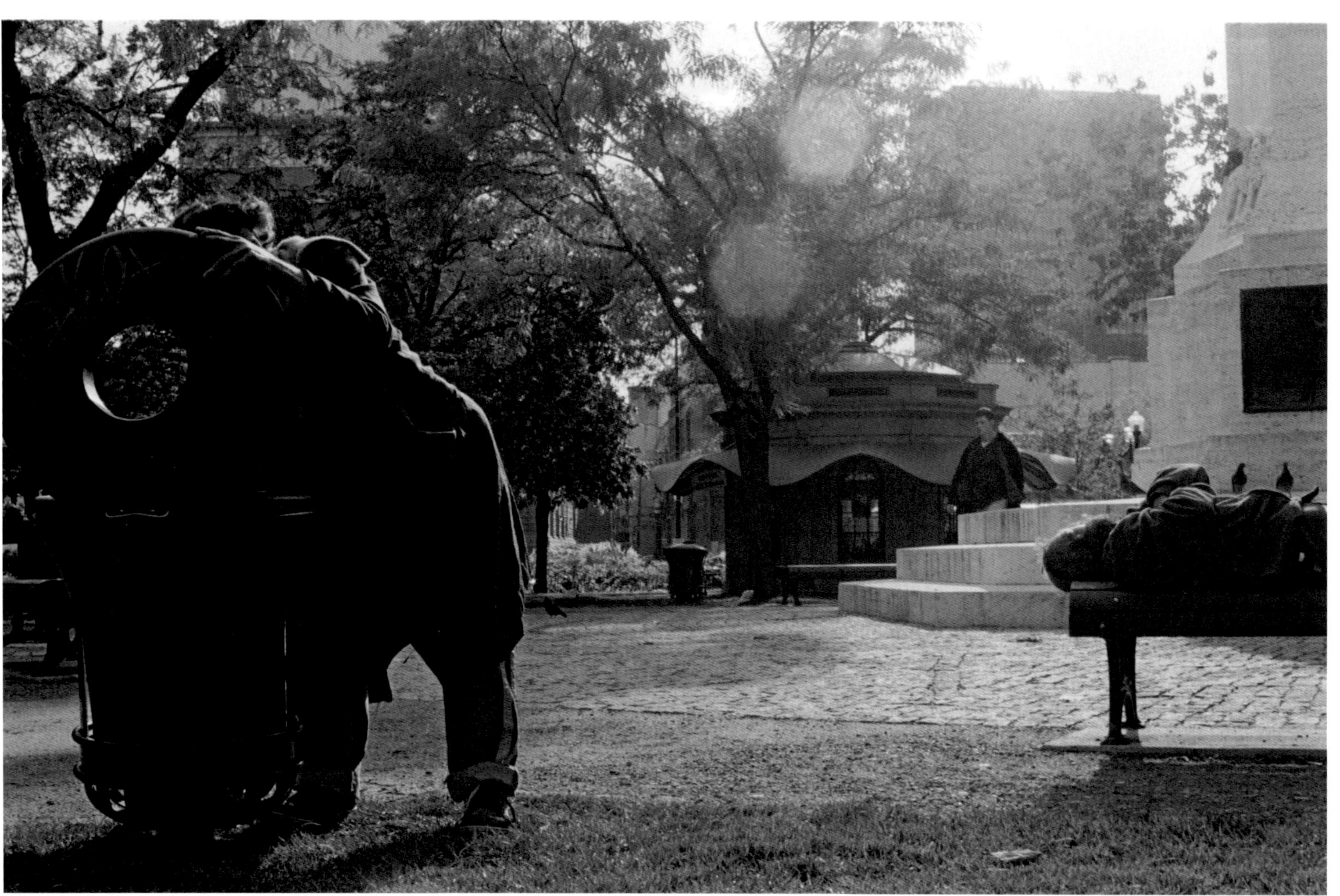

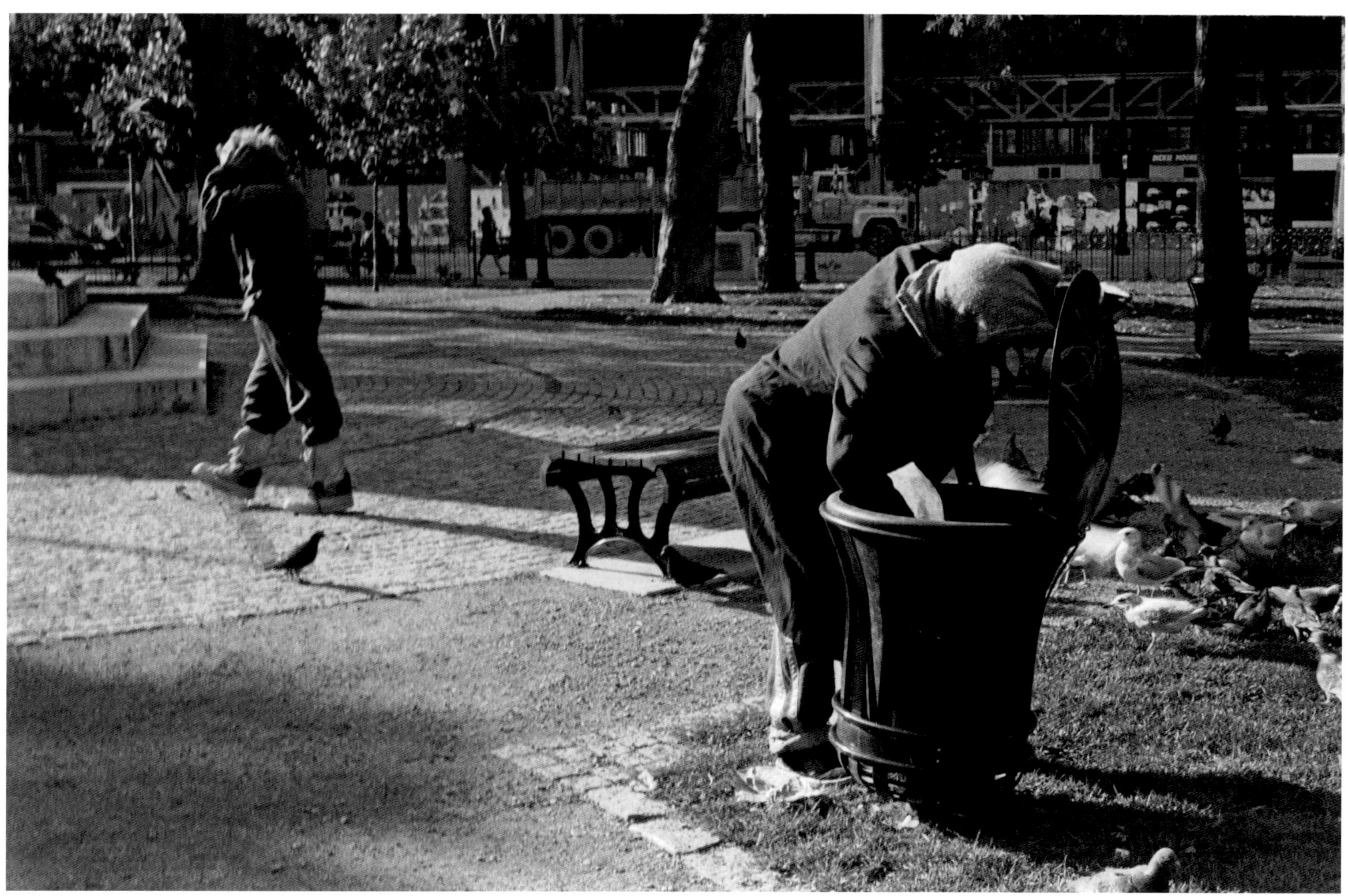

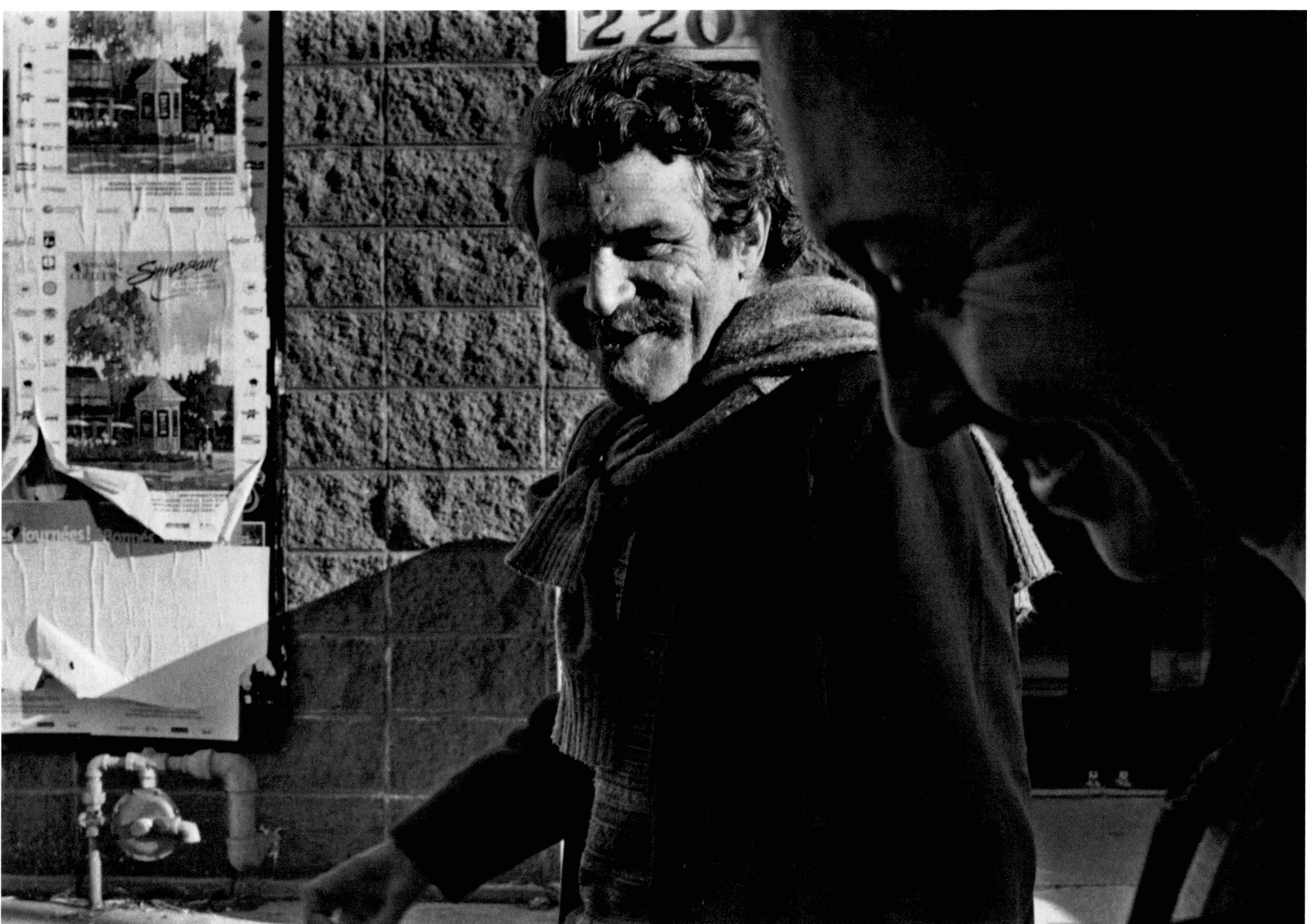

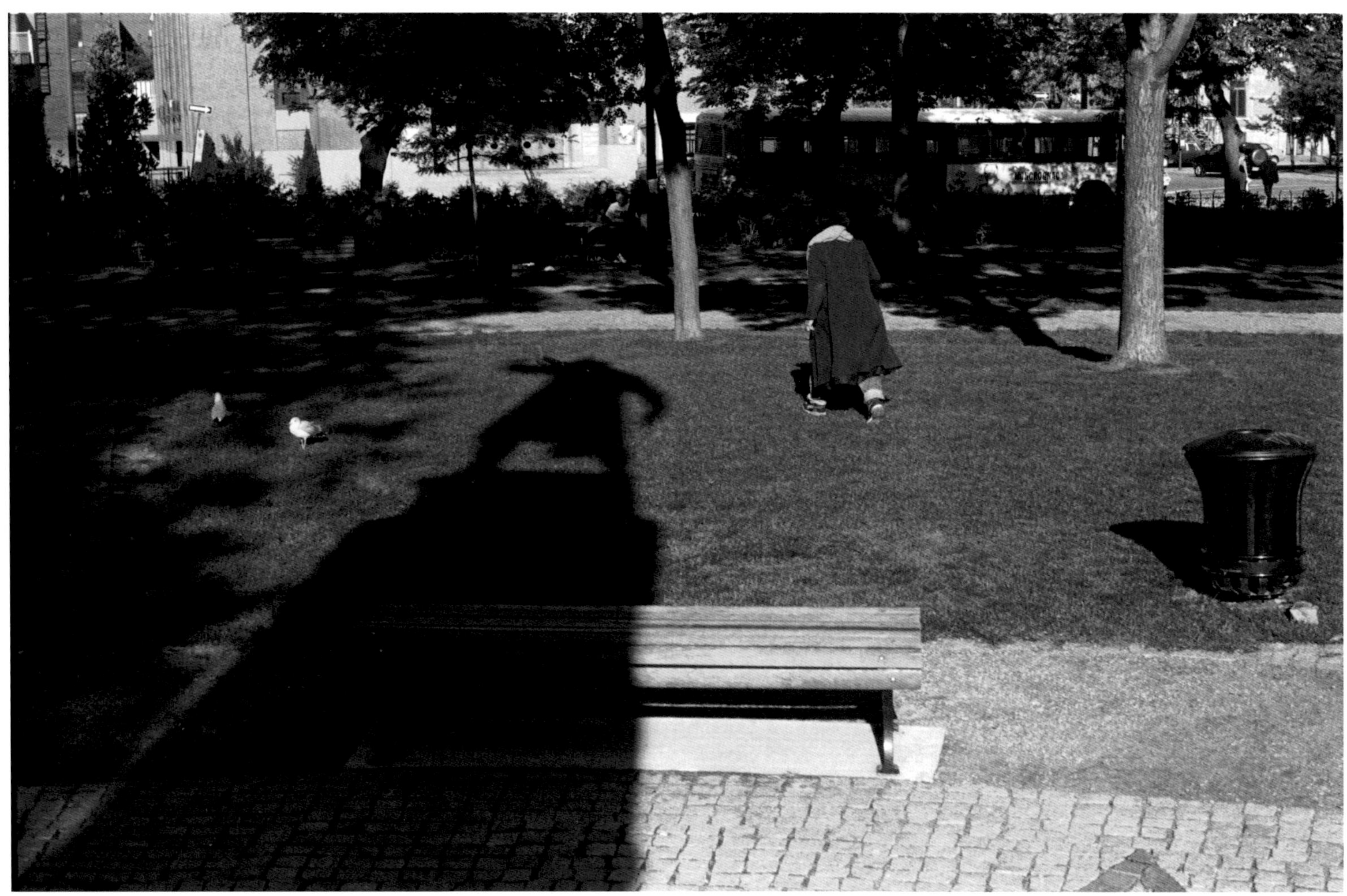

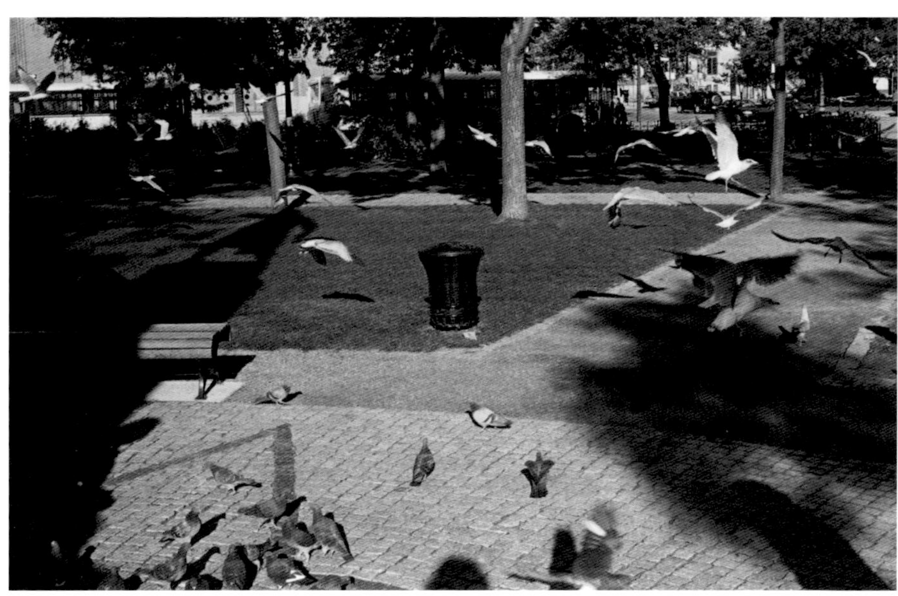

Philip Tétrault

POETRY

THE GREATEST FEAR OF THE EVERYDAY
THAT   POSSESSES ME
IS   NOT   THE   COLD OF DAYS
NOR   THE   POVERTY, WHICH IS A FROST OF THOUGHT
IN   MY   CASE
THAT,   OF   ALL THE   TRIALS
I   HAVE   HAD   TO   SUFFER
            THAT   I   PUT   CHAINS
        ON   MY   MIND
    that   WOULD   ENTHRALL   ME
IN   A   WORLD   OF   KARMA
NOT   TO   BE   ABLE   TO   SEE   THROUGH
        ALL   THAT
            ....   COMES   TO ME
THE   COLD   IS   COME
            FOR   A   FEW   MONTHS   ANYWAY
    EVERY   YEAR, AROUND THIS   TIME
            IT   IS   THE   SAME
        . ....
THE   GIRLS   OF   THE   SMALL   CAFÉ
                REMEMBER   ME
    EVERY   MONTHS, LIKE   A   GLASS   BEAD   CLEAR
        I   COME   TO   HER,
"MONEY   AS   NO   OBJECT,"
        ....'HERE," SHE   SAYS
AND   I   BOW   TO   HER
        FOR   KNOWING   THAT
    THE   HELP   SHE   GIVES
            IS   BEYOND
            WHAT   I   can   say....

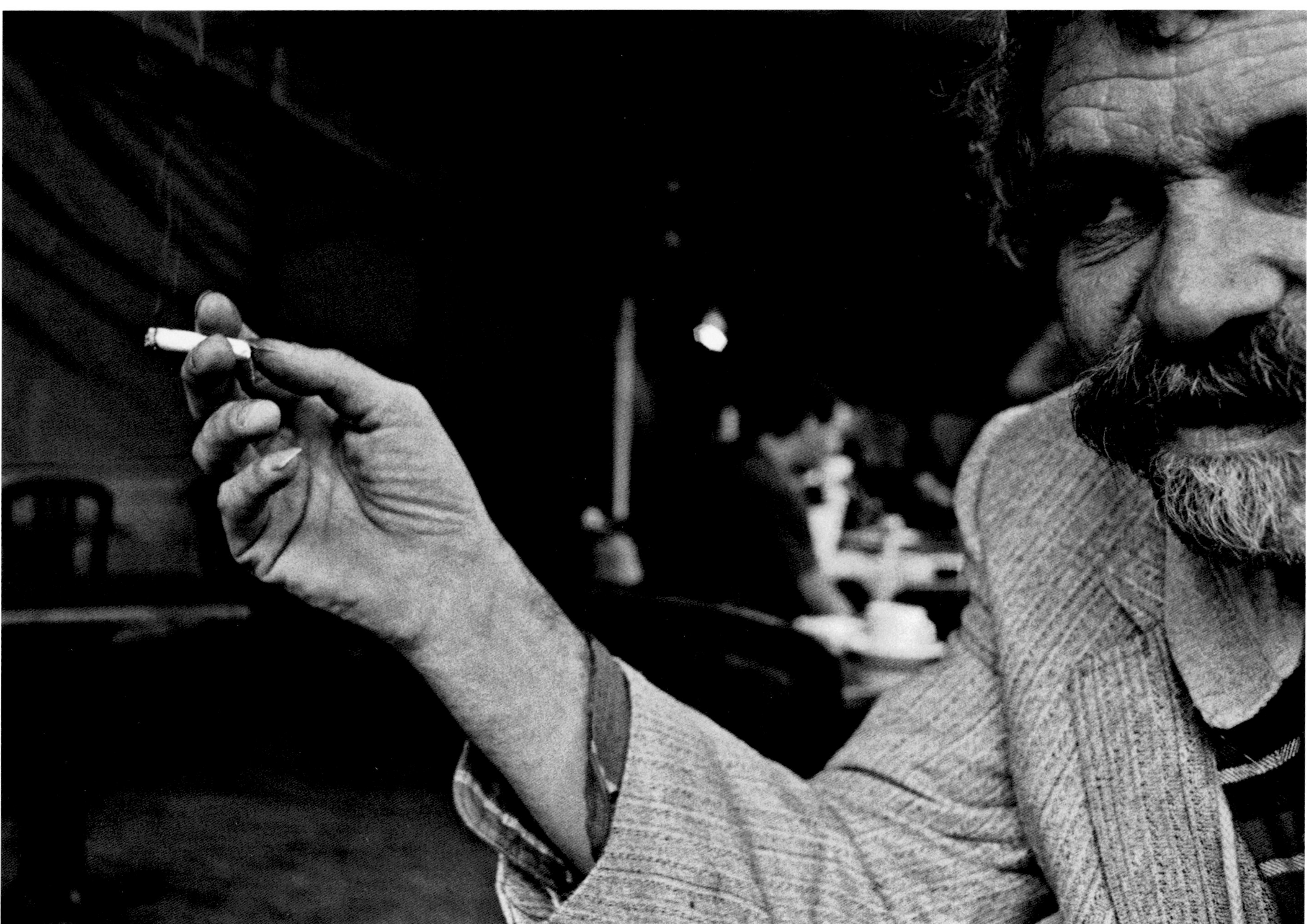

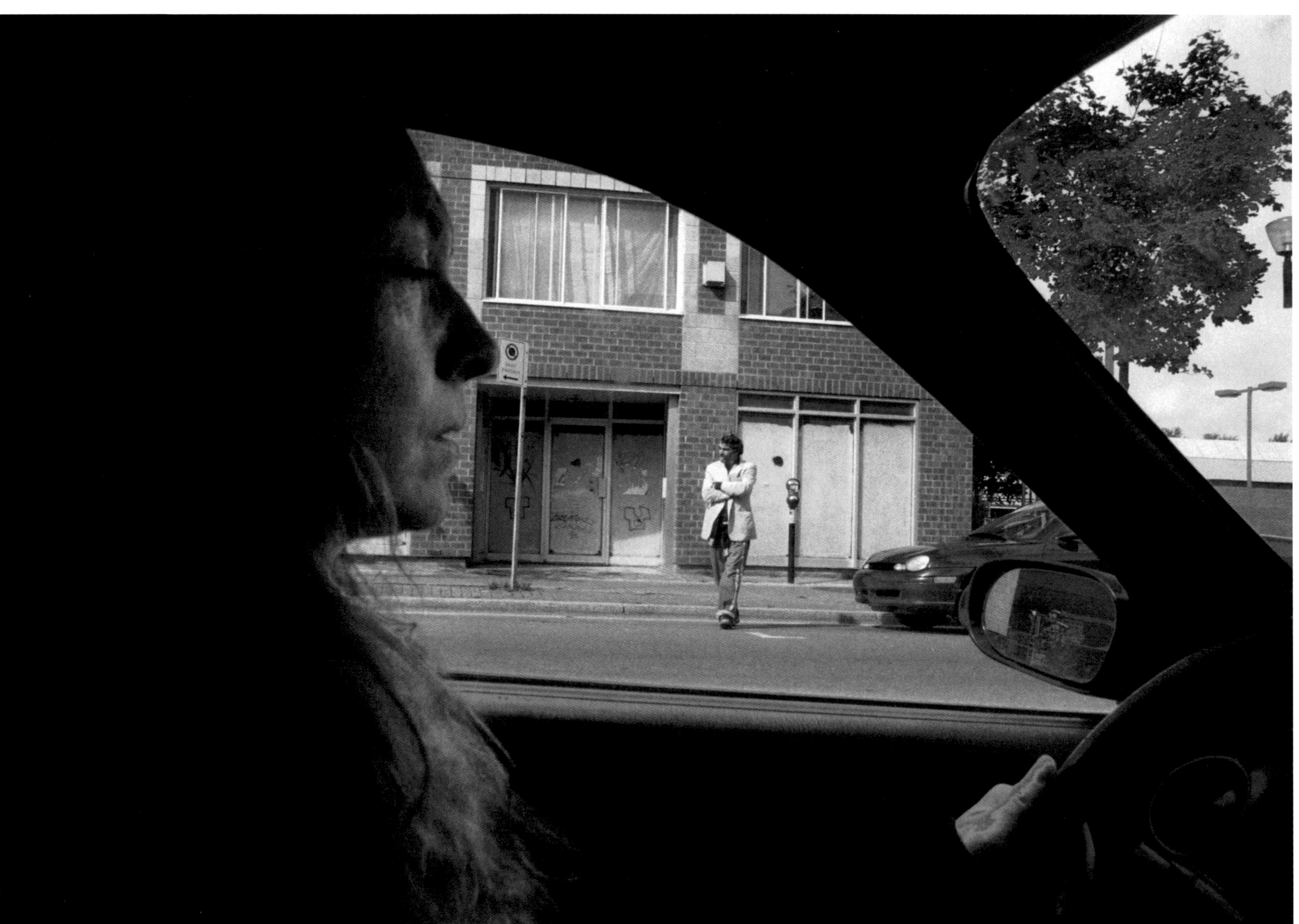

It is an hodour
to believe
that the sleep, that
I feel;
has to do with you;
My dreams, although
totally impossible
to understand;
remind me of you;
This is to say;
this is Love;
and, I shall distribute
it everywhere; until
we meet again.

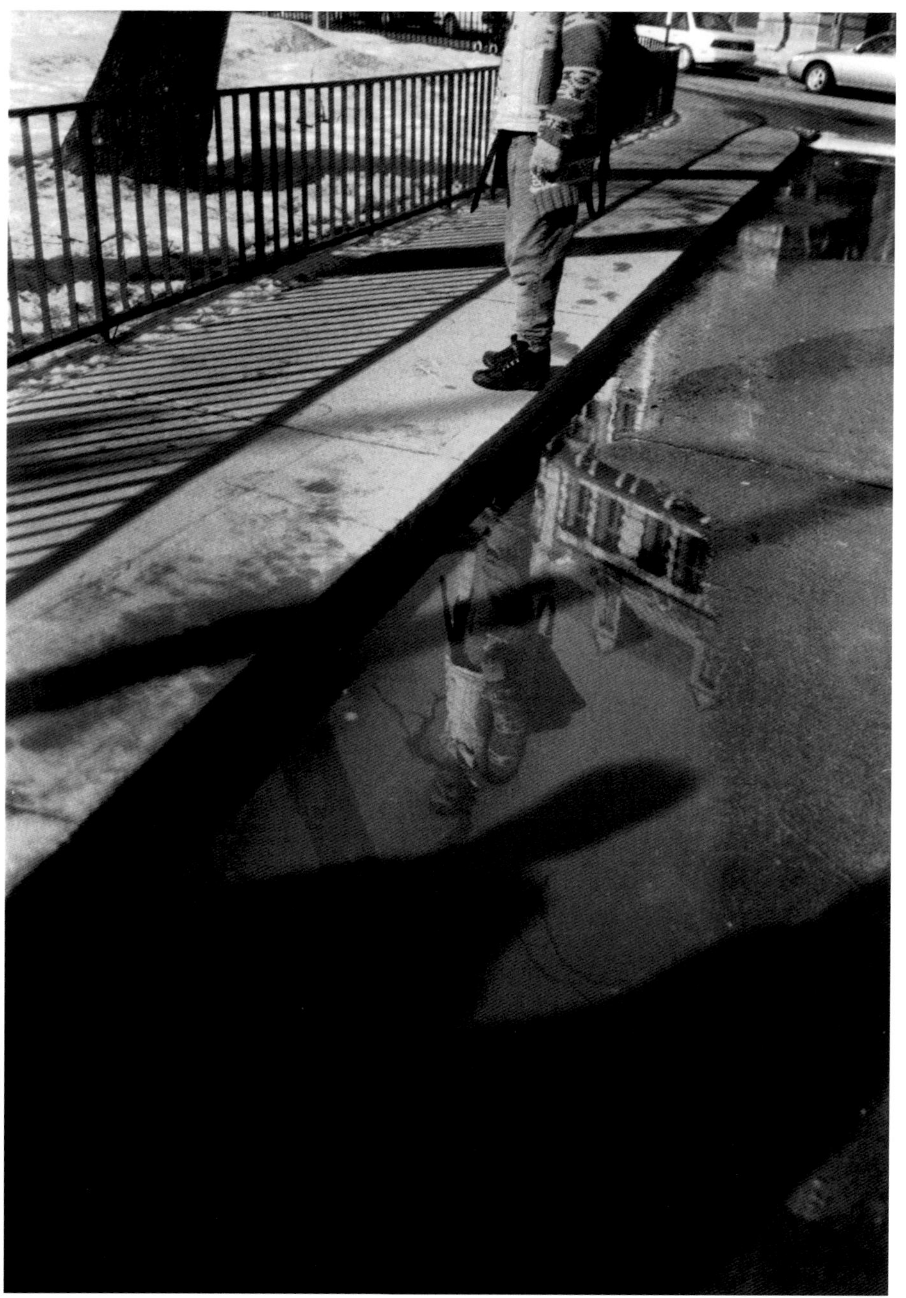

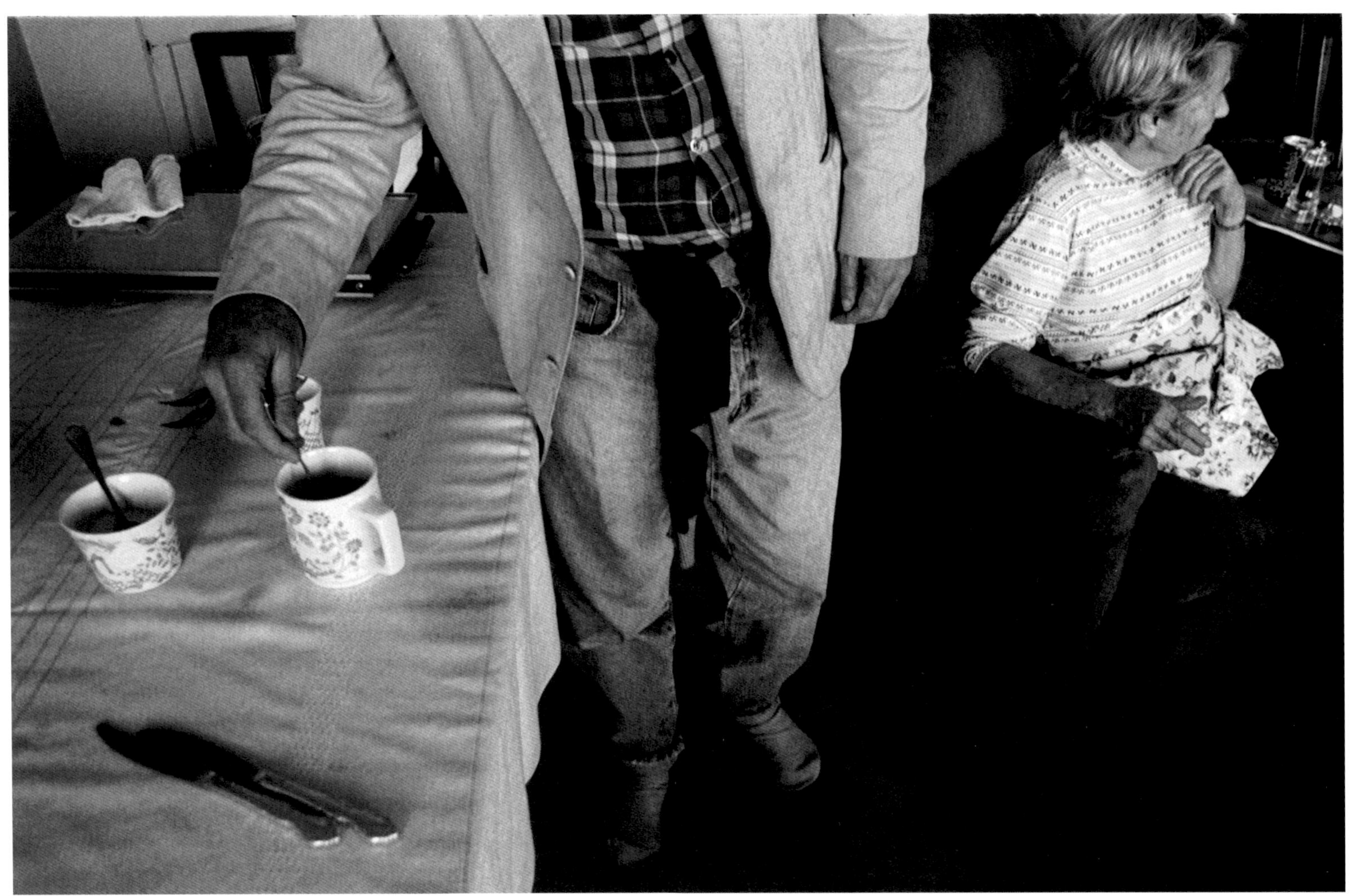

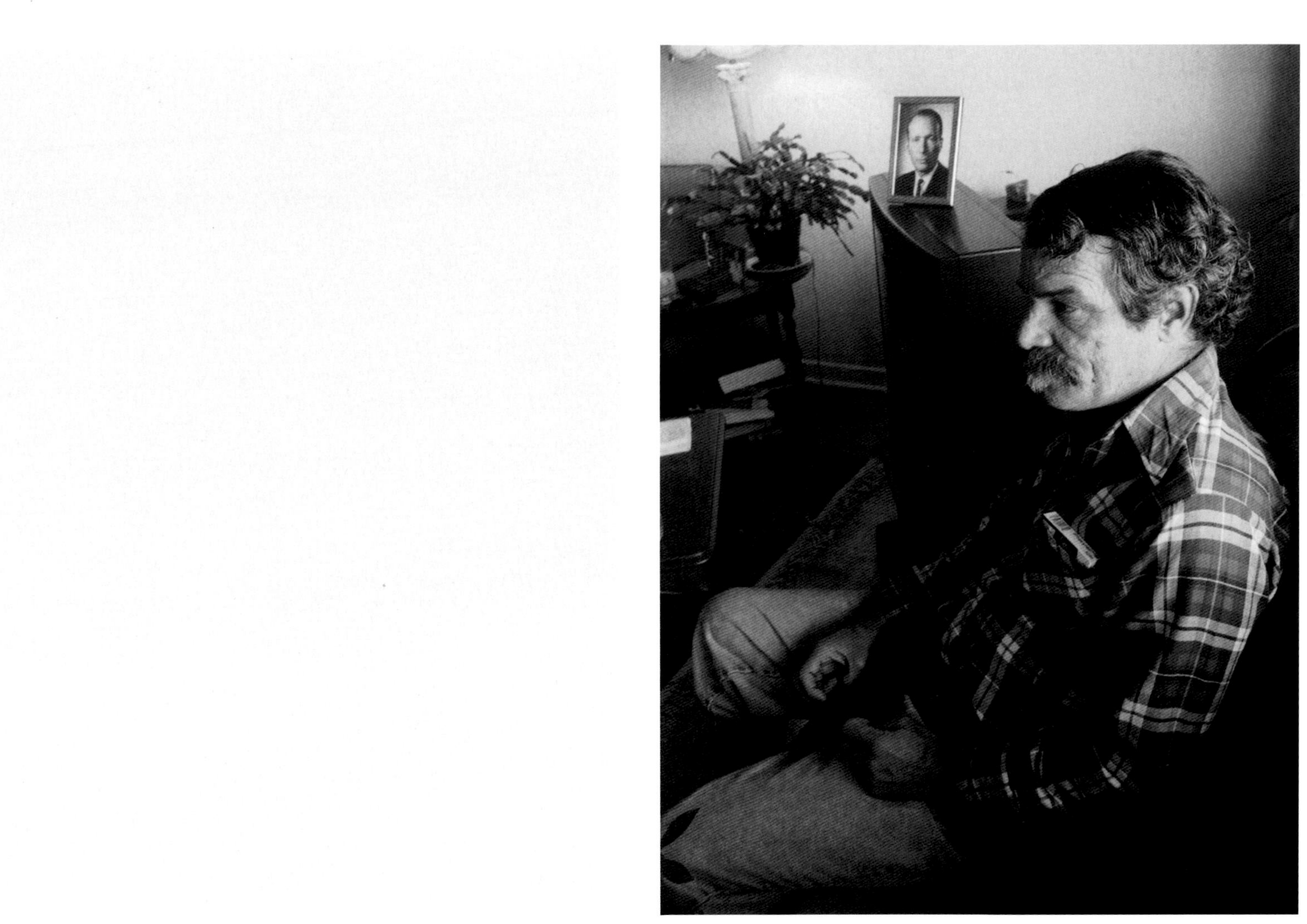

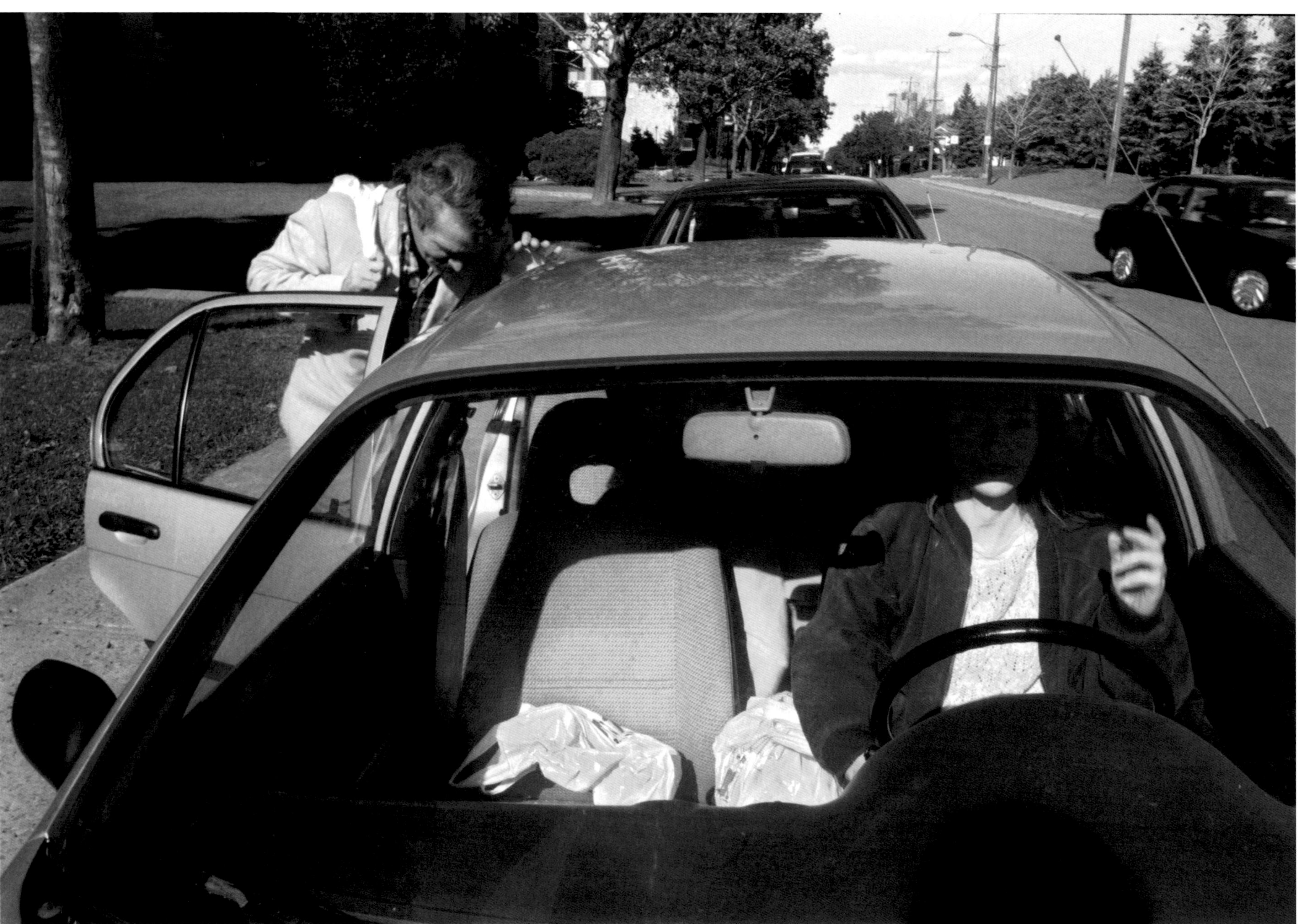

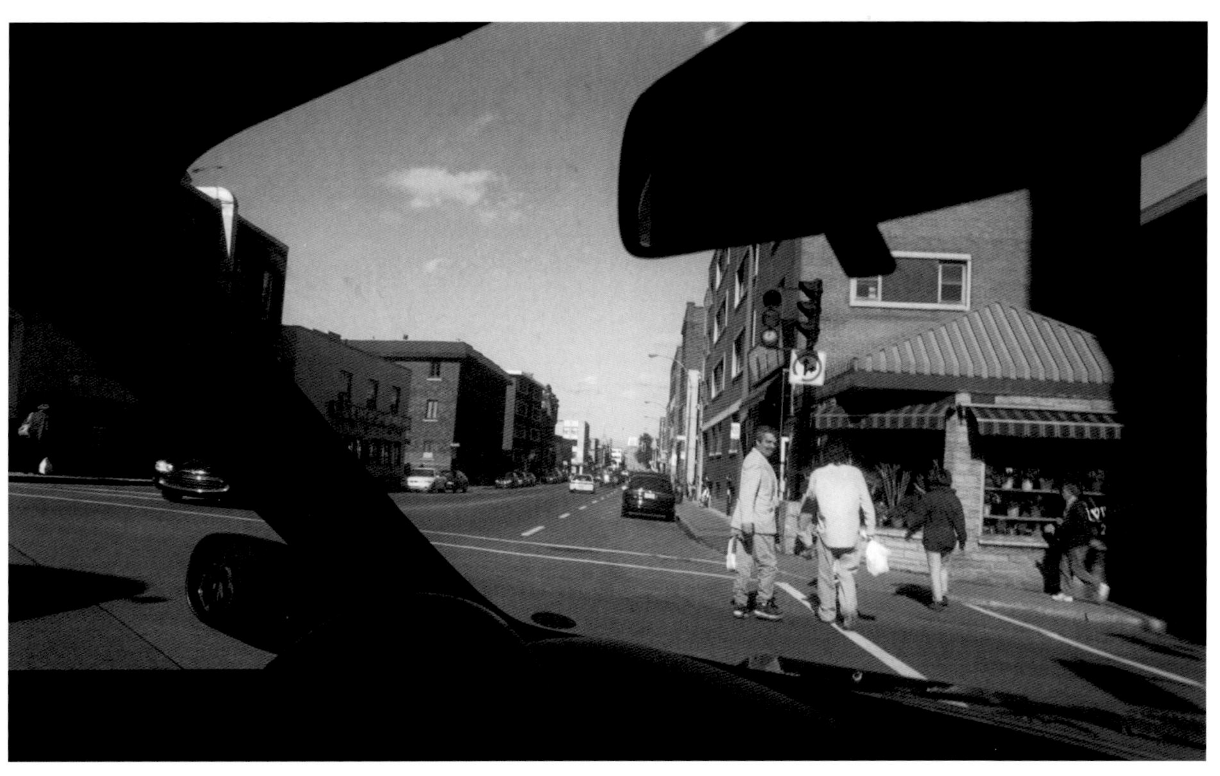

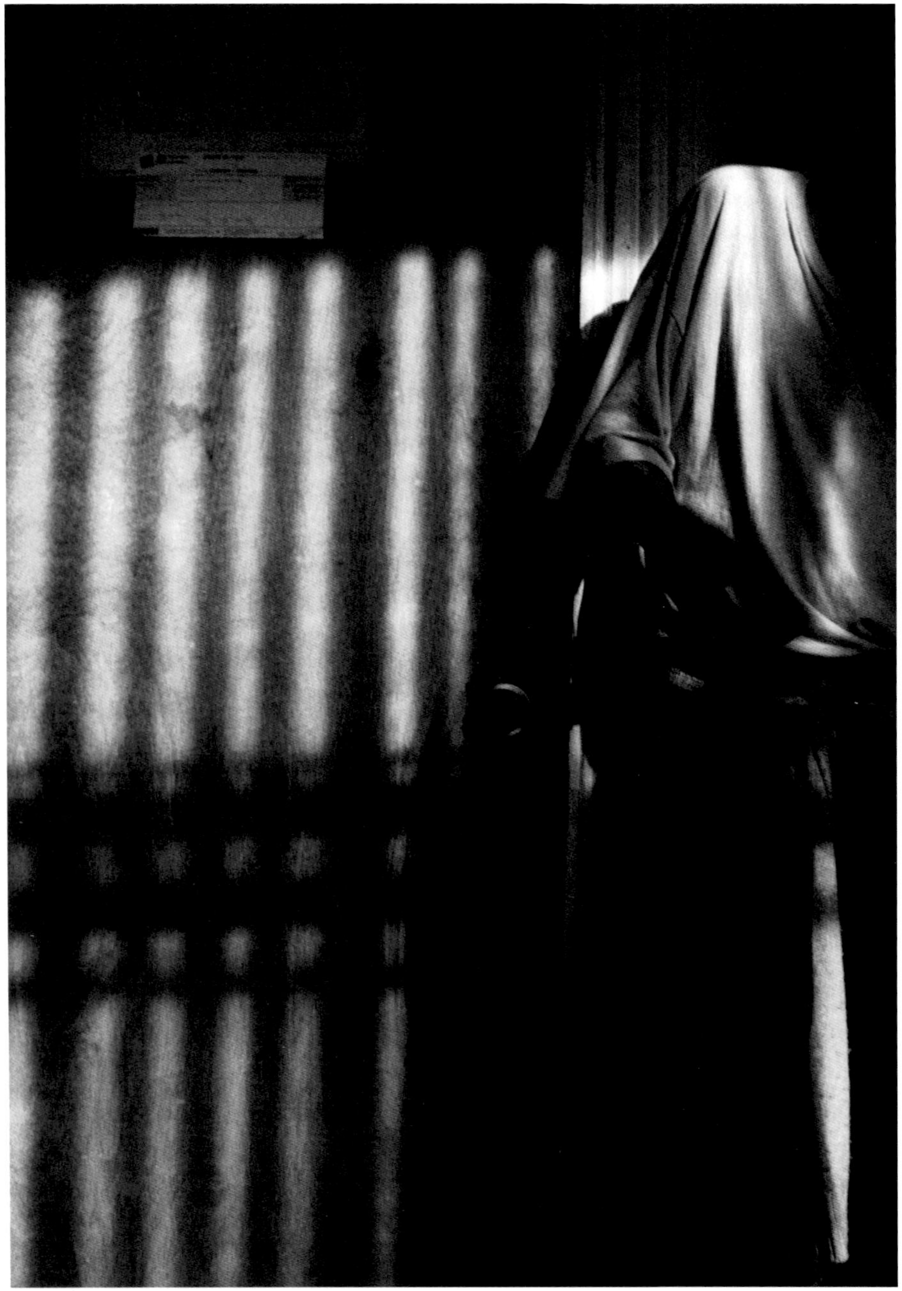

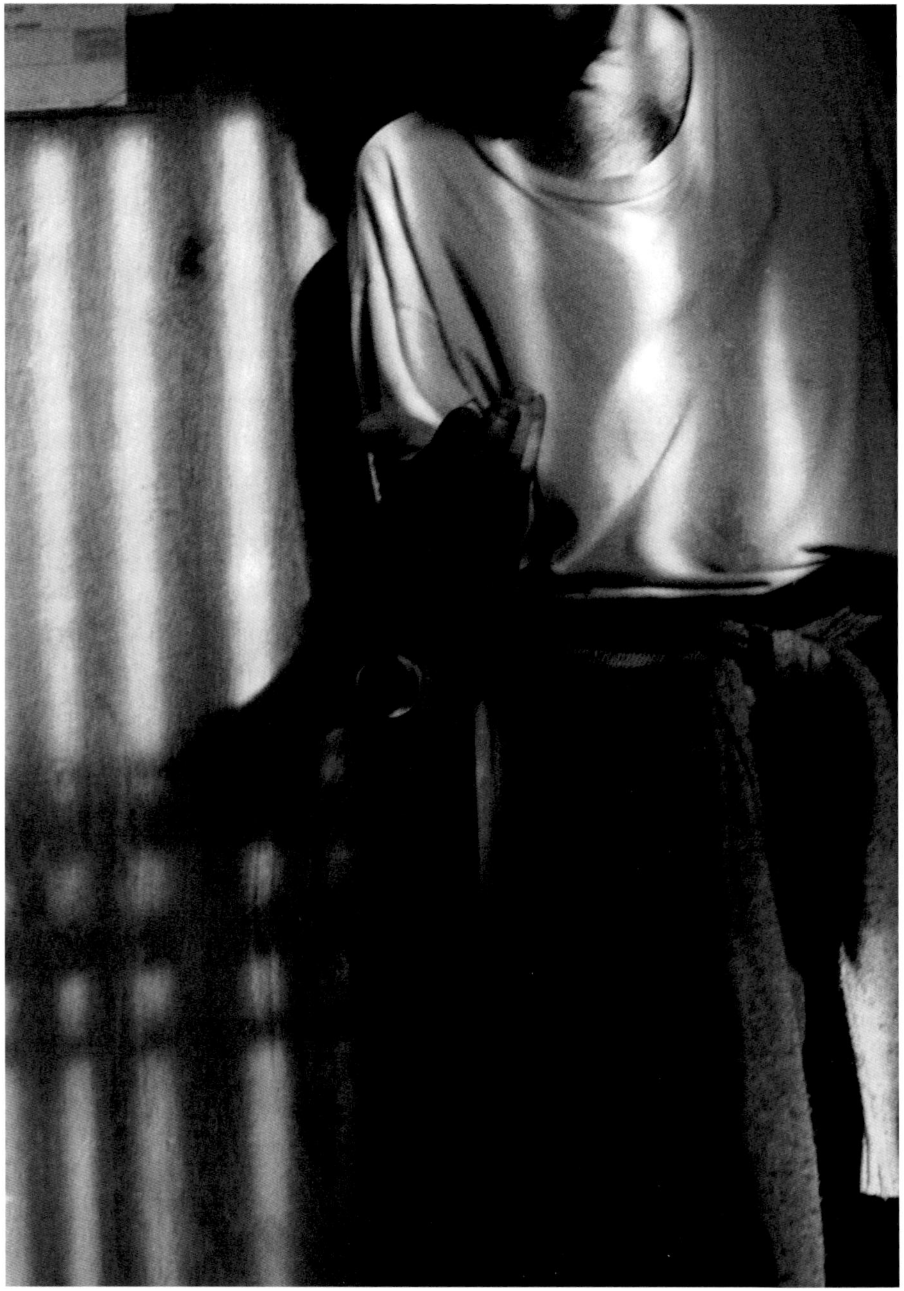

THERE IS LOVE,
  and it is long + generous
IT WATCHES THE LOVER
  with careful eyes;
NOT trying to assess
  the value of the
emotion;
  not anticipating to deny;
There is love, that is
  new, sometimes forbidden
that digs from the source
and scrunises upon the course
it will take
within the blinking of
  an eye;
if true love tends
  to forget,
then, it wasn't watching
  very closely.

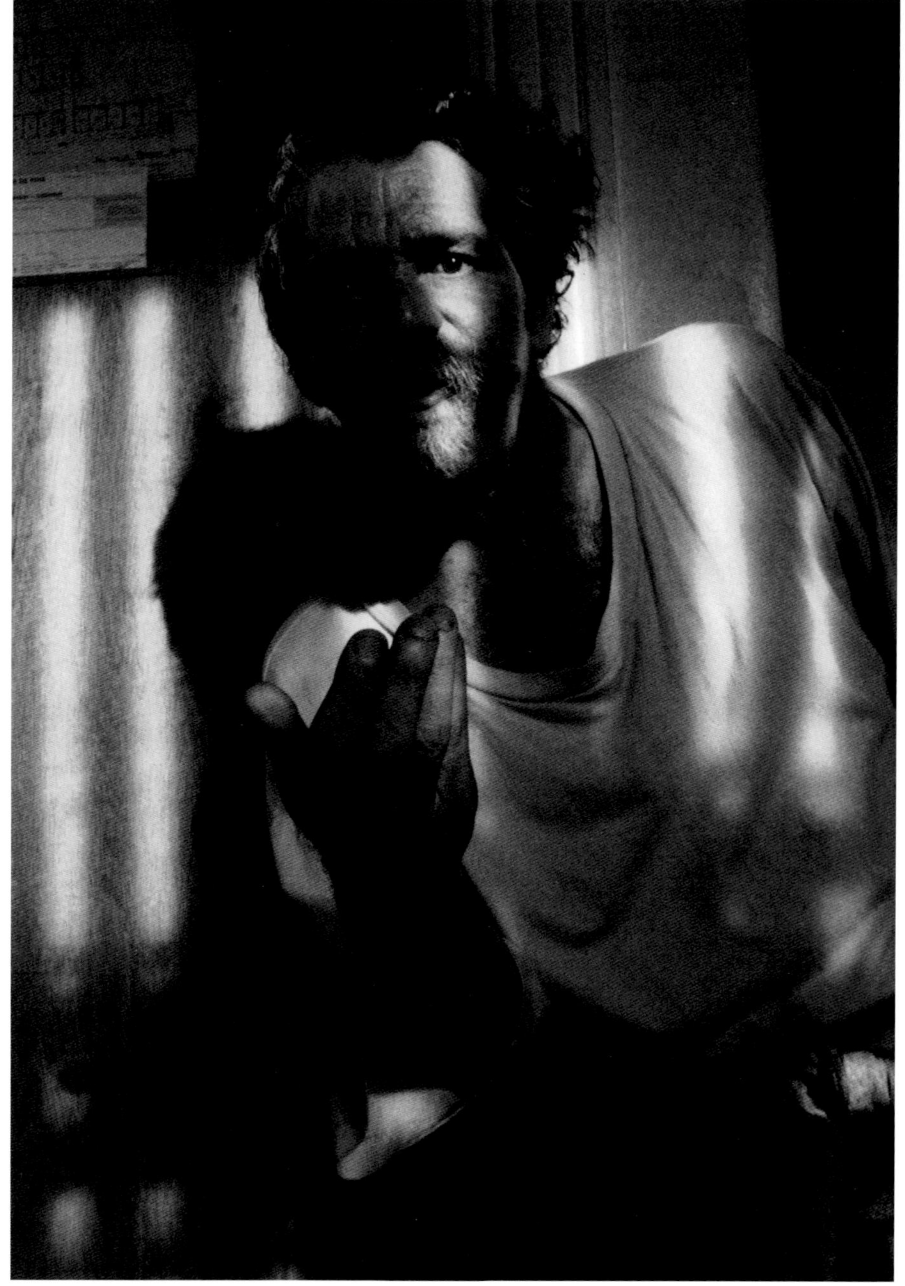

THERE is so,
many things
THAT will sink
beneath
the waves of
my understanding;
and still,
the great stars
roll in motion
against the
ethos;
that which is the
space between
the stars,
and most living things:
Ugliness rises up
and completes ~~the~~
perfection,
sometimes I see
ugliness, I think
it is perfect.

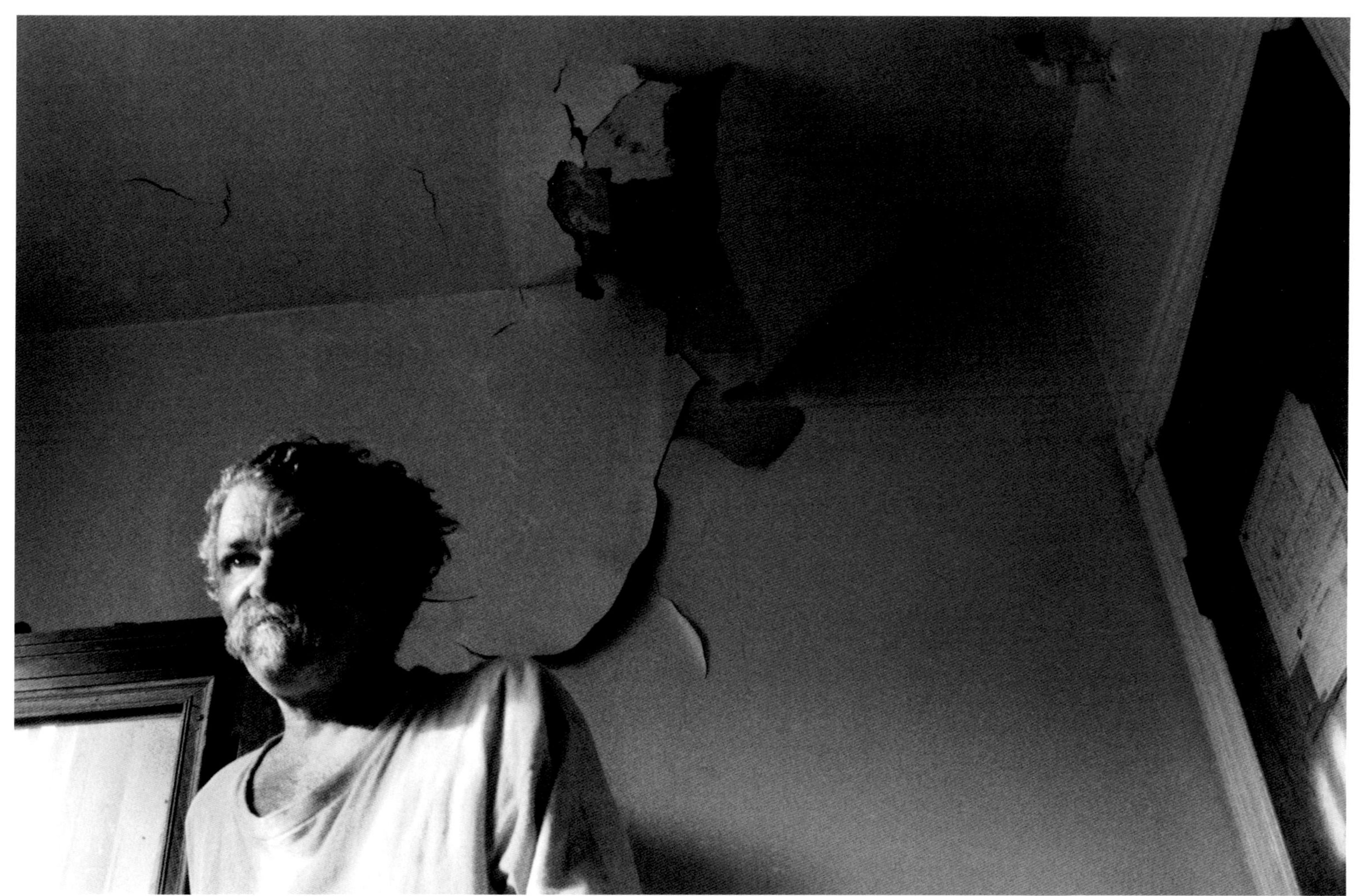

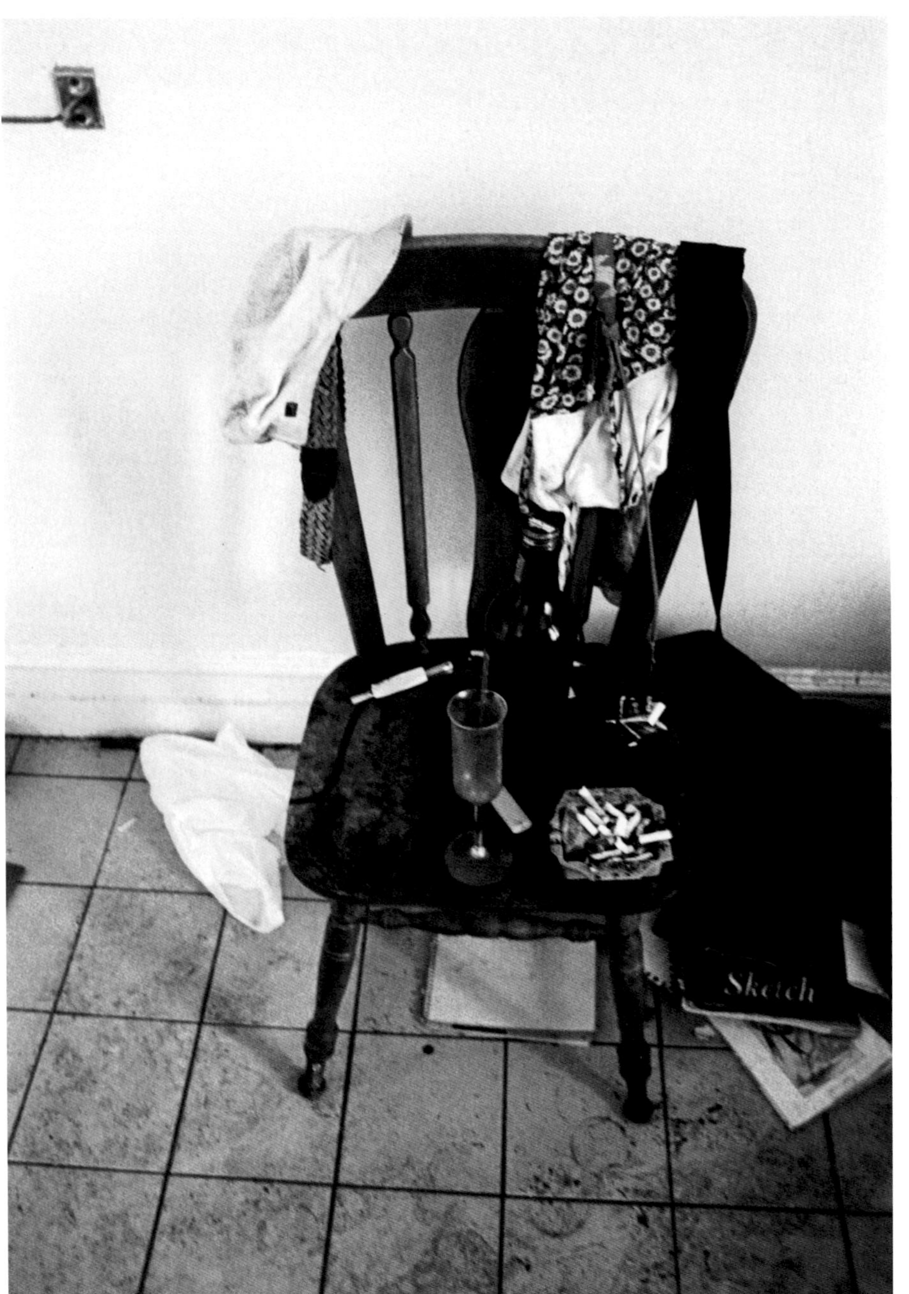

To stare darkness
in the face;
oh, what I do
not understand;
black on white;
there is a RAiNbow
that tells me;
that darkness;
my mis-understanding
will pass;
and I will

pass-over
all the other
estimates
that under-estimate
me;
the sky has clouds;
Does the sky like
this? No....
but they are there.

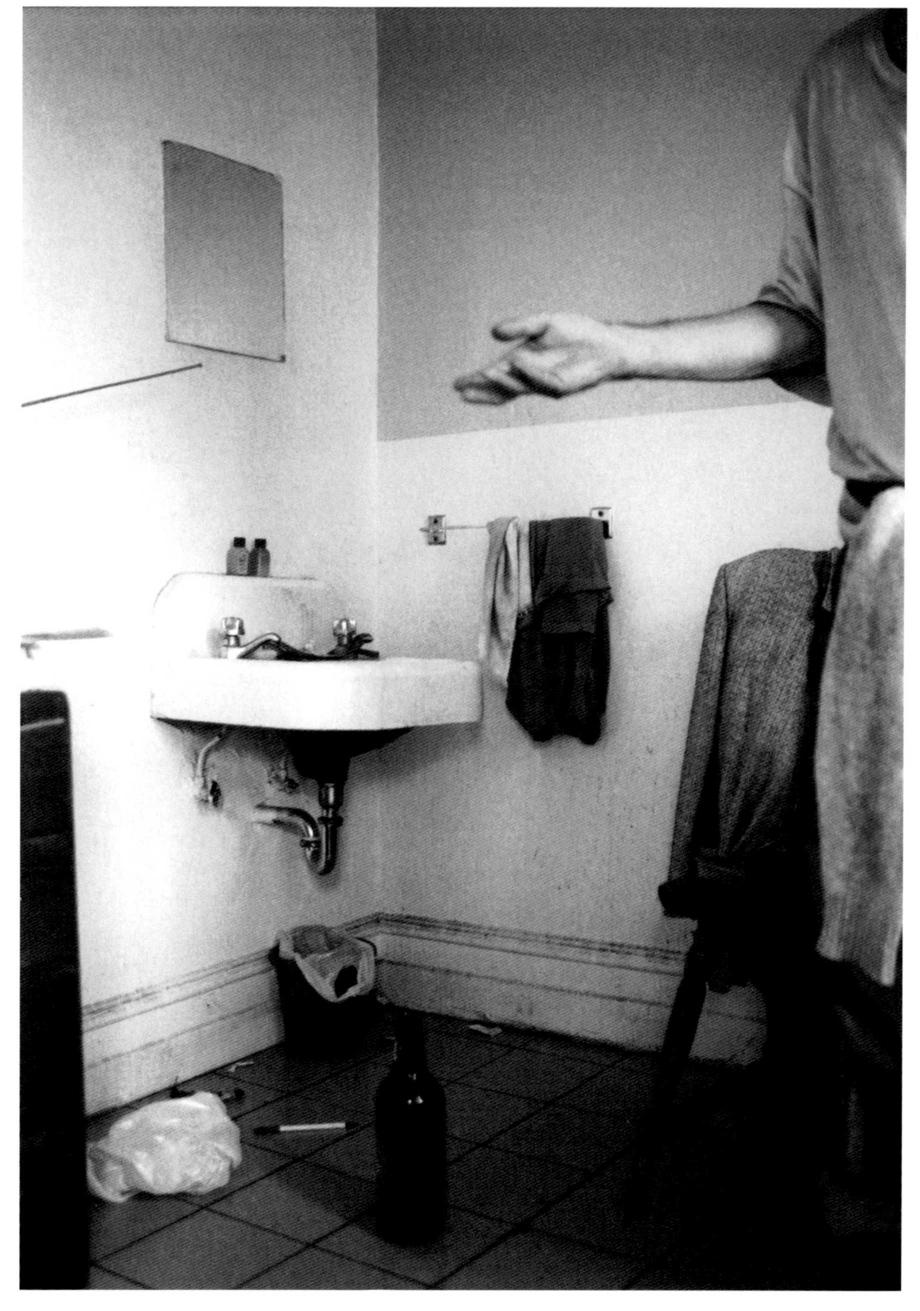

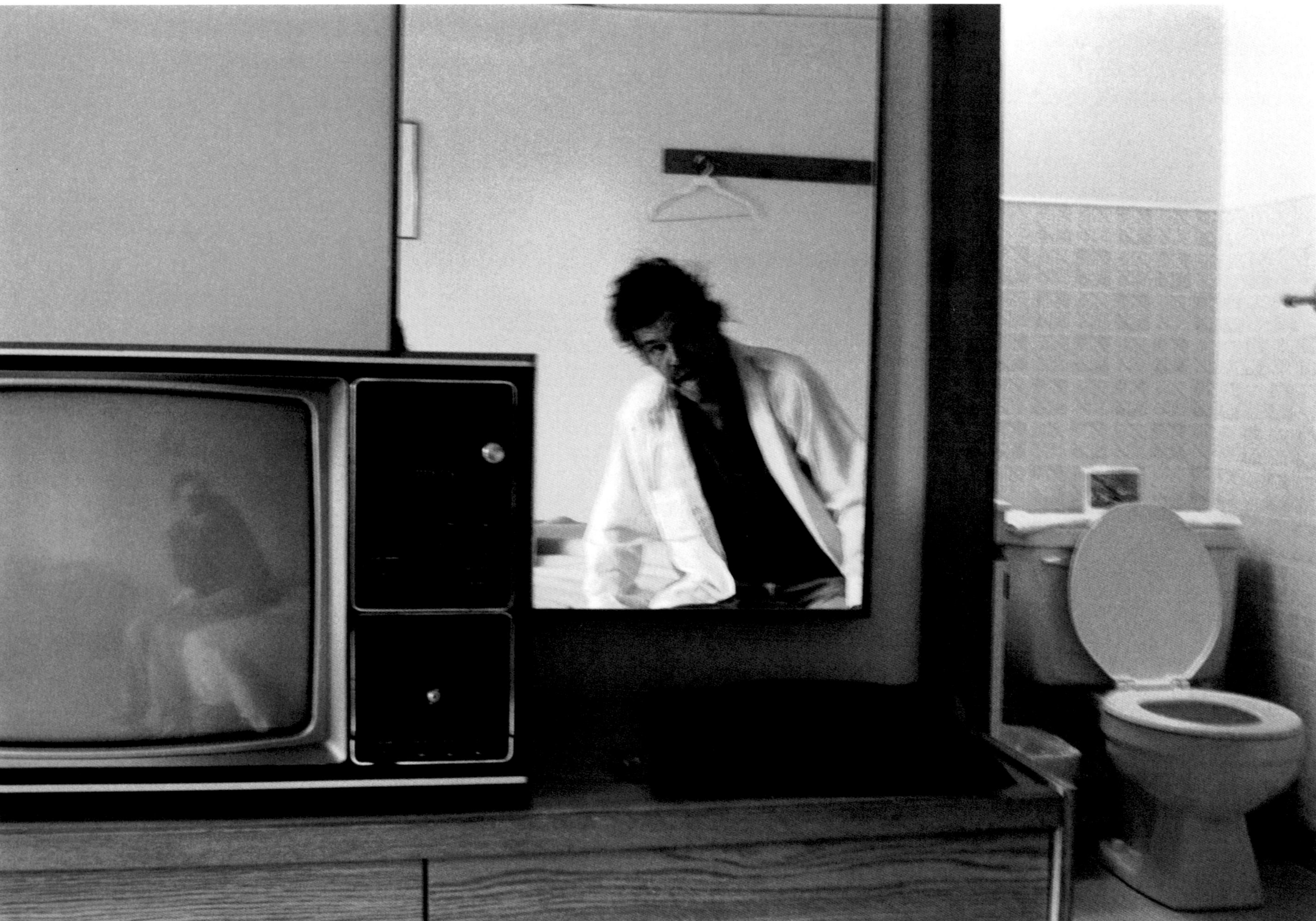

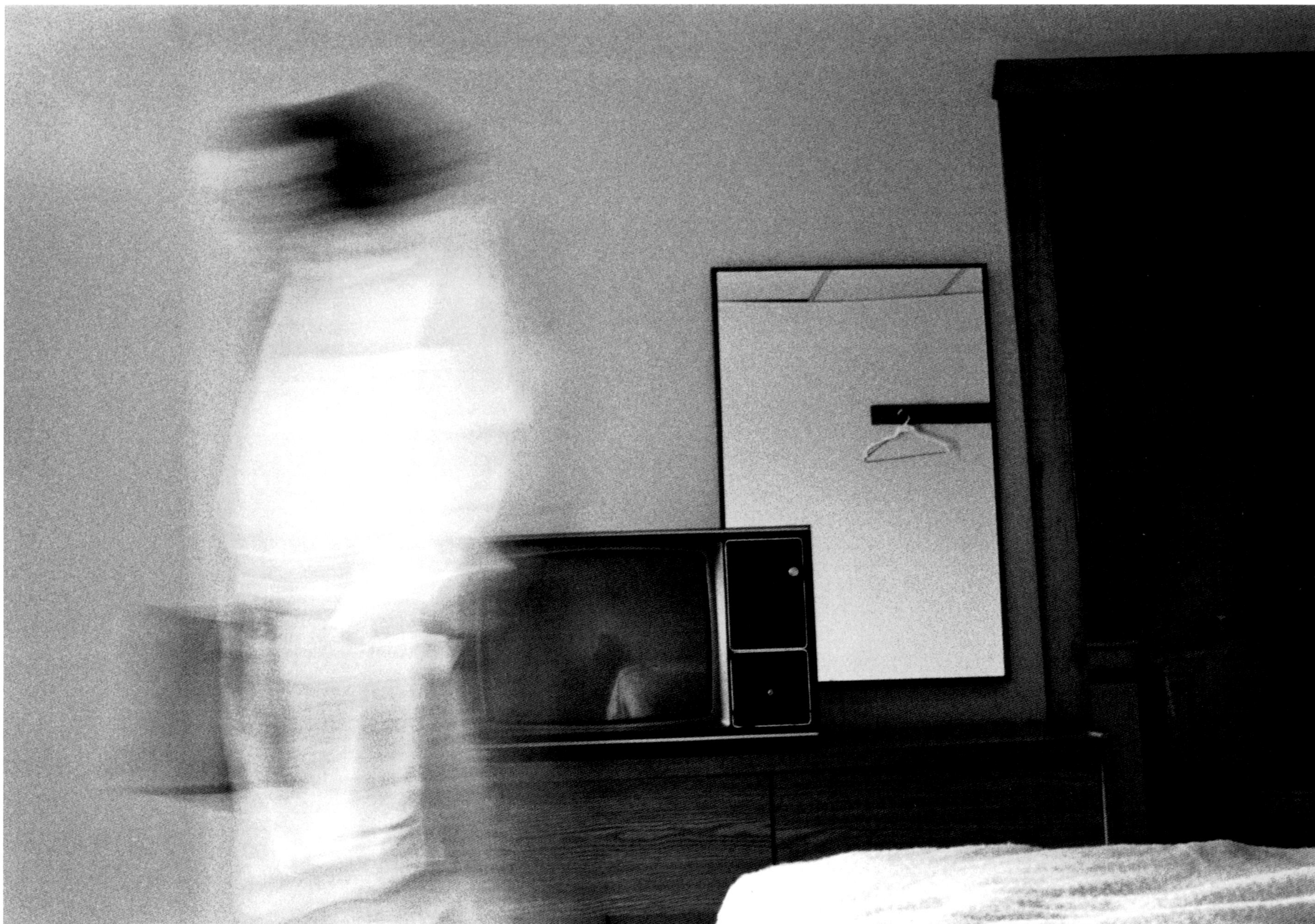

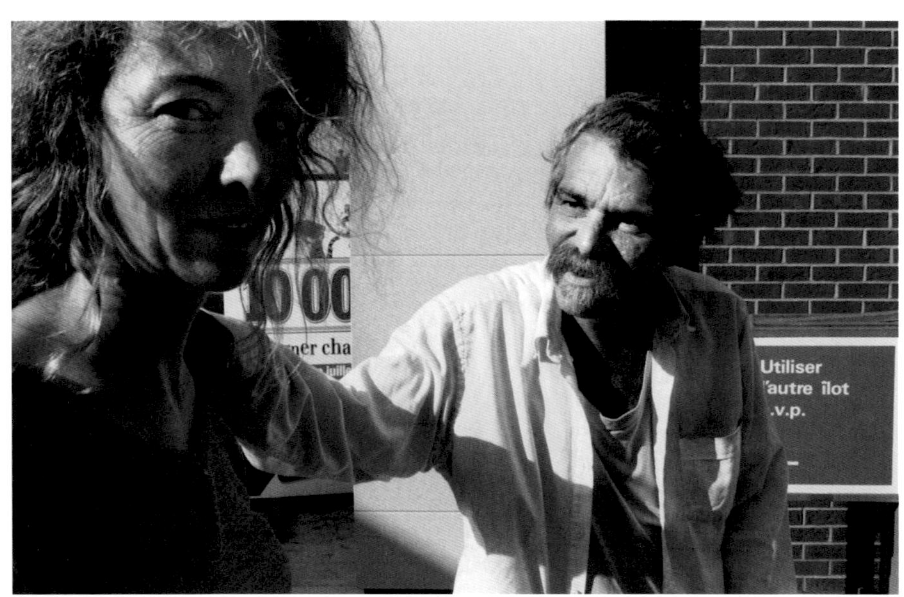
Utiliser
l'autre îlot
.v.p.

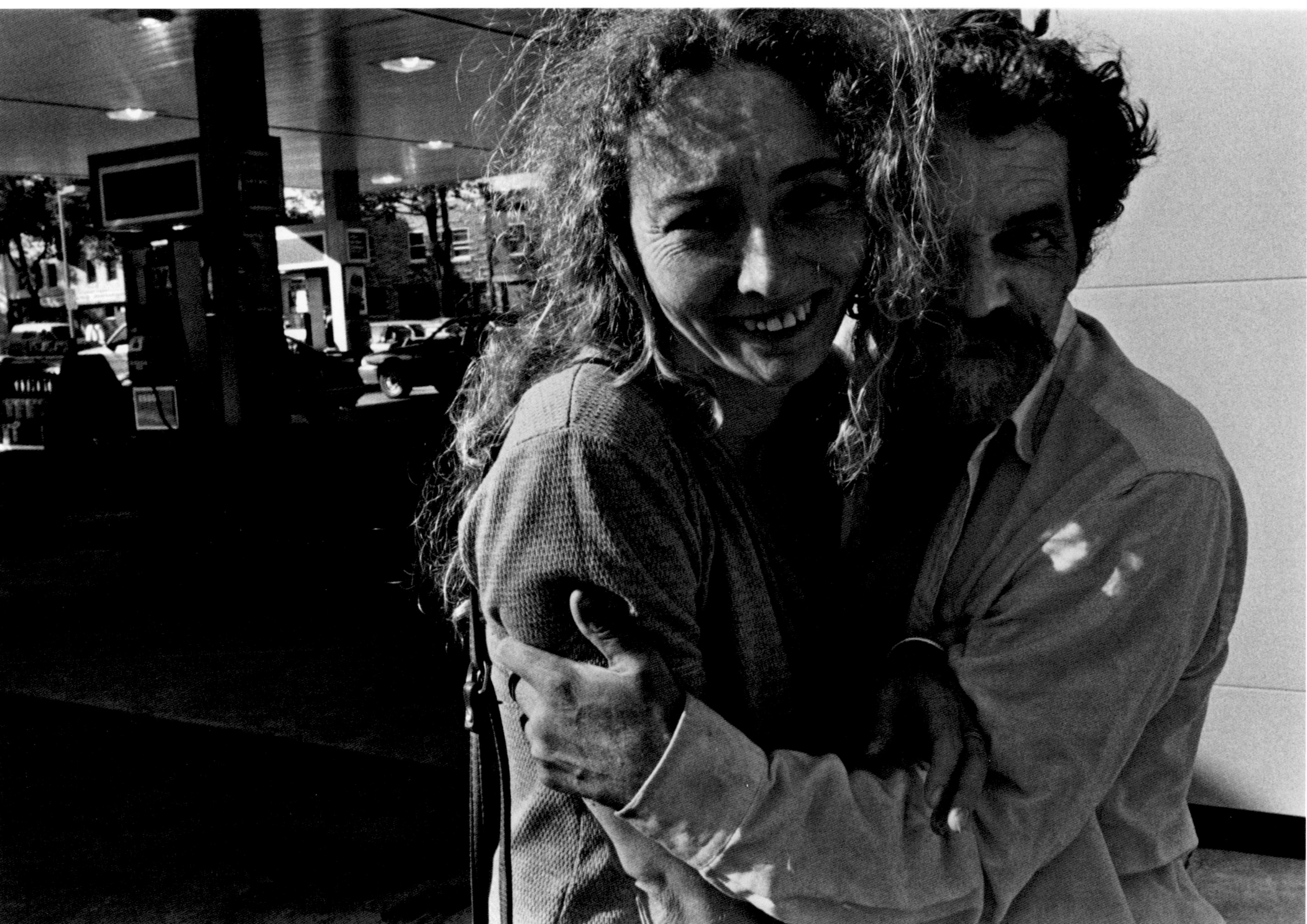

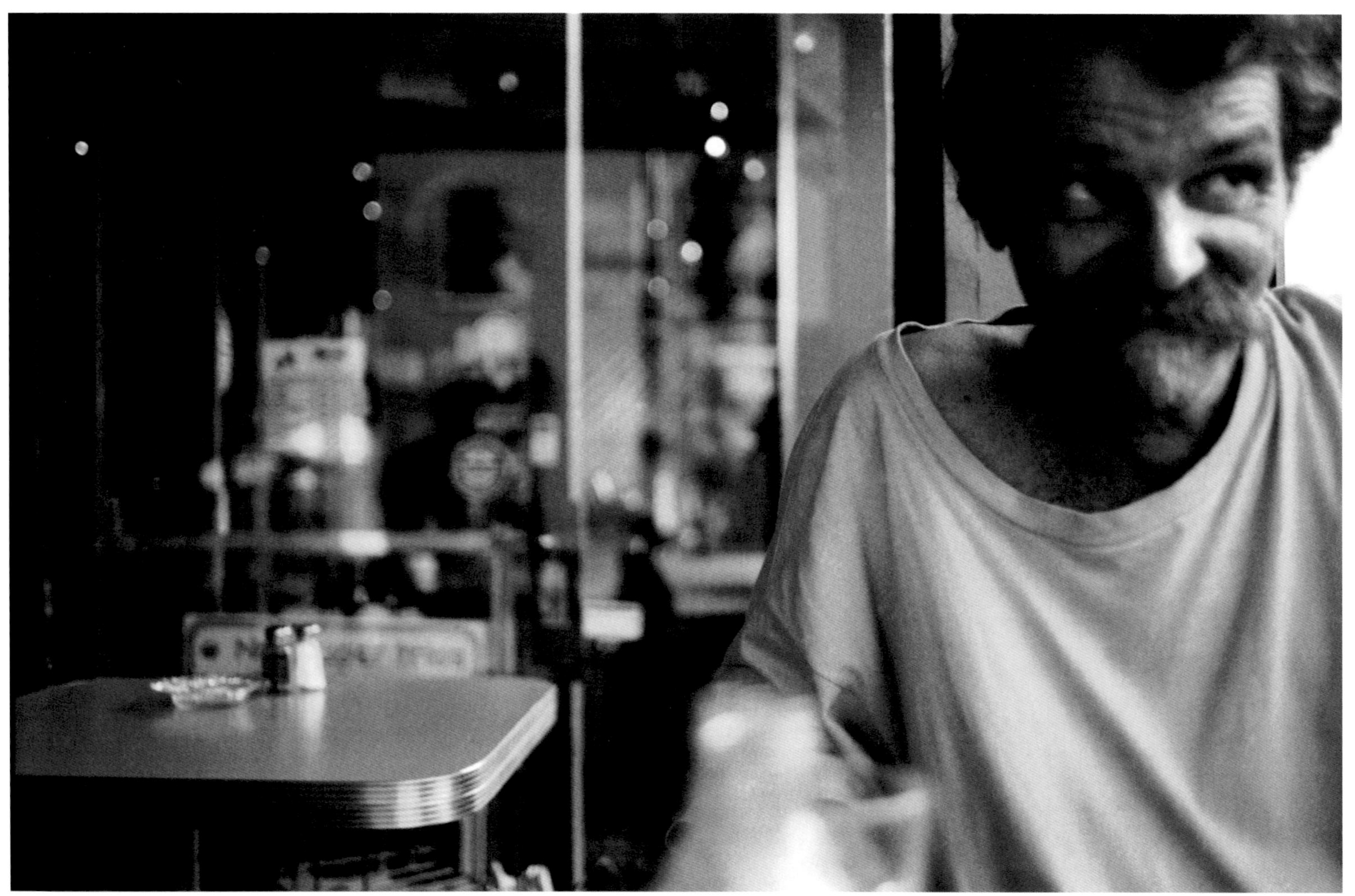

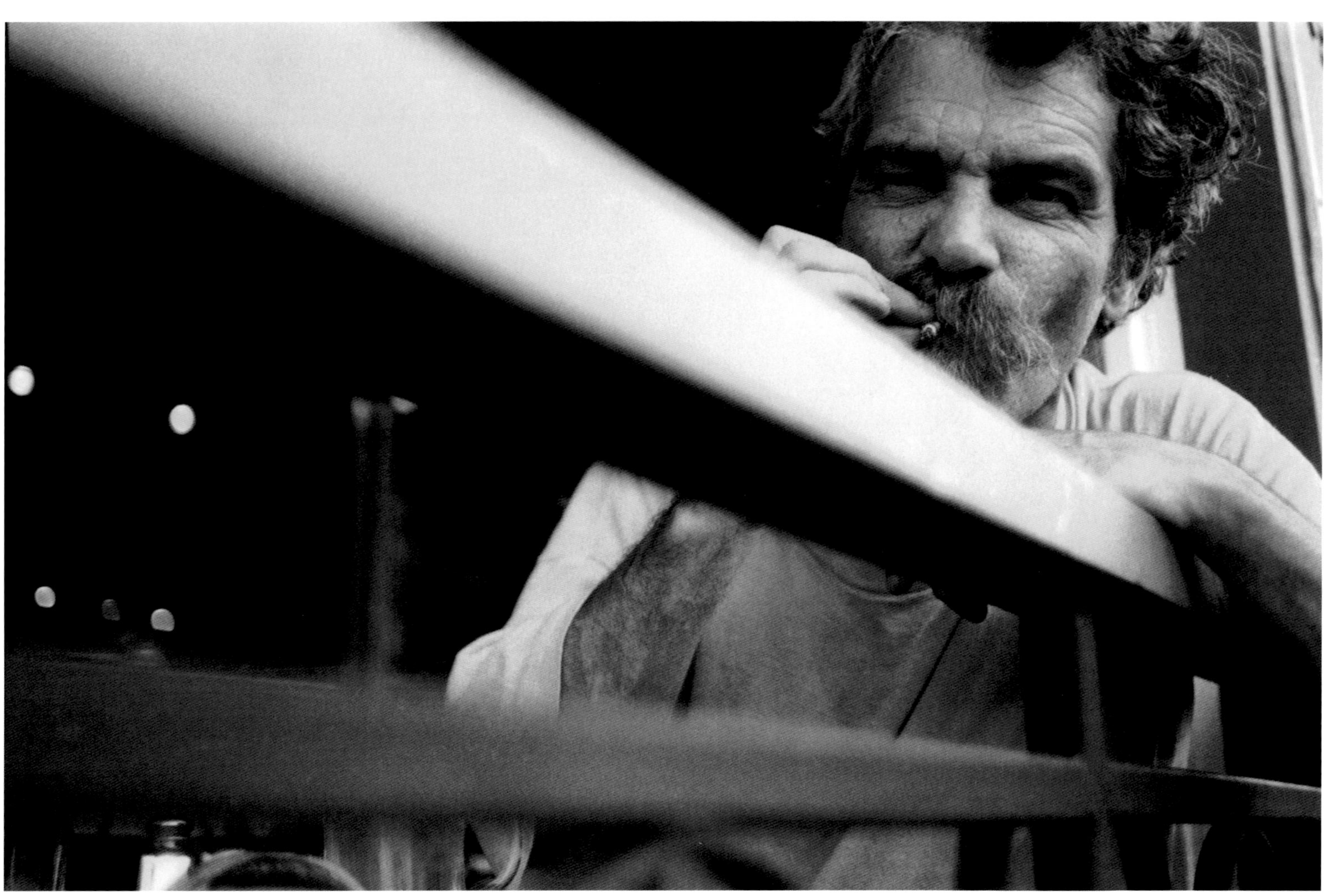

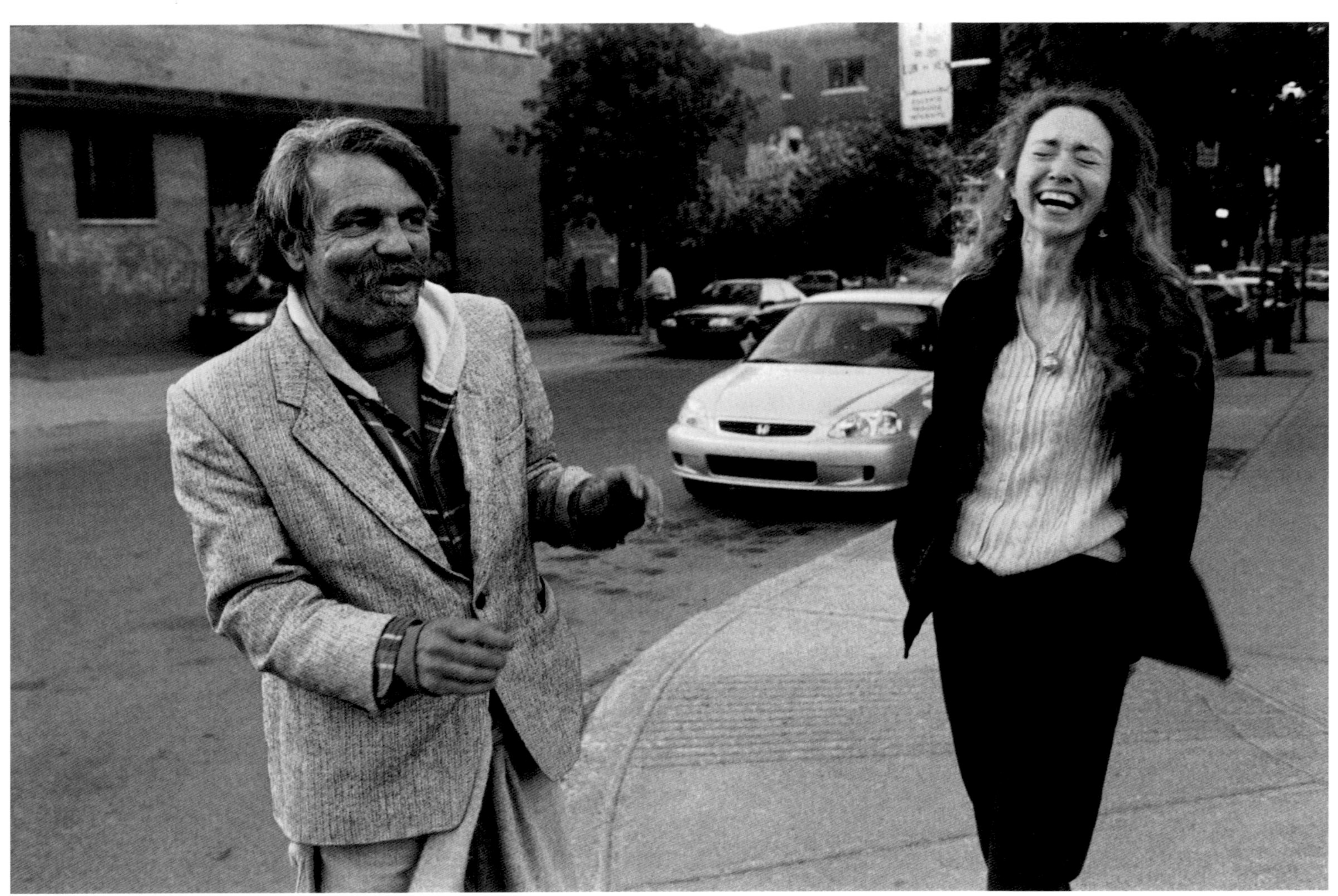

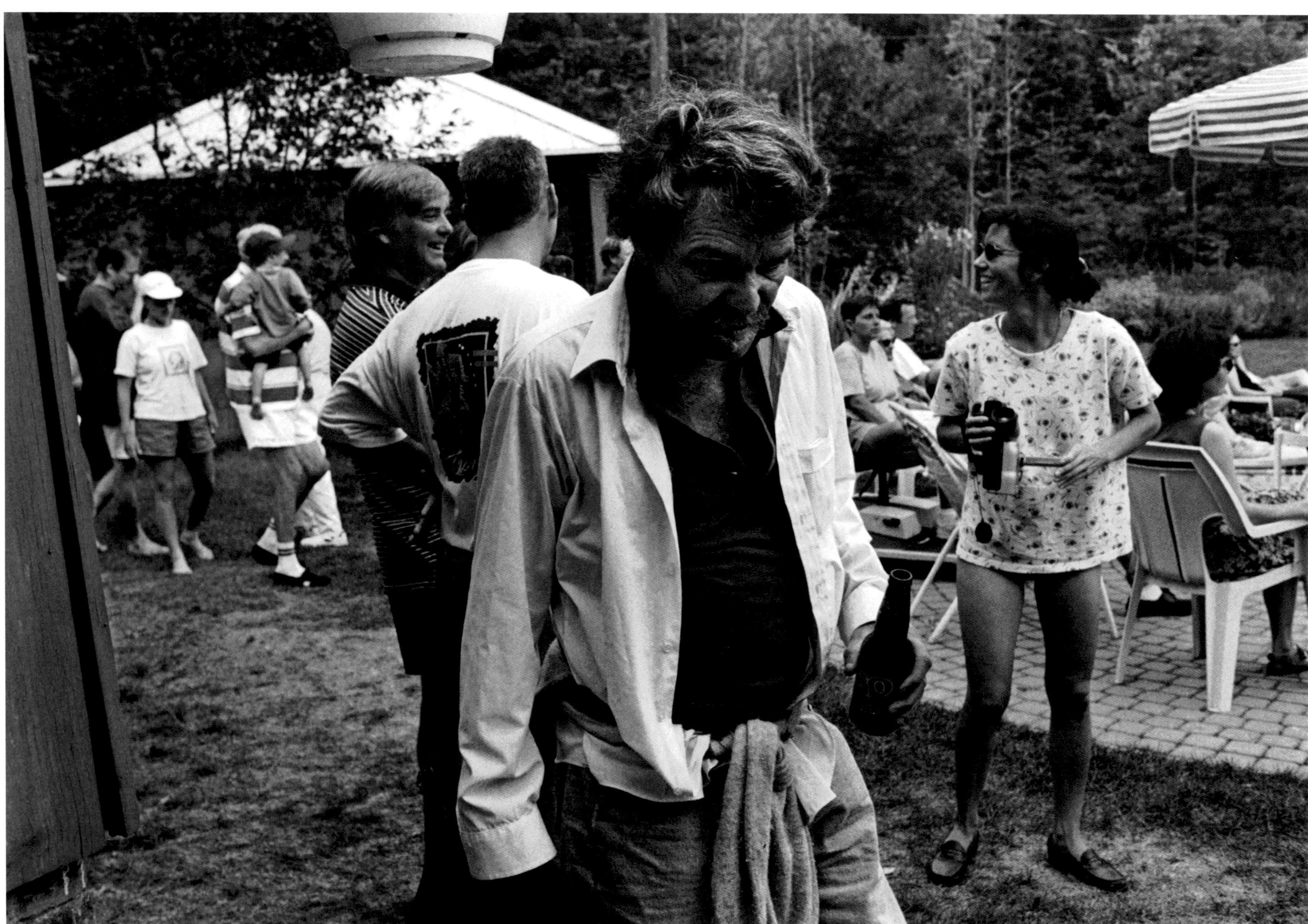

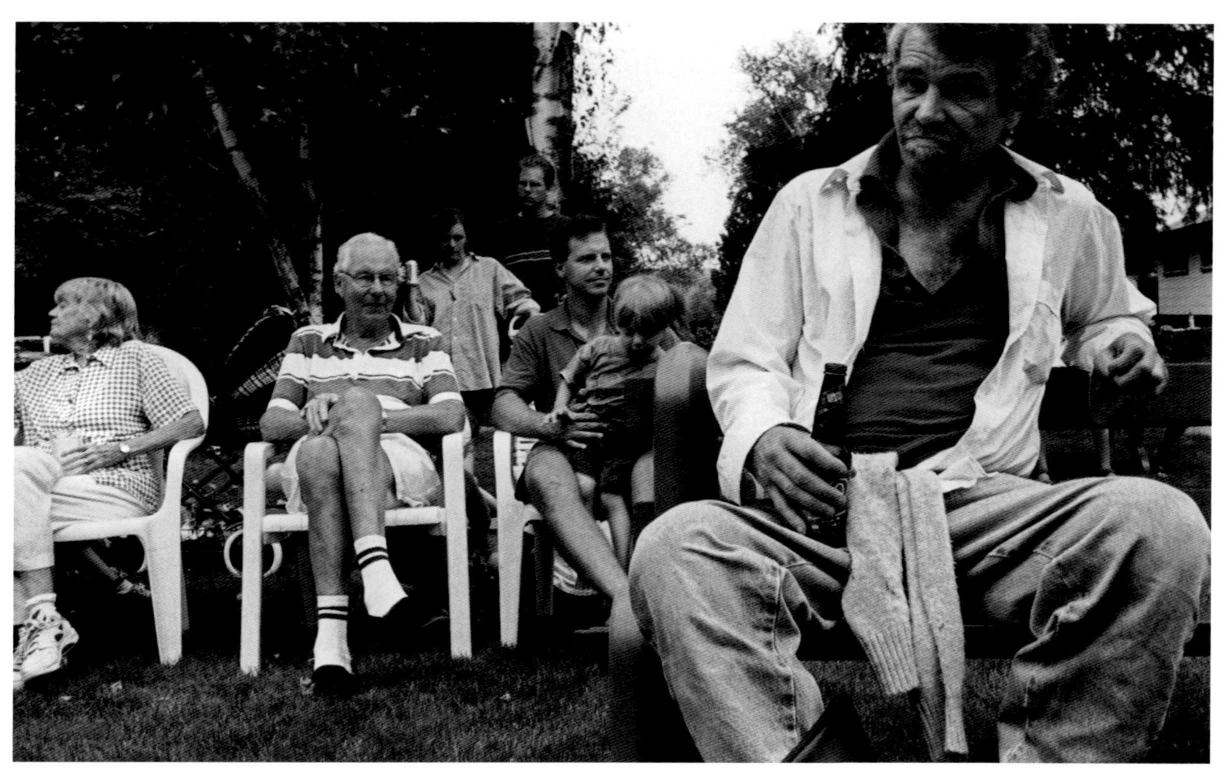

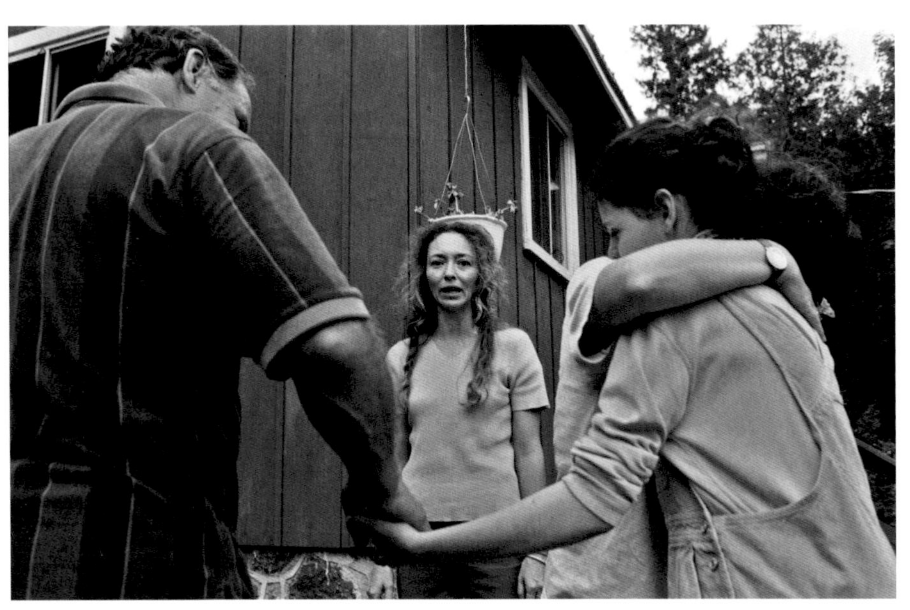

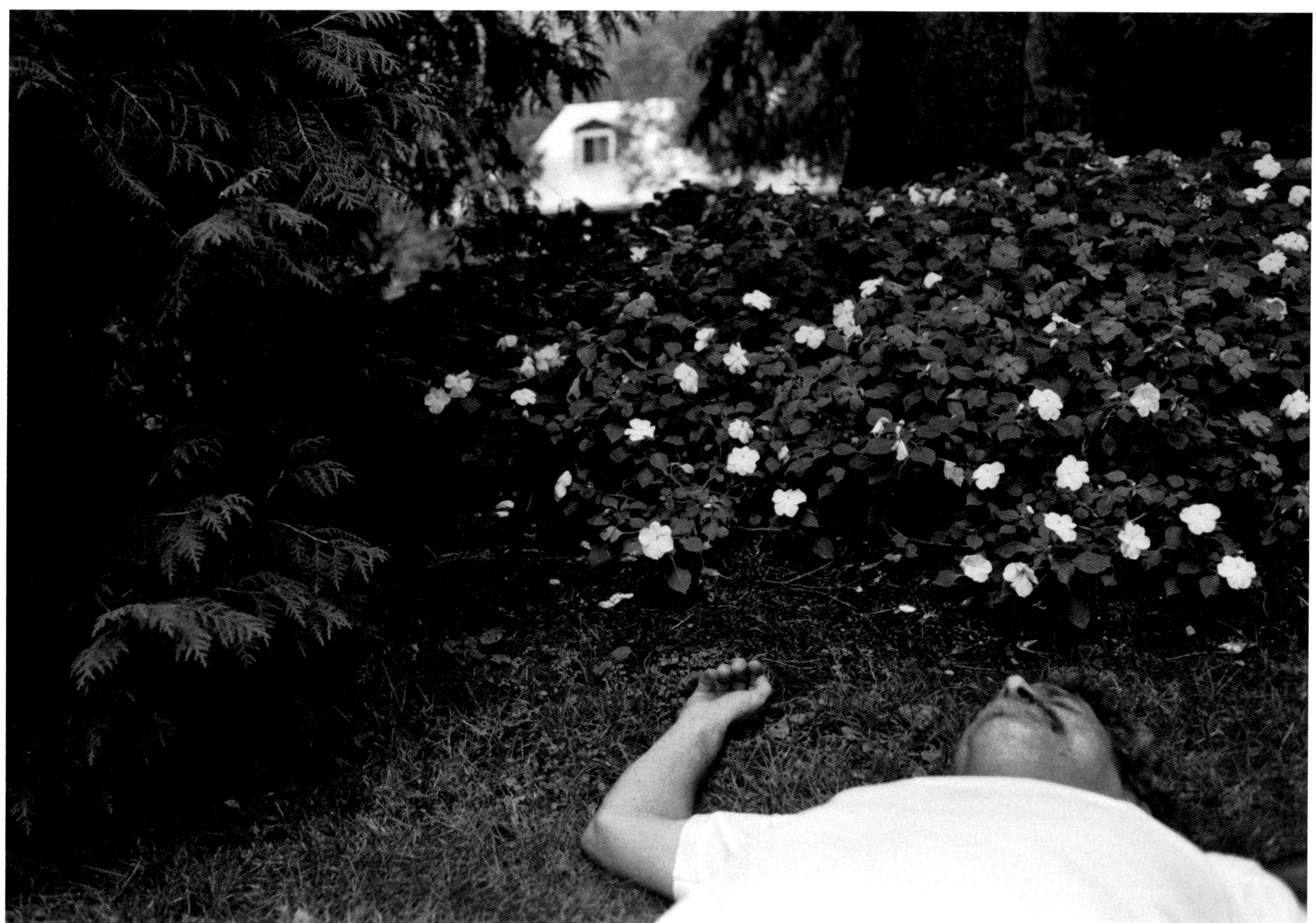

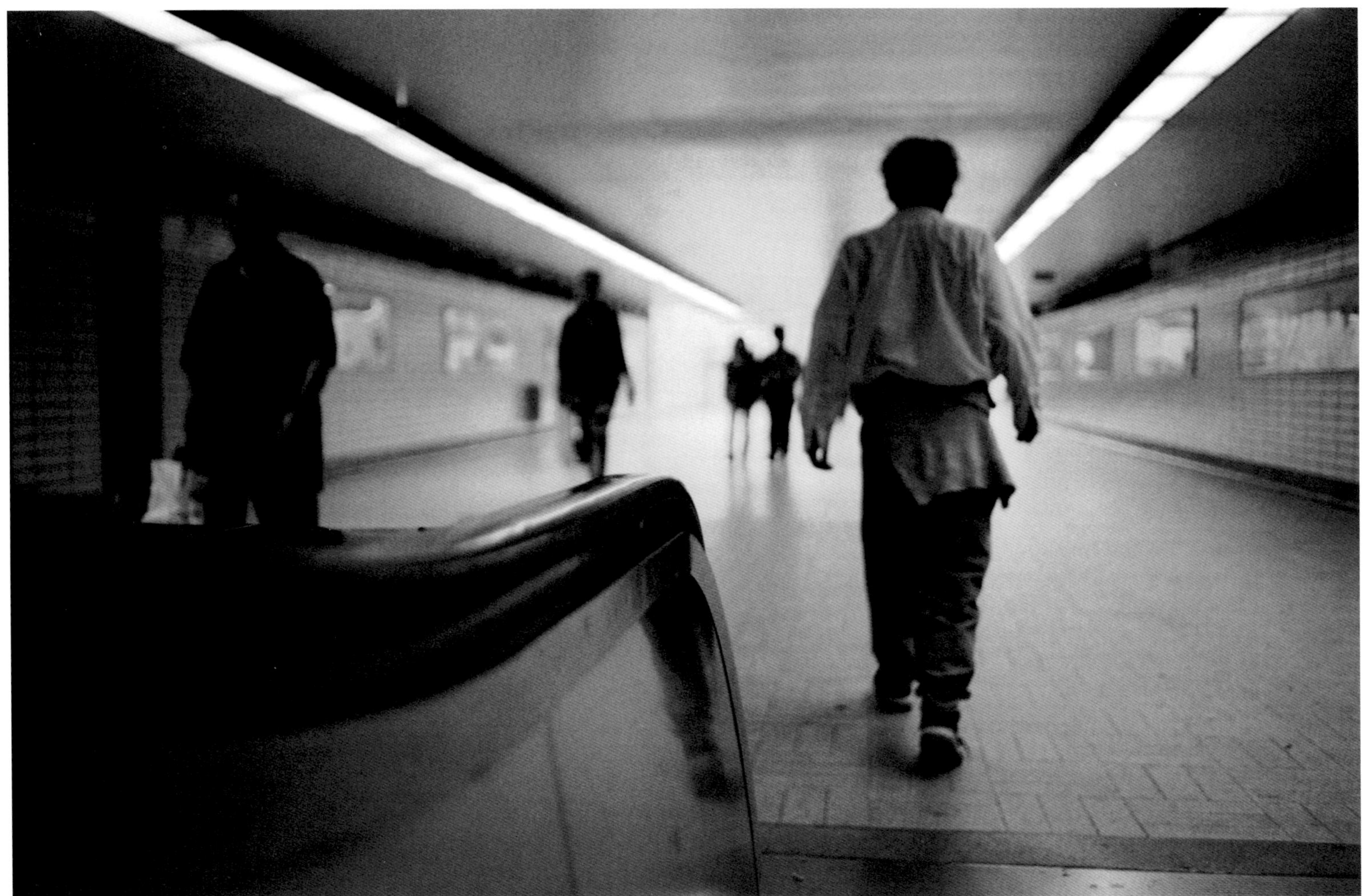

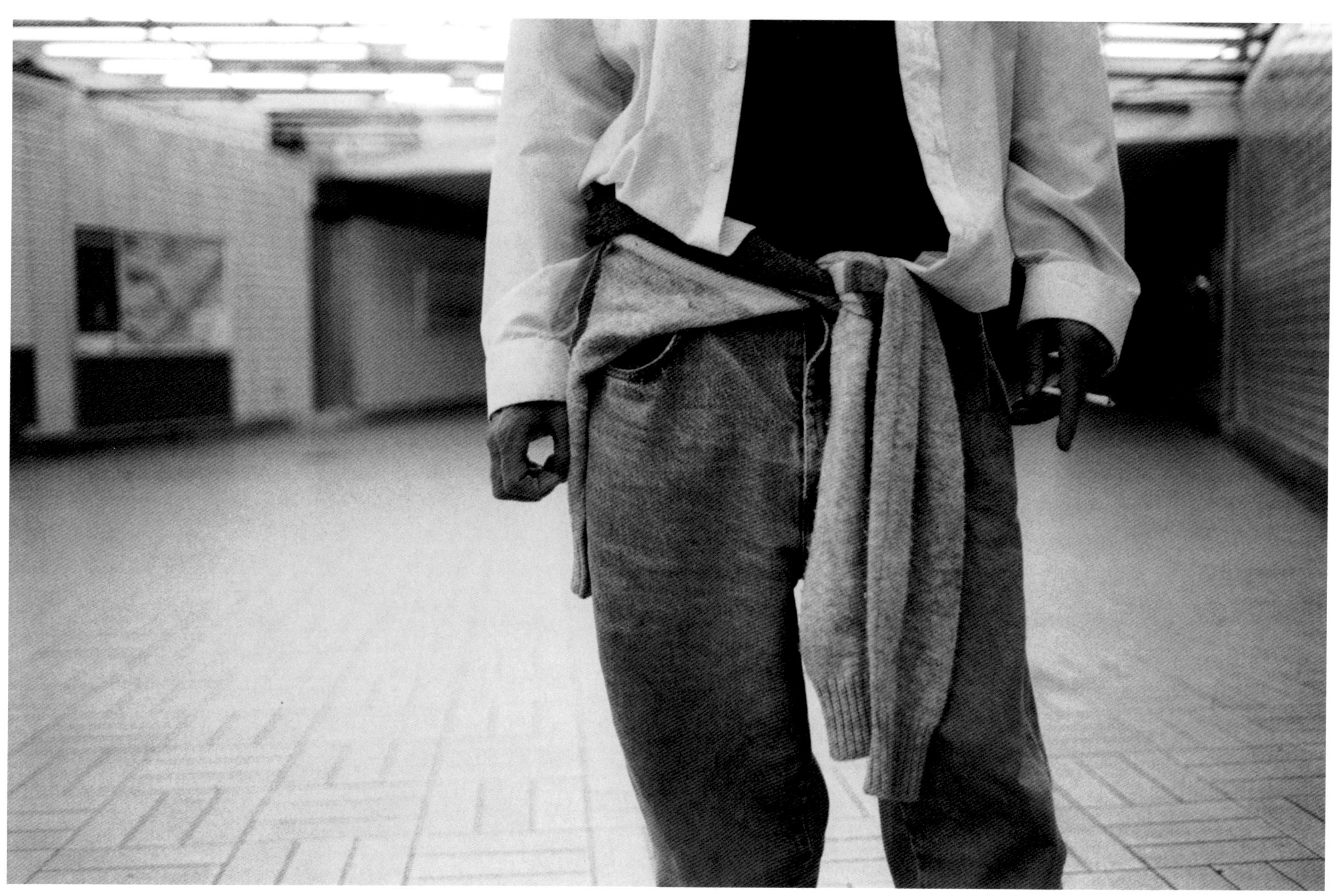

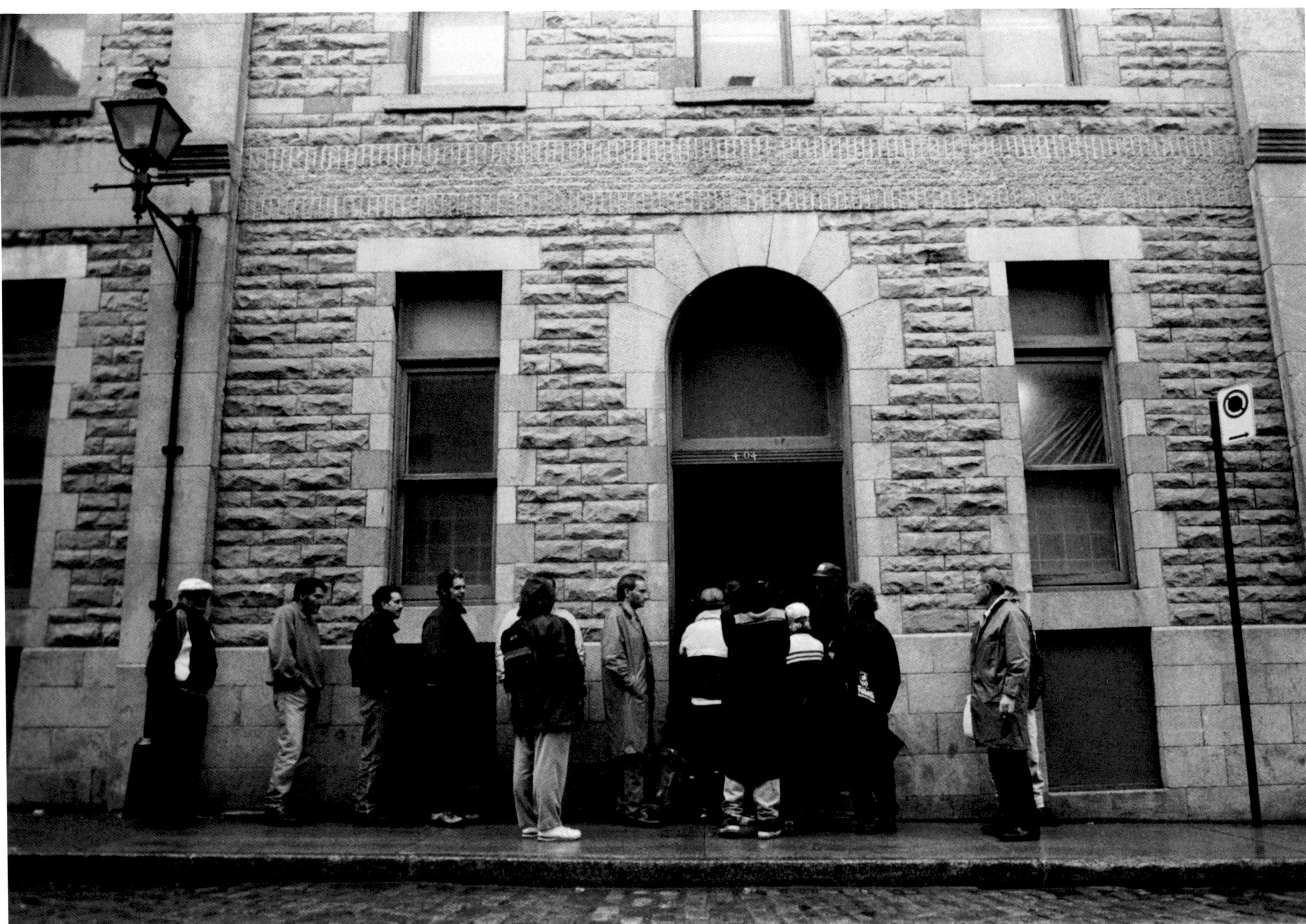

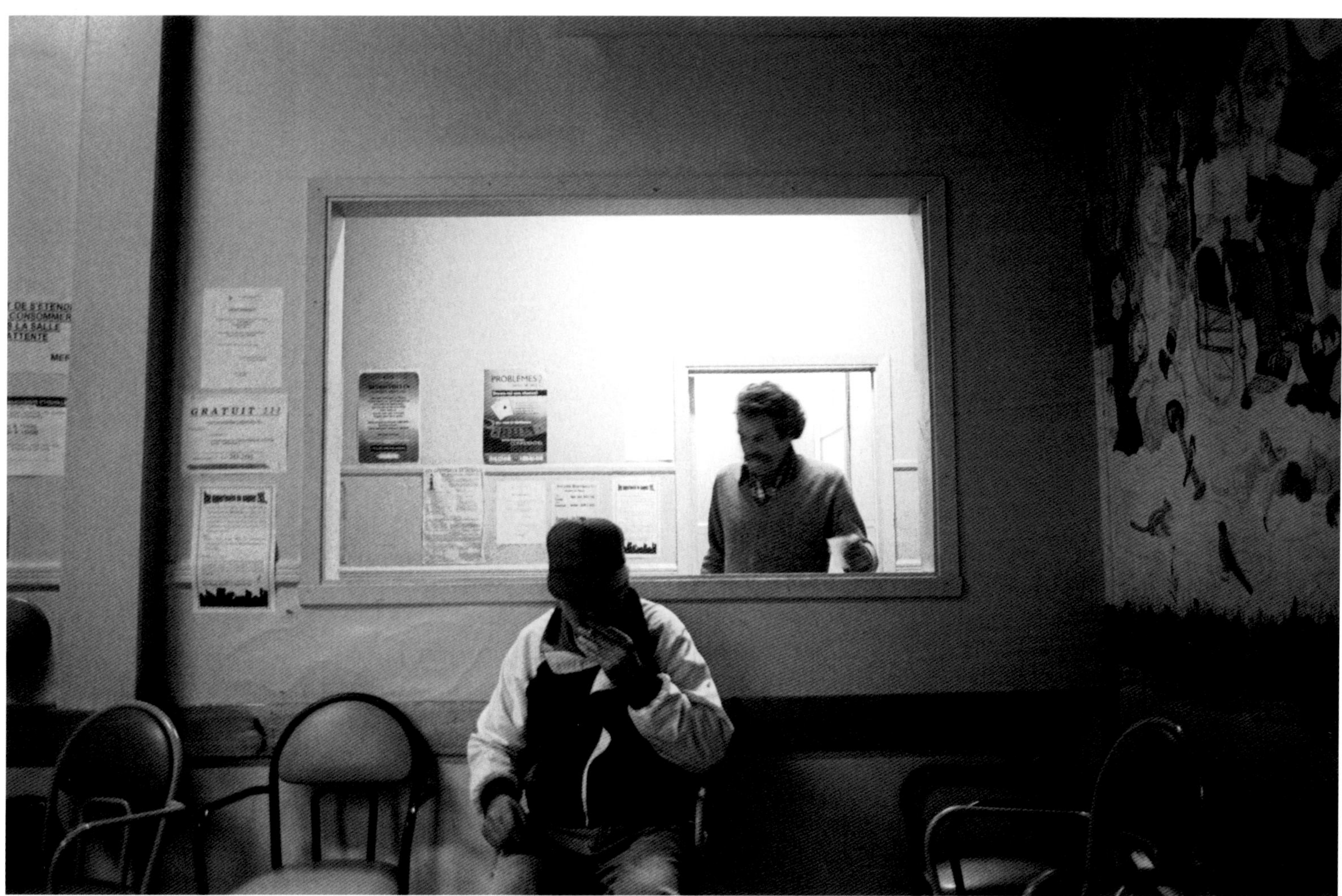

between the
   thoughts;
and, the sounds
of you and me;
there is a space;
space is the lover
    of the silence;
silence is the lover
that sootles your
    thoughts;
captures the sounds
    of you and me;
when we are
    talking.

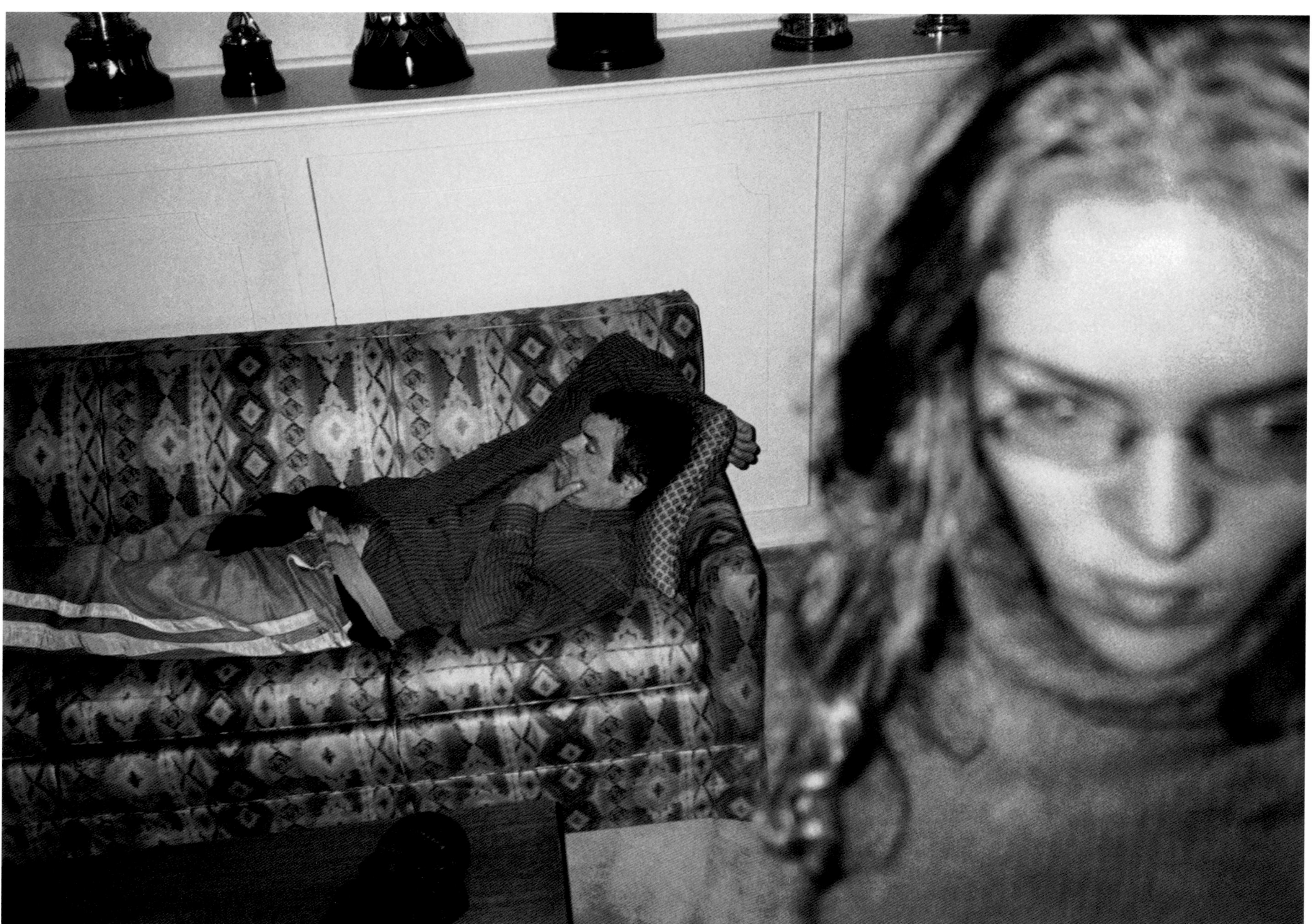

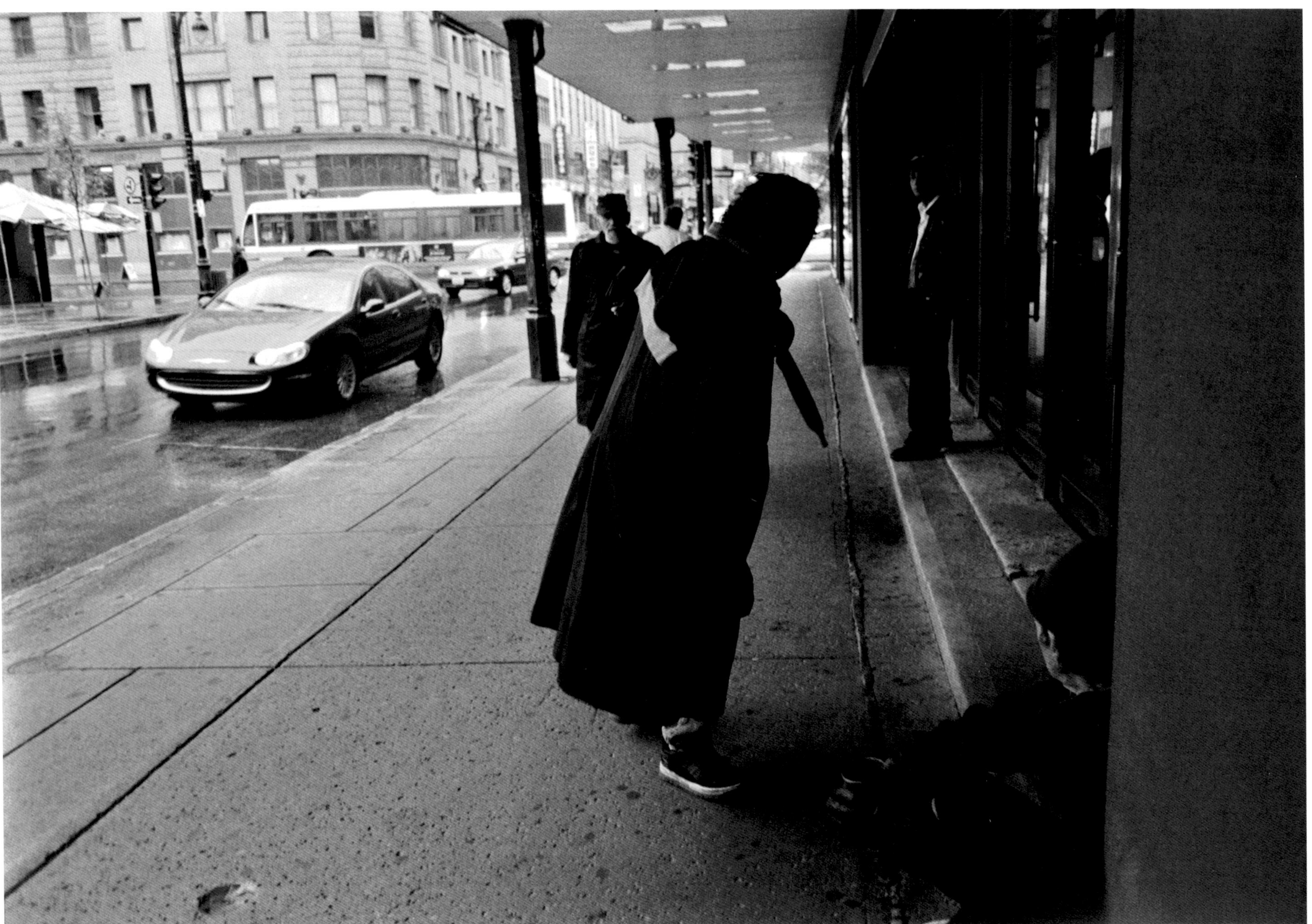

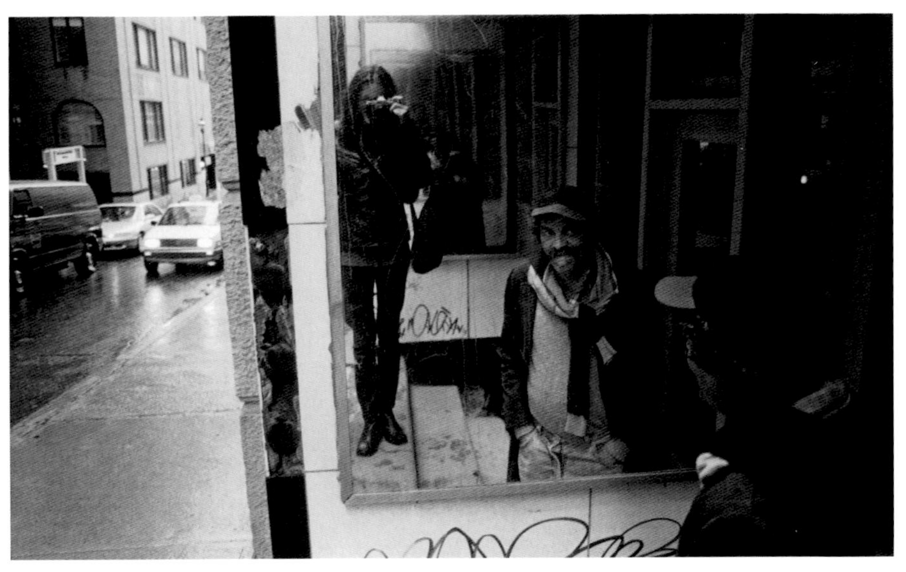

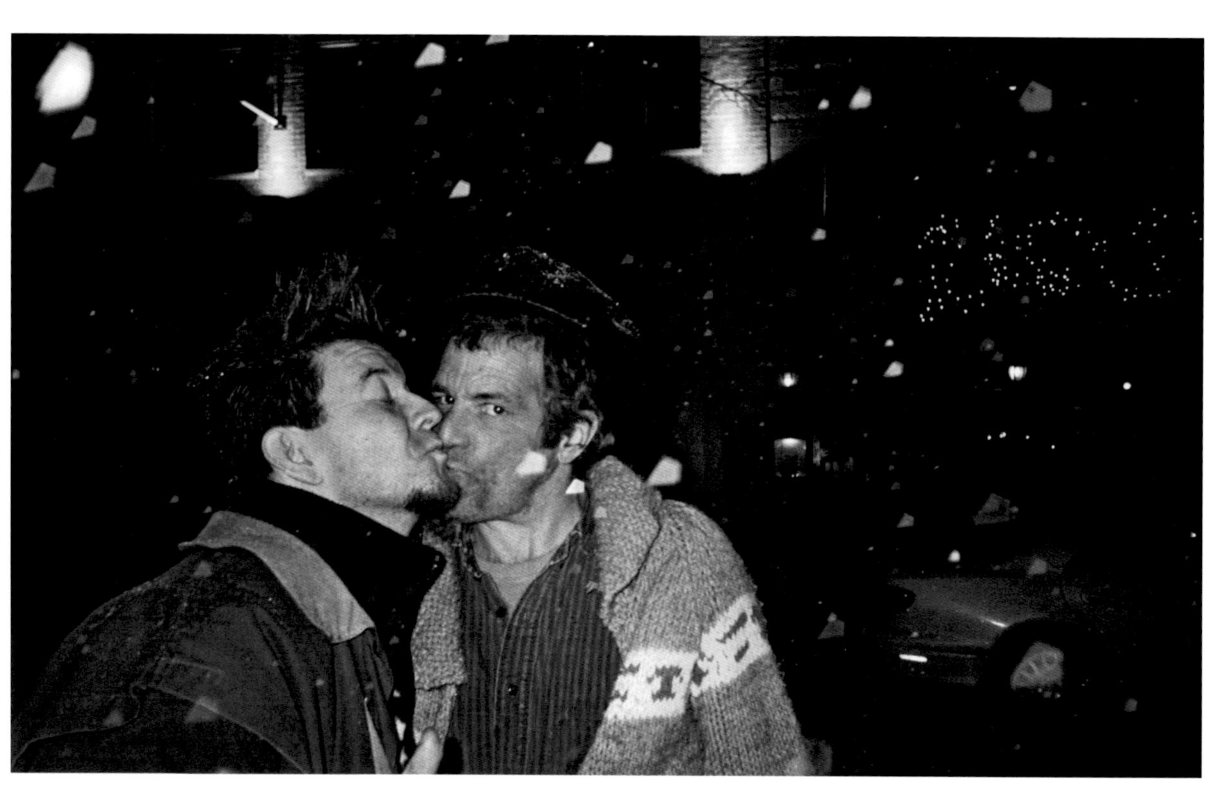

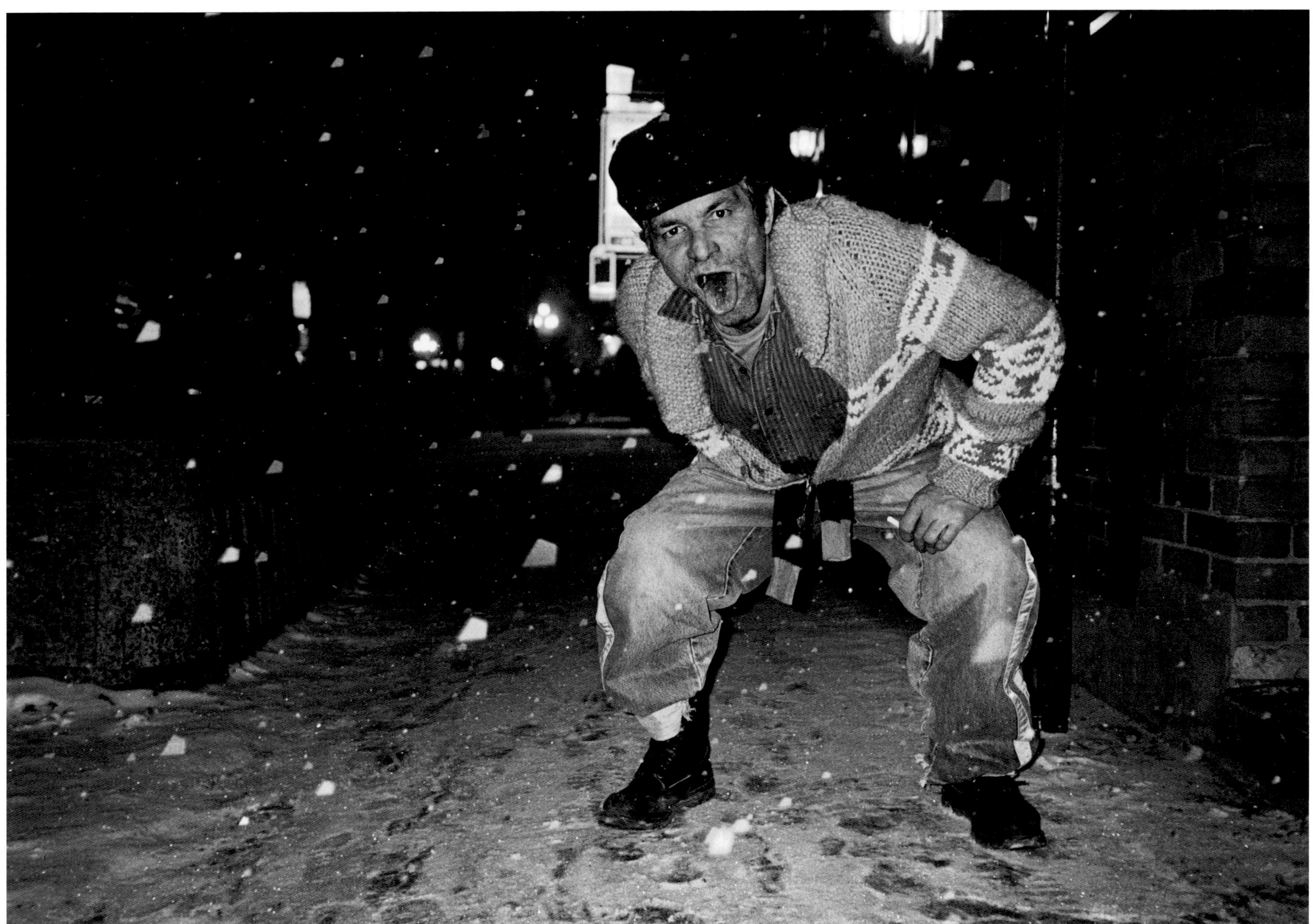

As I measure this
awareness,
the snow falls in a
milder chime;
so the consciousness
softens
        towards
the atmosphere, the changing
    times;
compared to God, to the balance
of morality;
Introspective in the frozen
cold;
Forgiveness comes easier;
and suffering is eased;
in the sorrow of the
strangers' eyes.

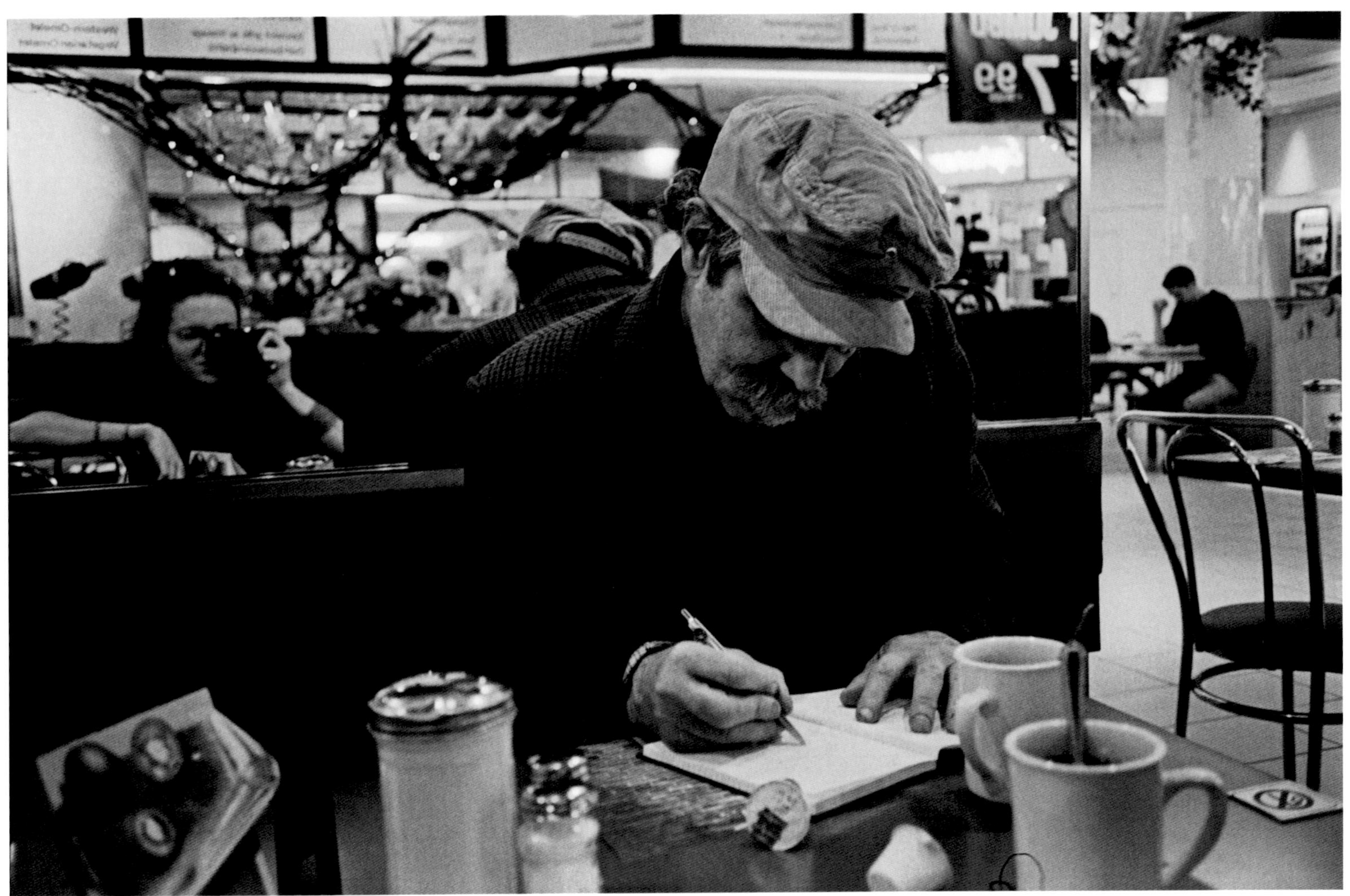

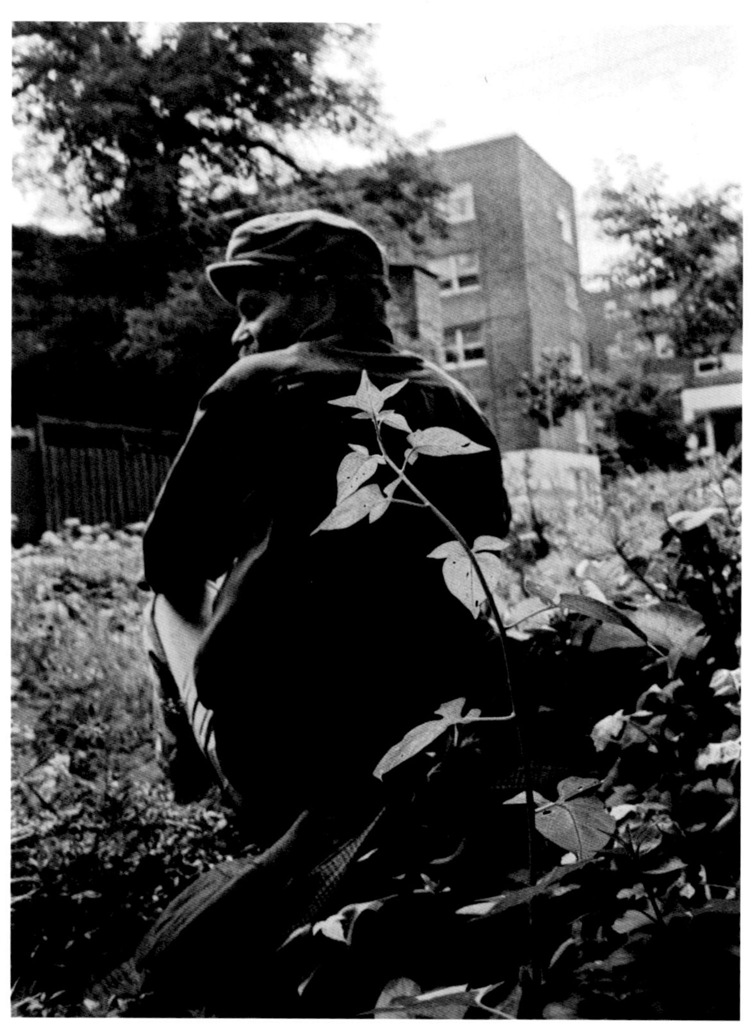

THE MOMENT OF THE SPARROWS

Sitting in a common field
on the university grounds
Sucking slowly at apple wine
        beneath the trees
I had been banished from
   the religious garden
     a day before;
Christ knows why; Christ
            forgives.
     Thats all I know.
   I was angry, seething in
         a strange silence
When the brethren came,
What amounted to forty sparrows
     surrounding me.
I never loved a sparrow
         until now
until I realised
   what affection they endow

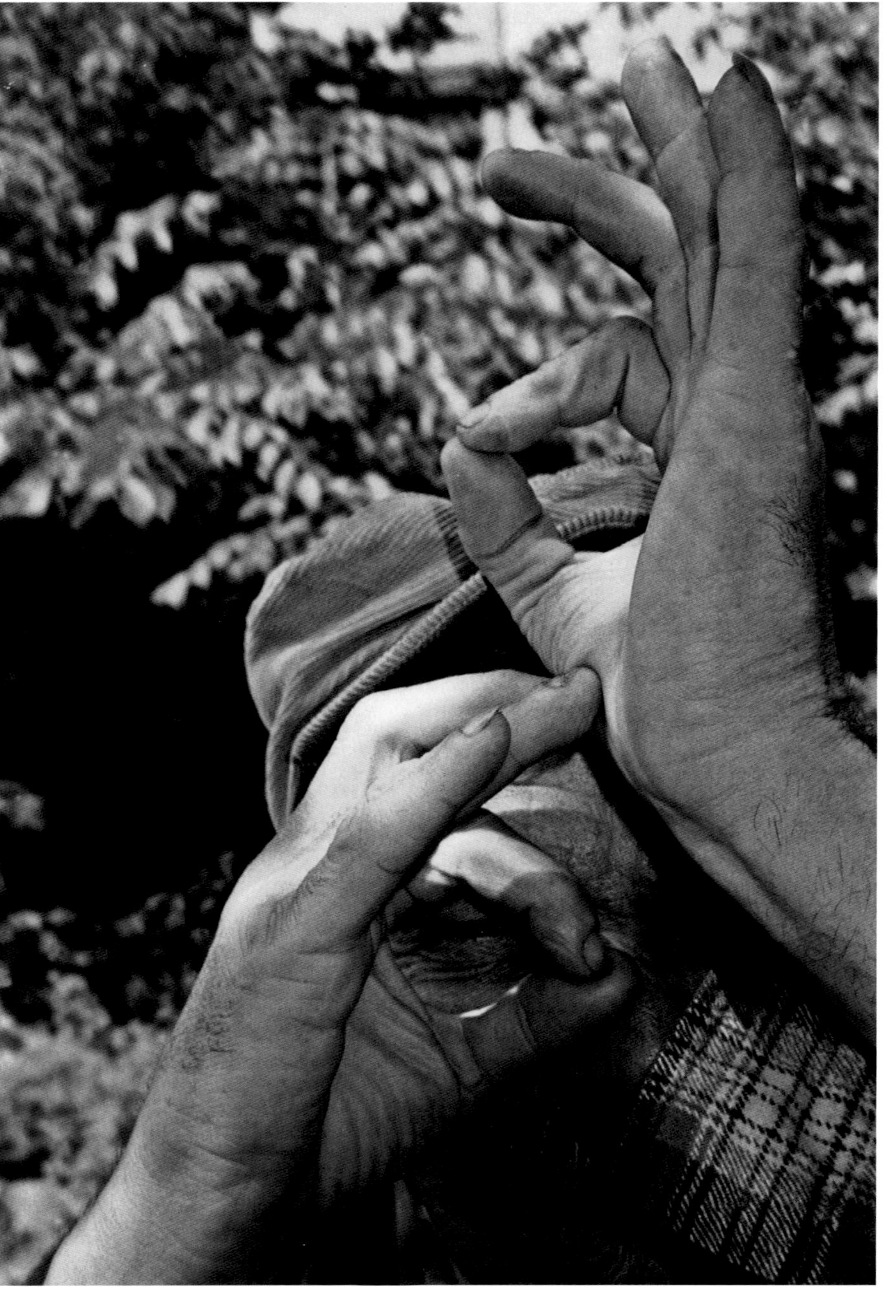

My integrity is a
star or a light
flight; scouring the
universe for a
lover.

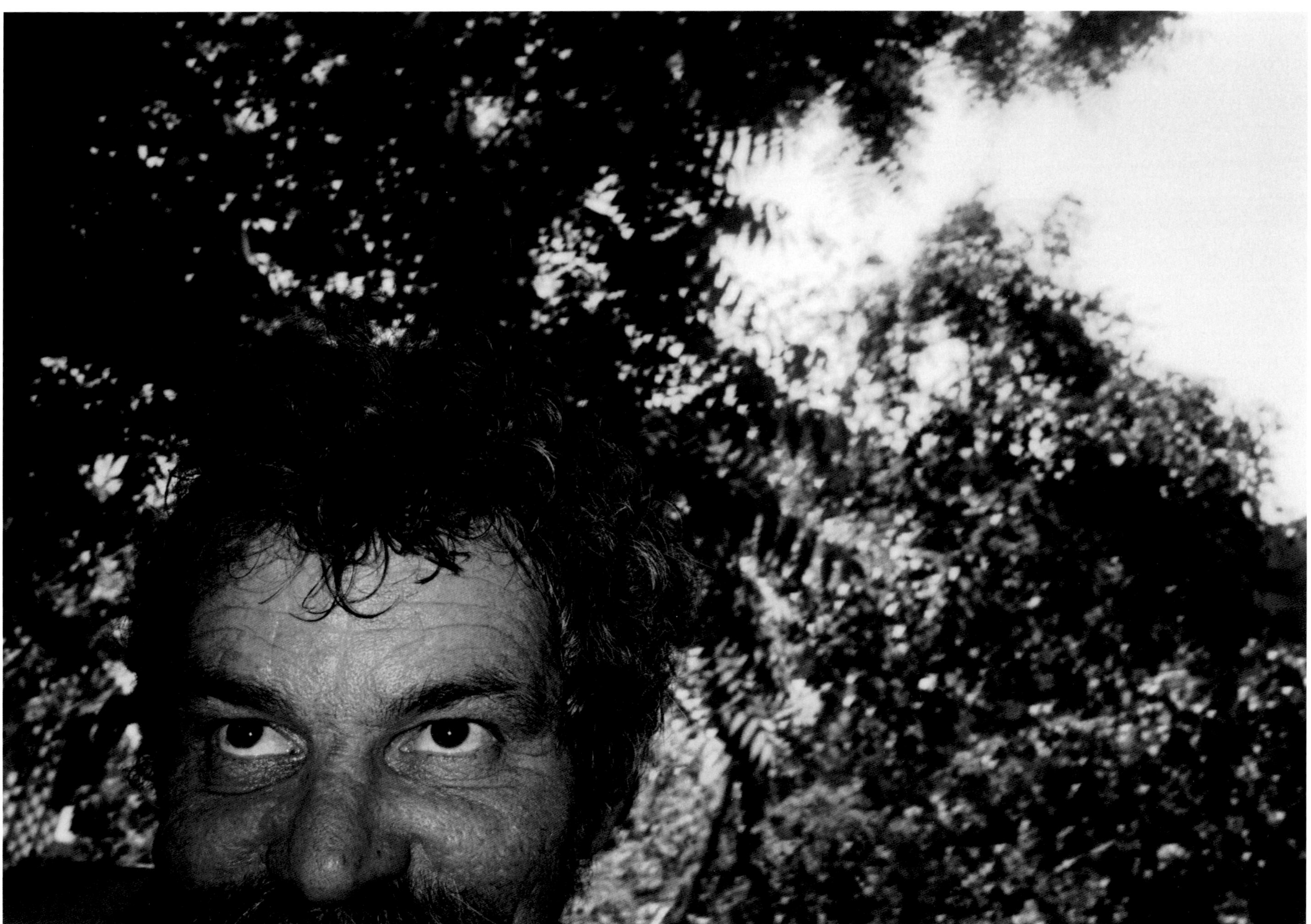

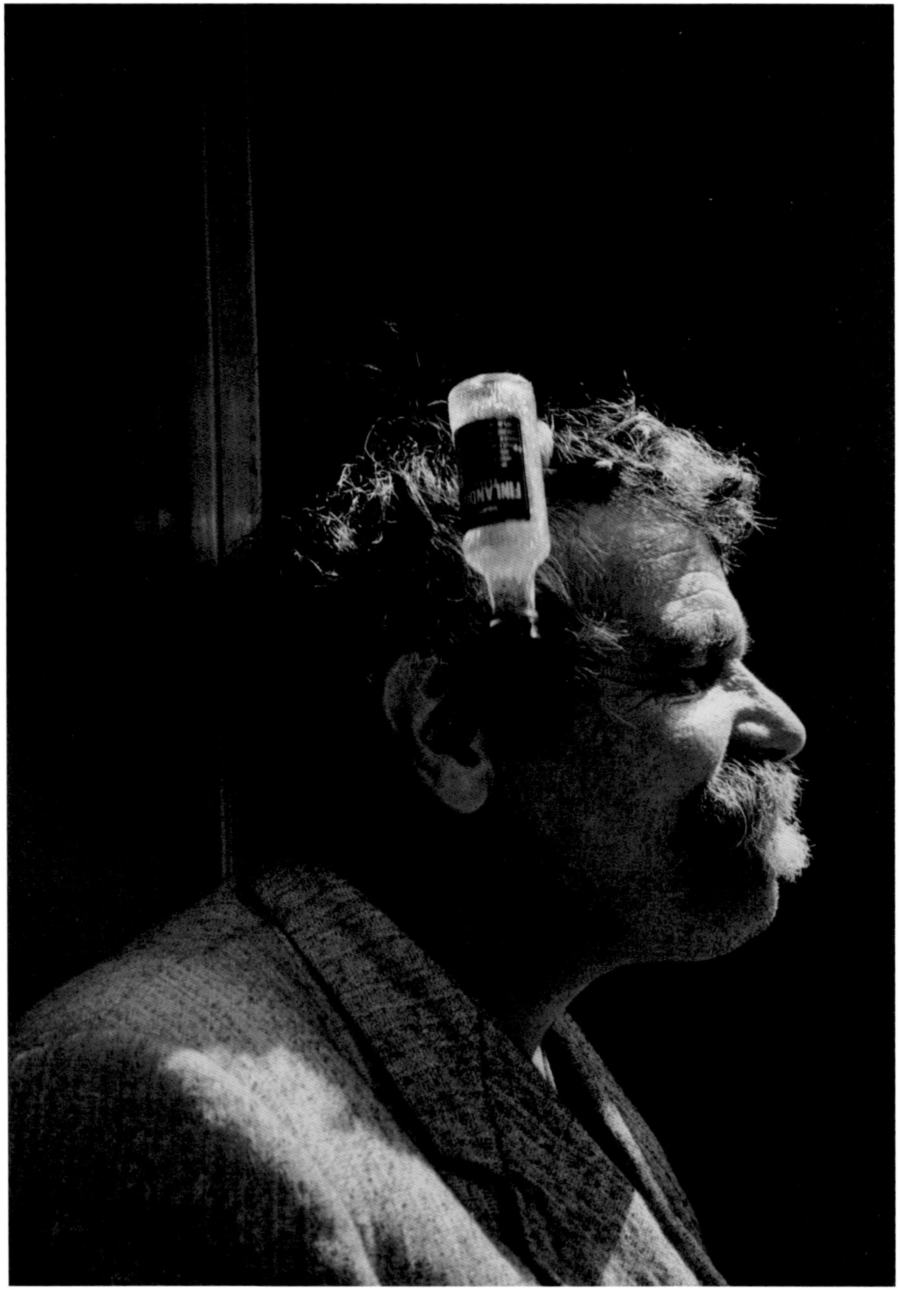

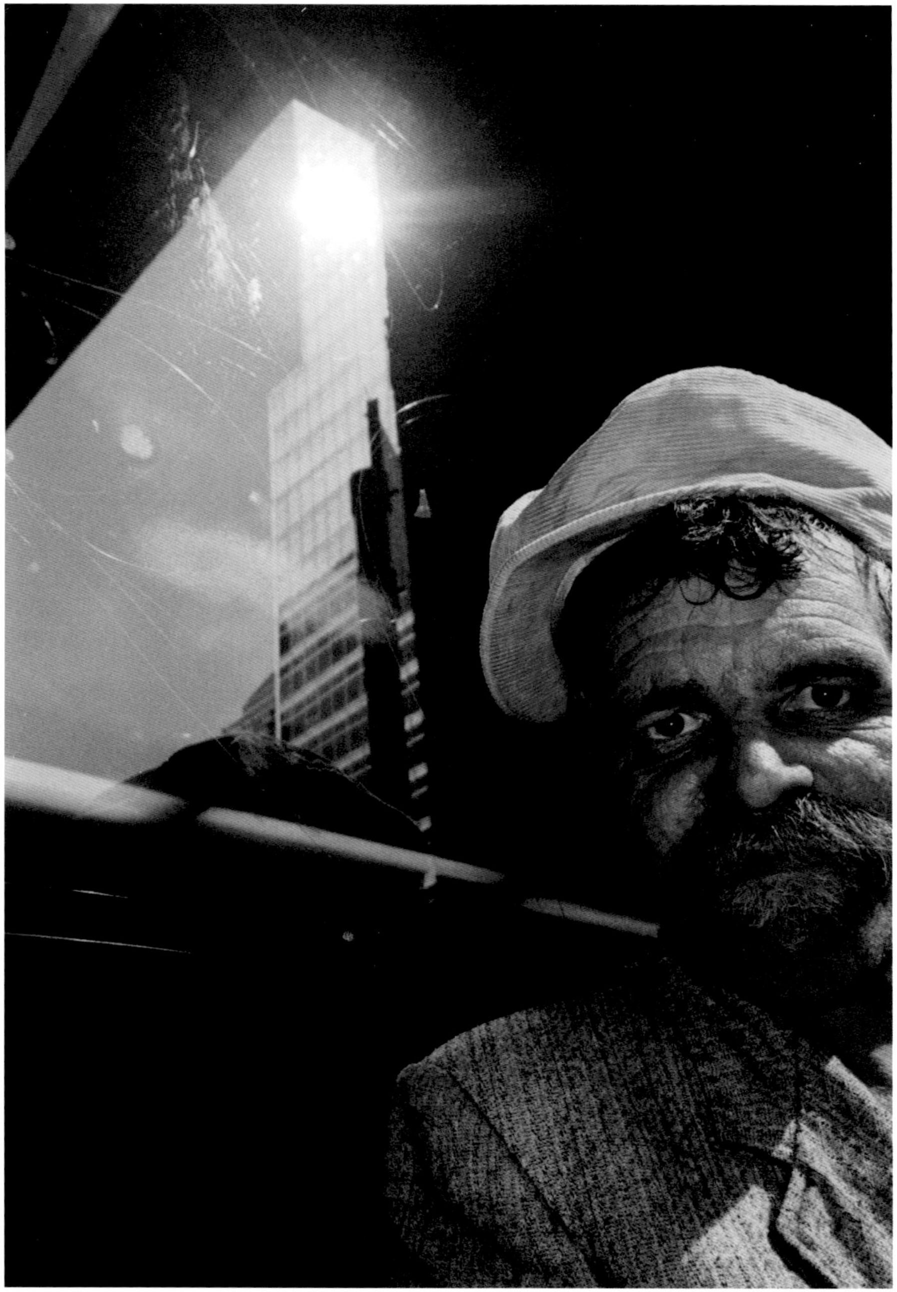

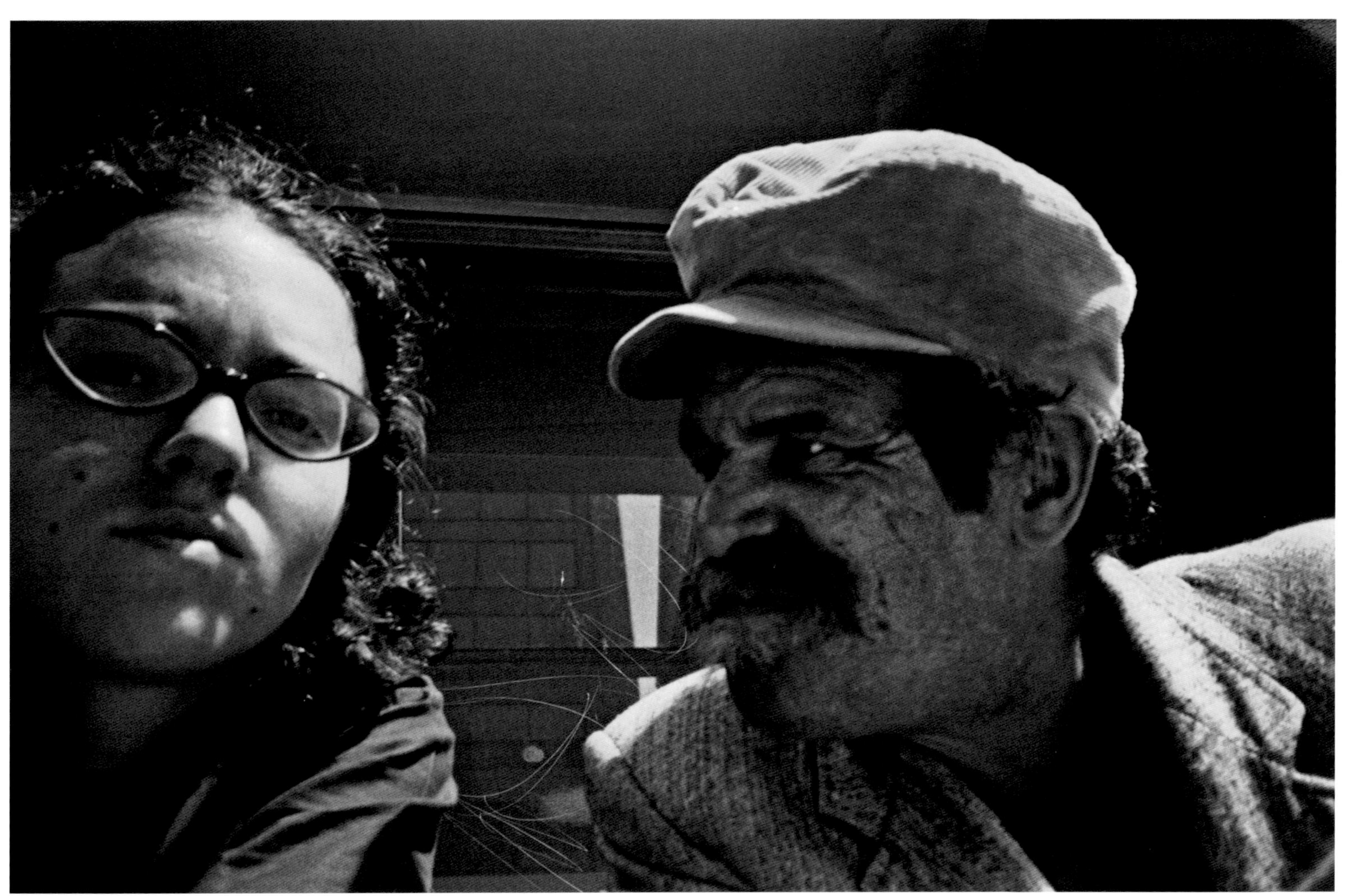

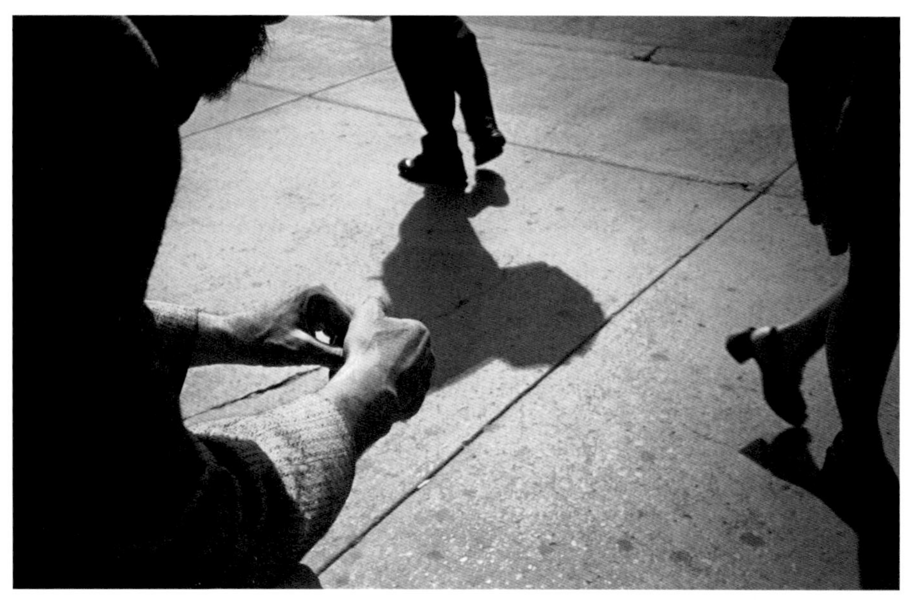

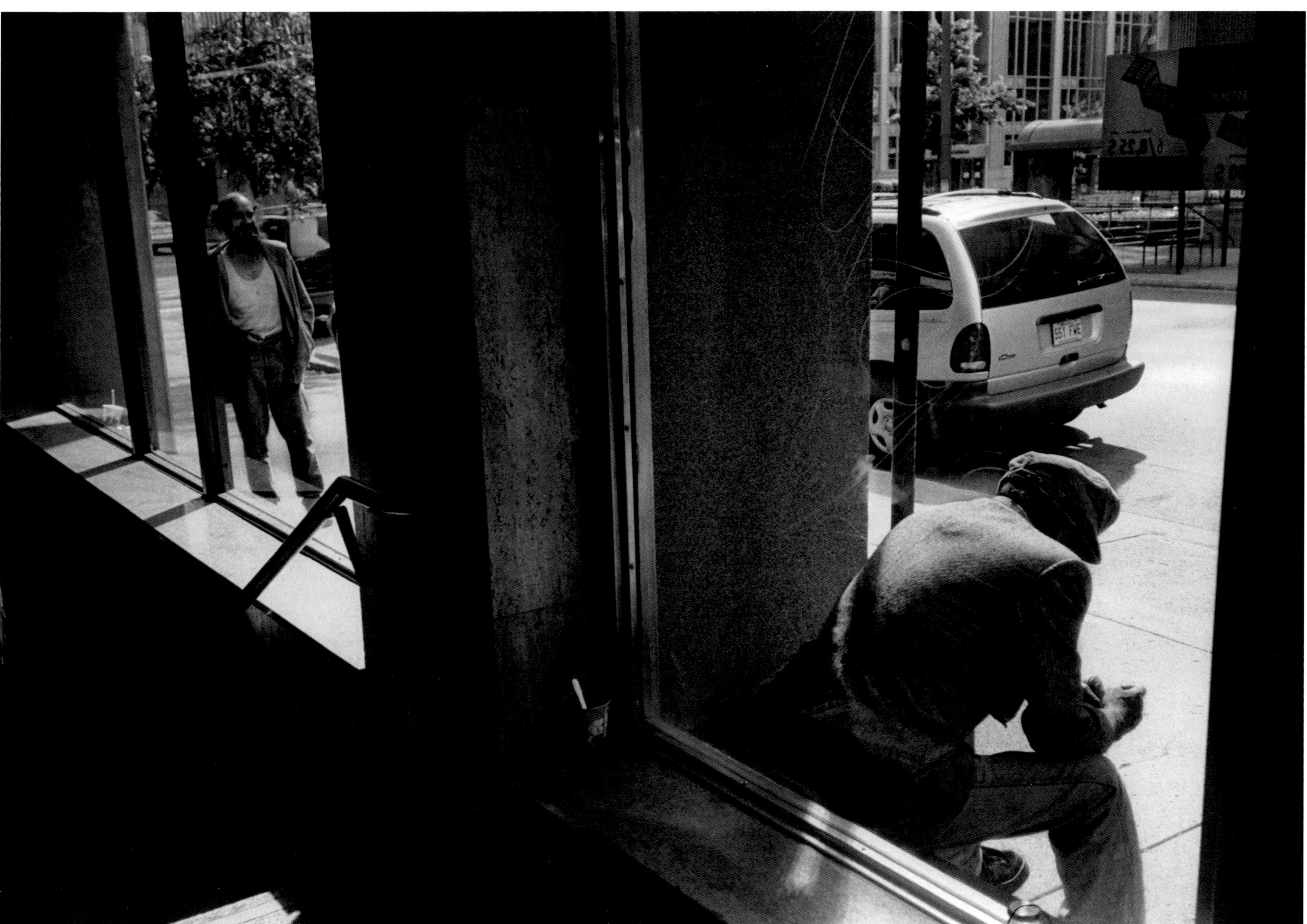

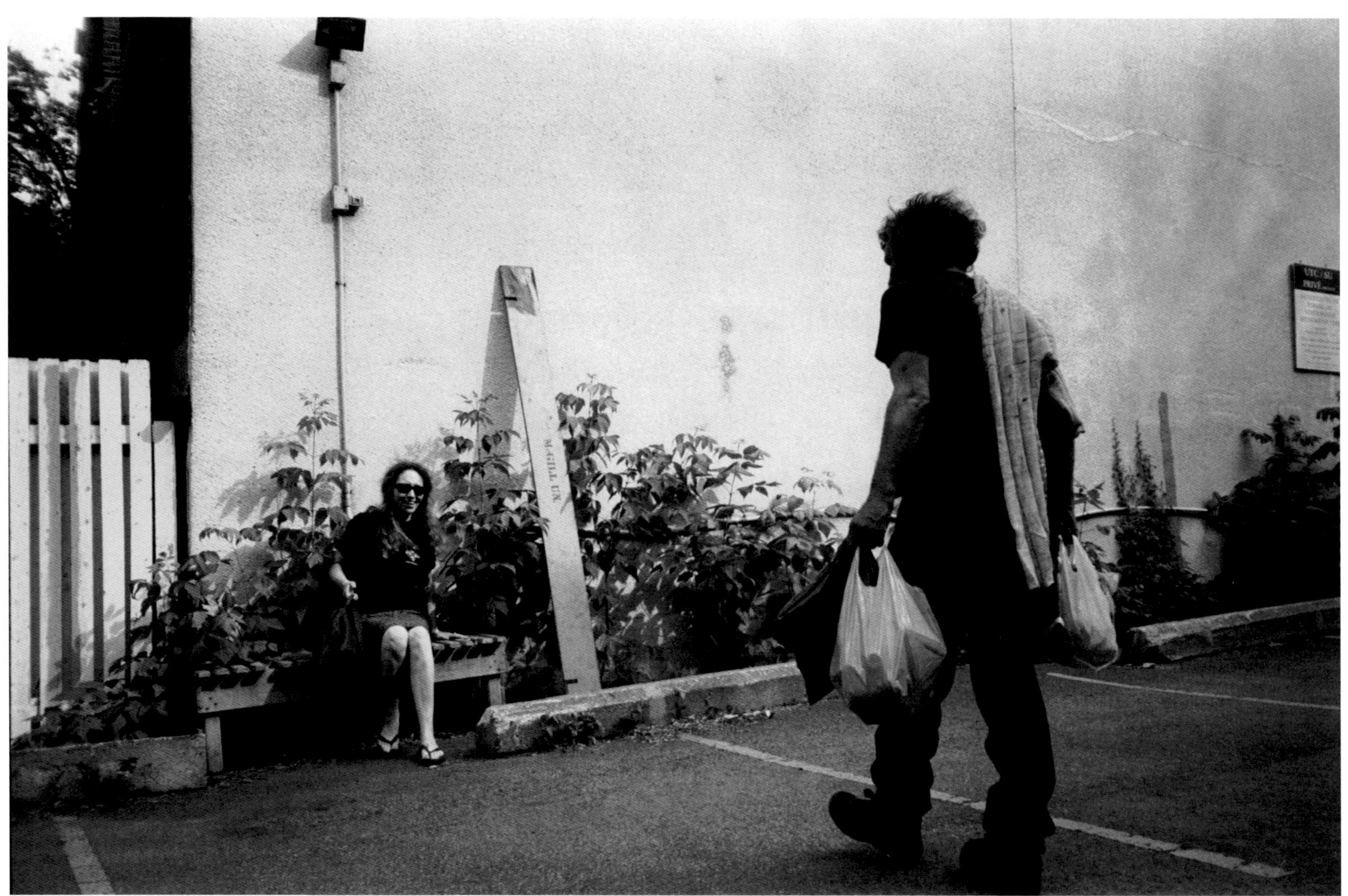

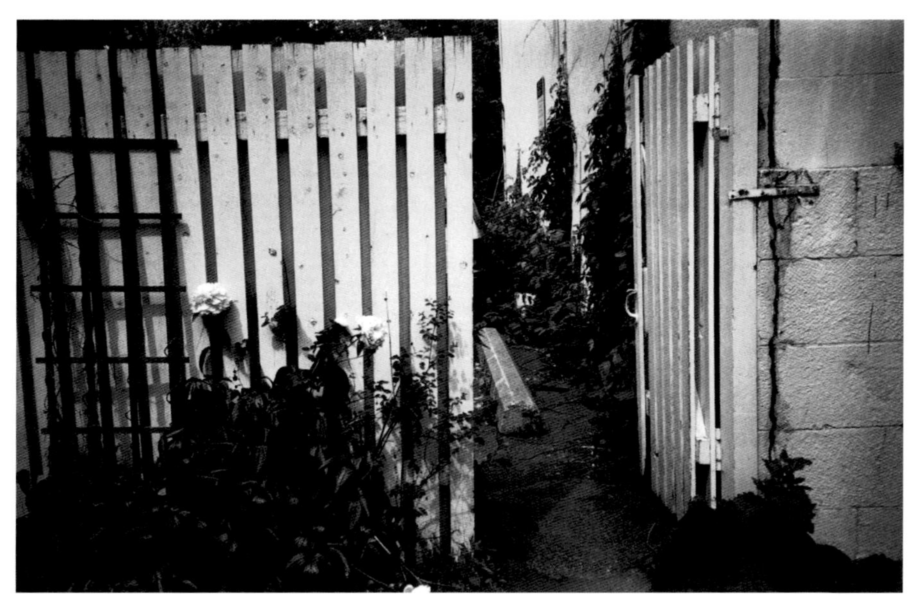

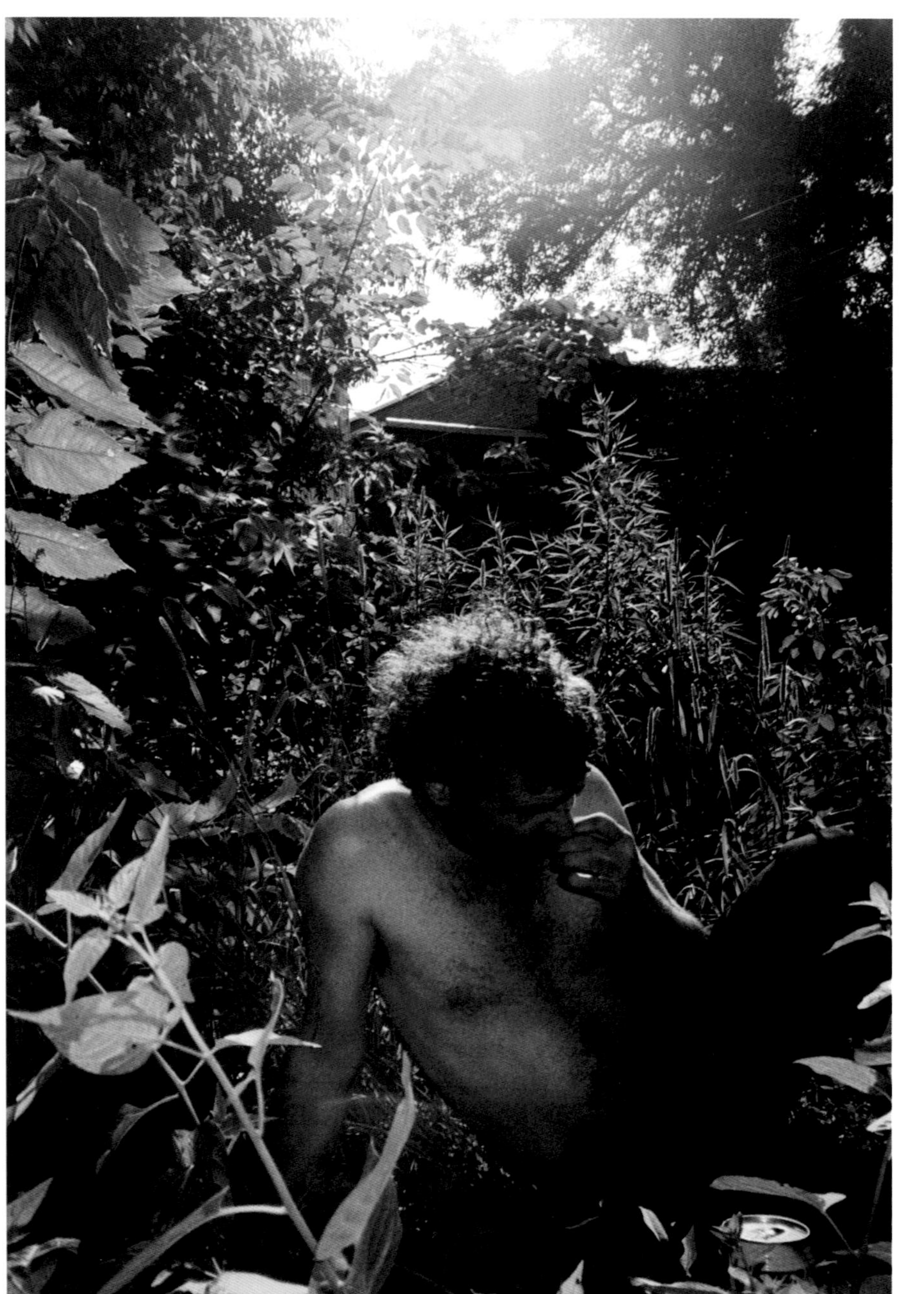

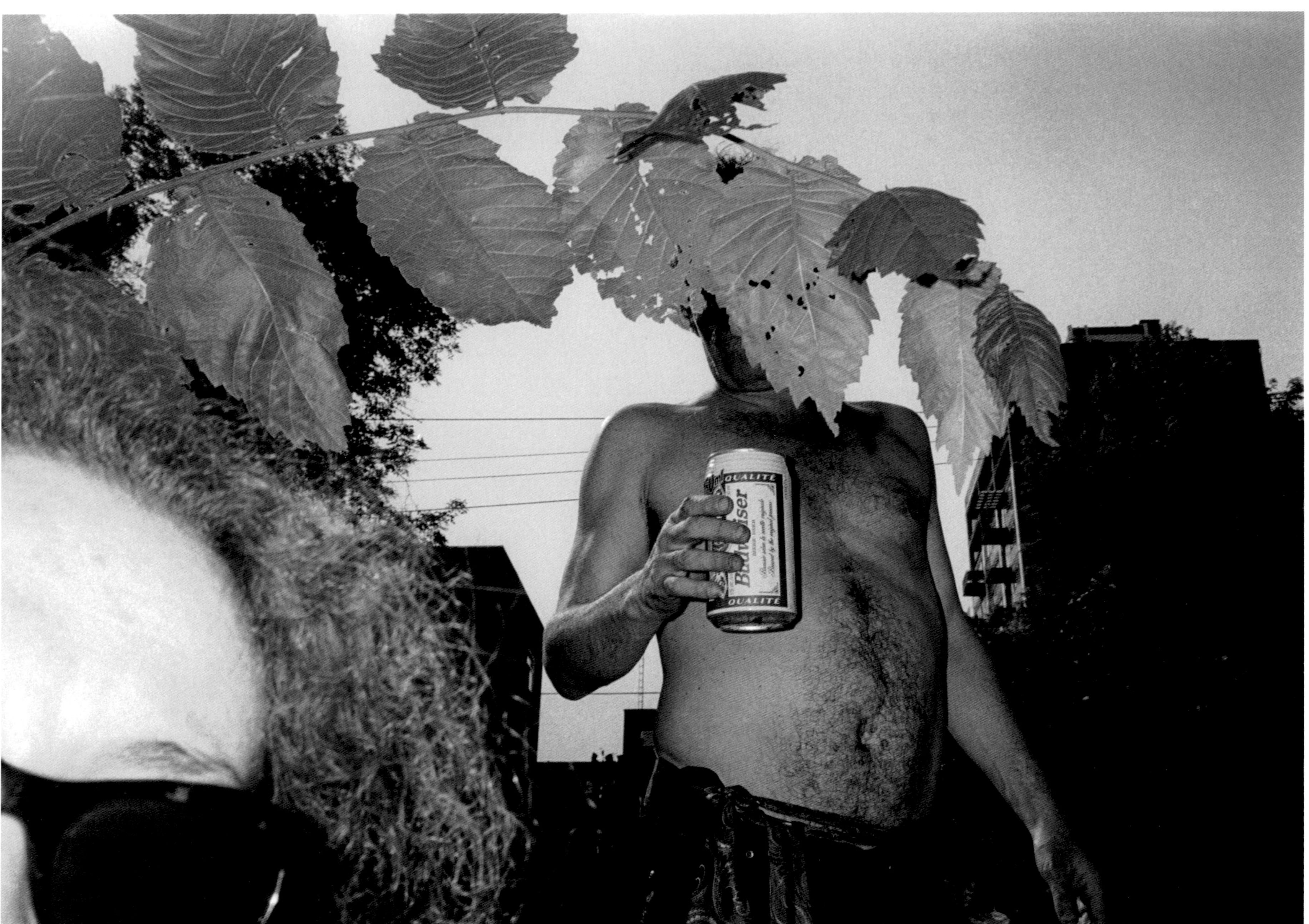

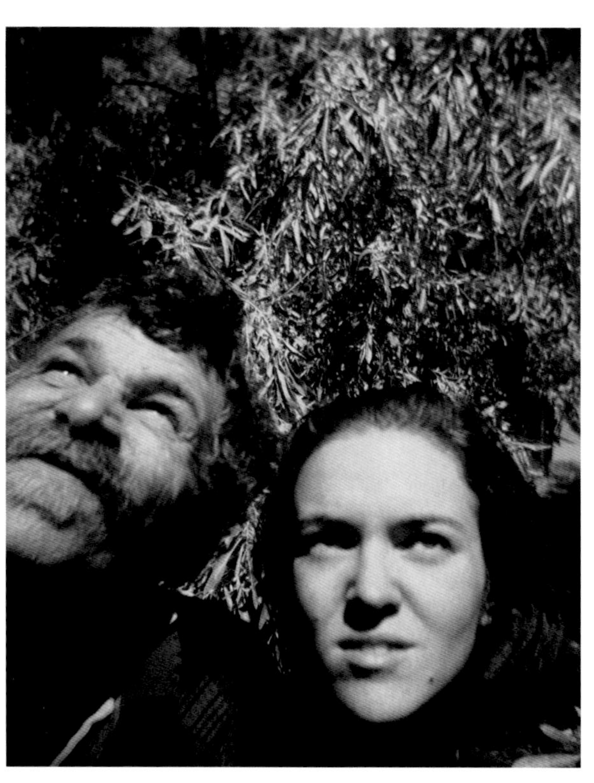

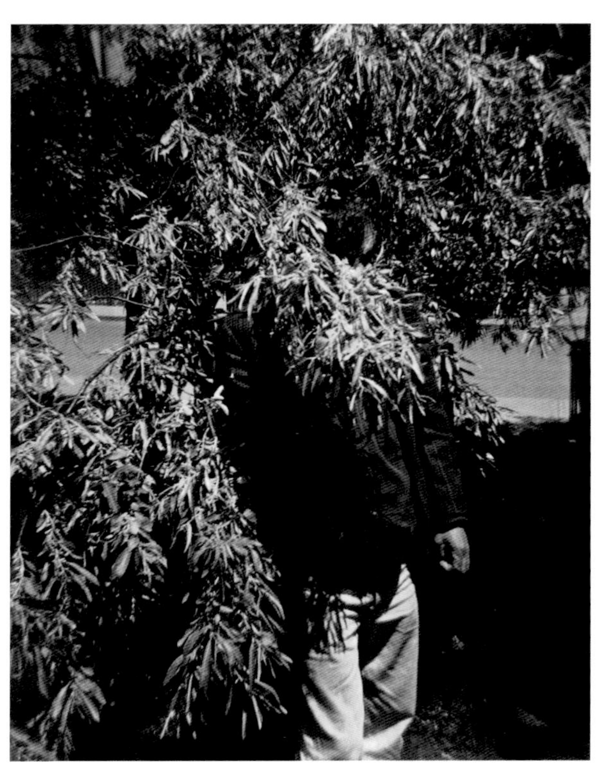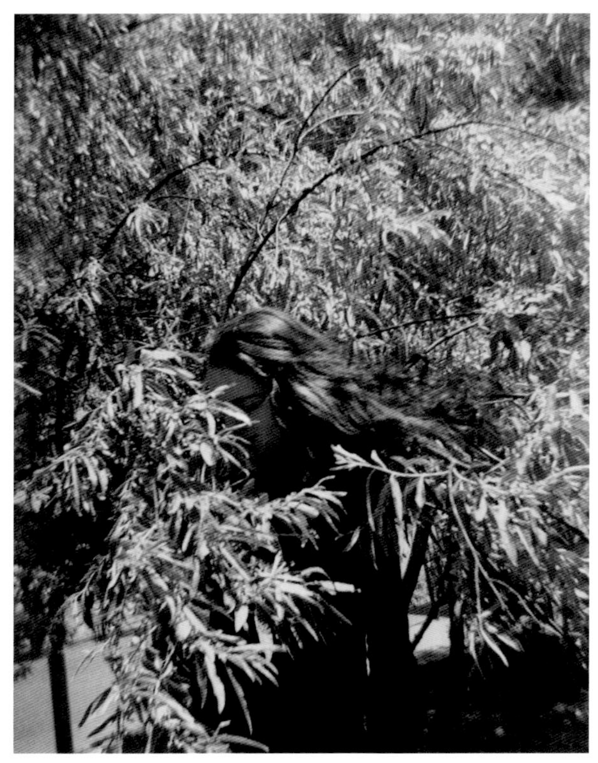

Mountain Song

There is something
    I'm not sure of;
There is a mountain Loves
me;
and, I could
    Die, there-upon;
How, when I
        Pass away
    in the metro
Or some other place;
or, not at all;
Because I might disappear
with No-one Knowing;
Like a mountain Lion,
which I
        Never saw....

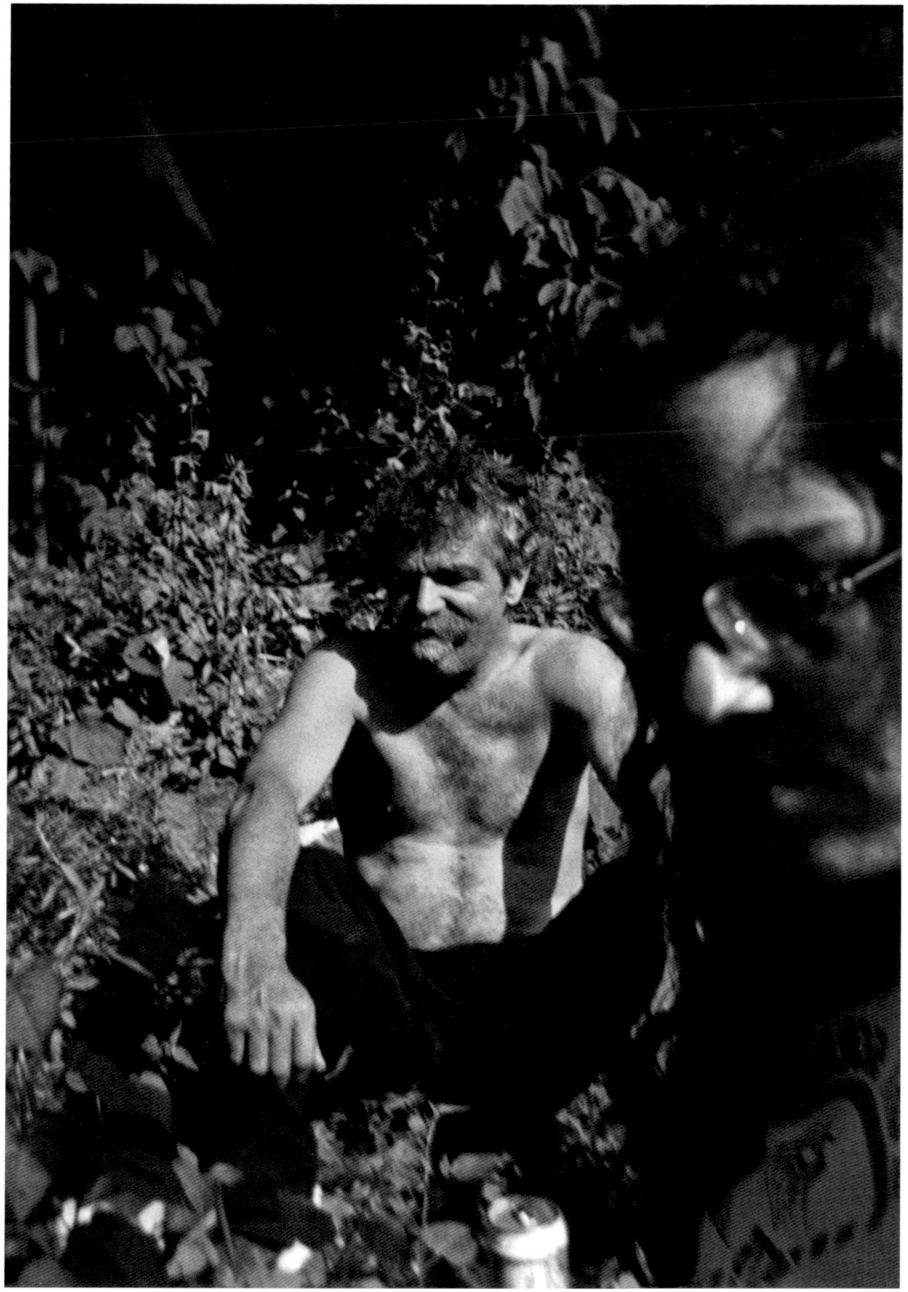

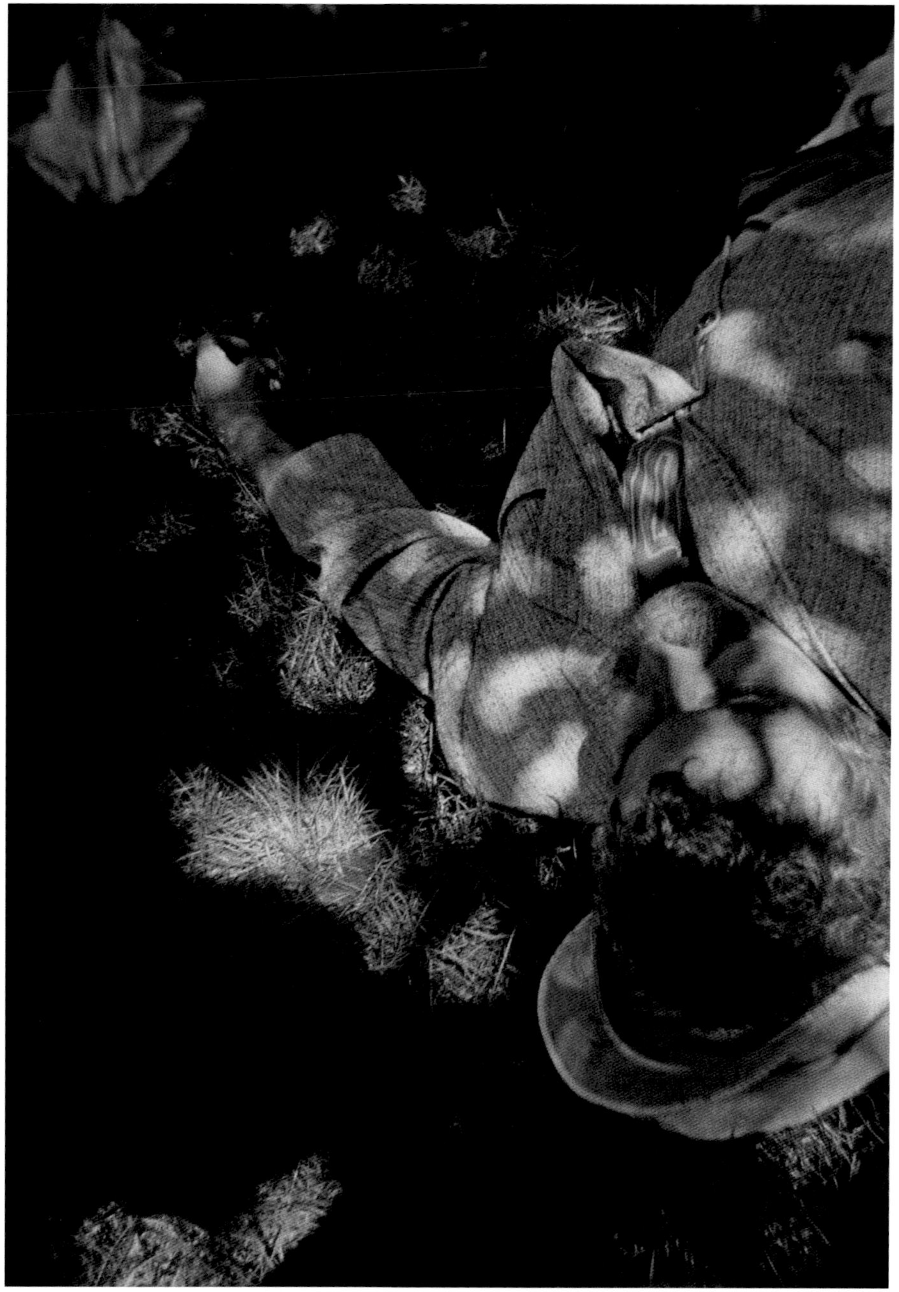

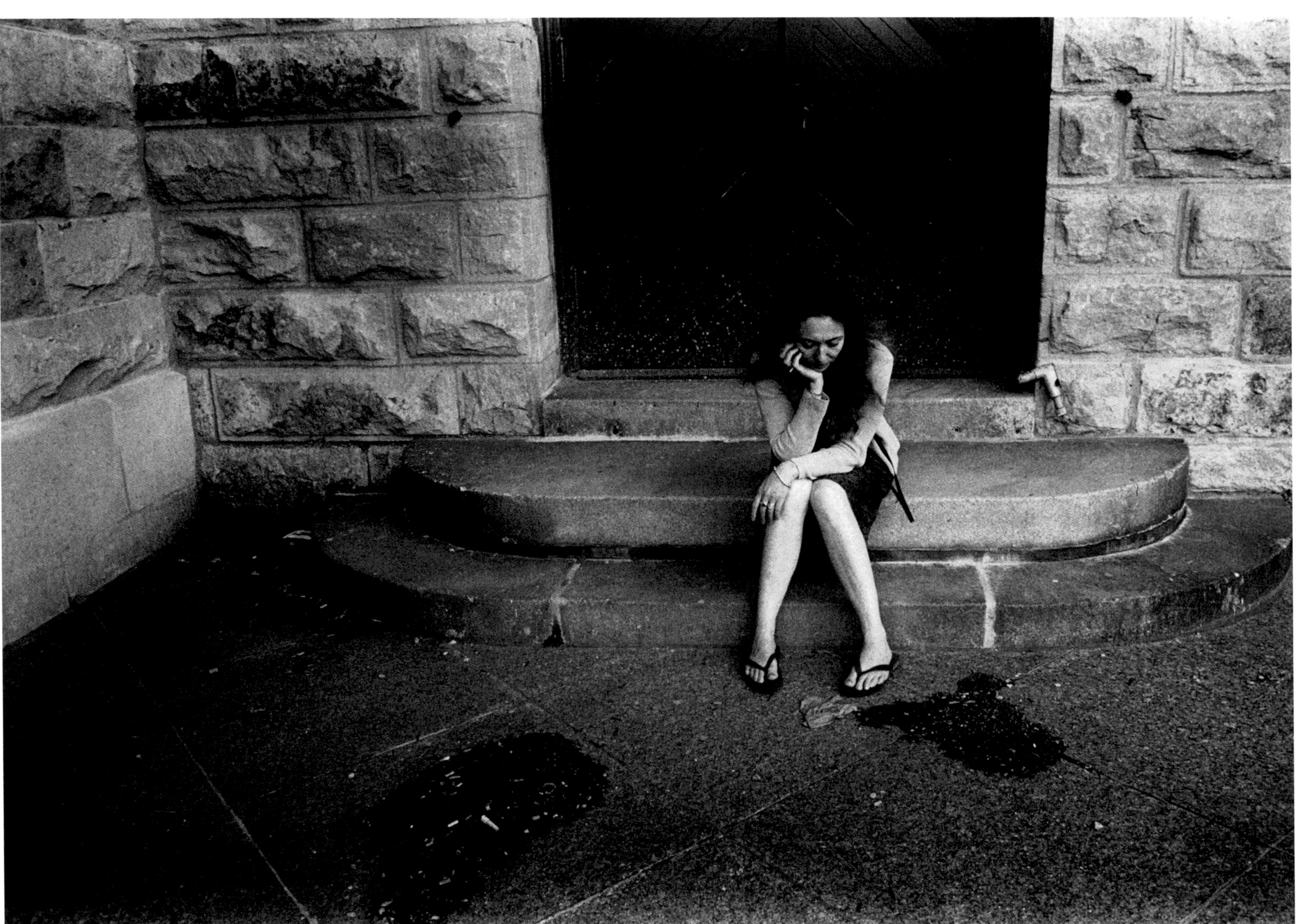

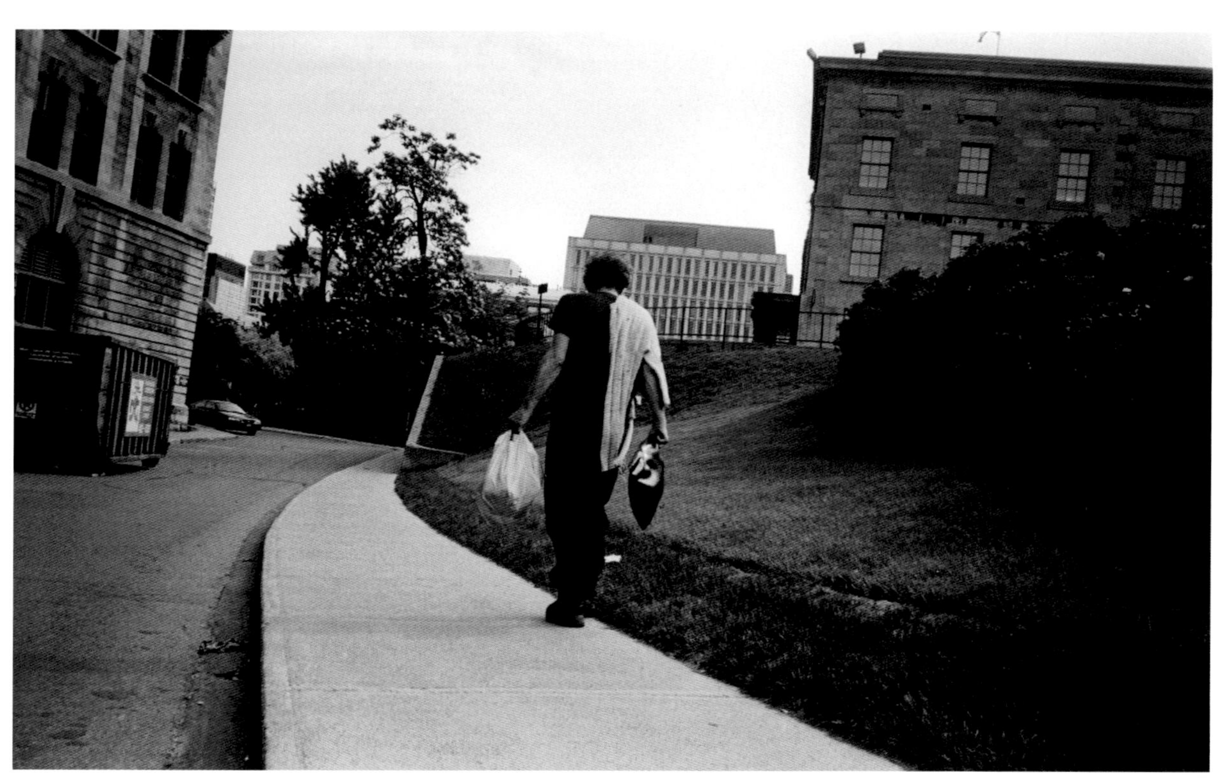

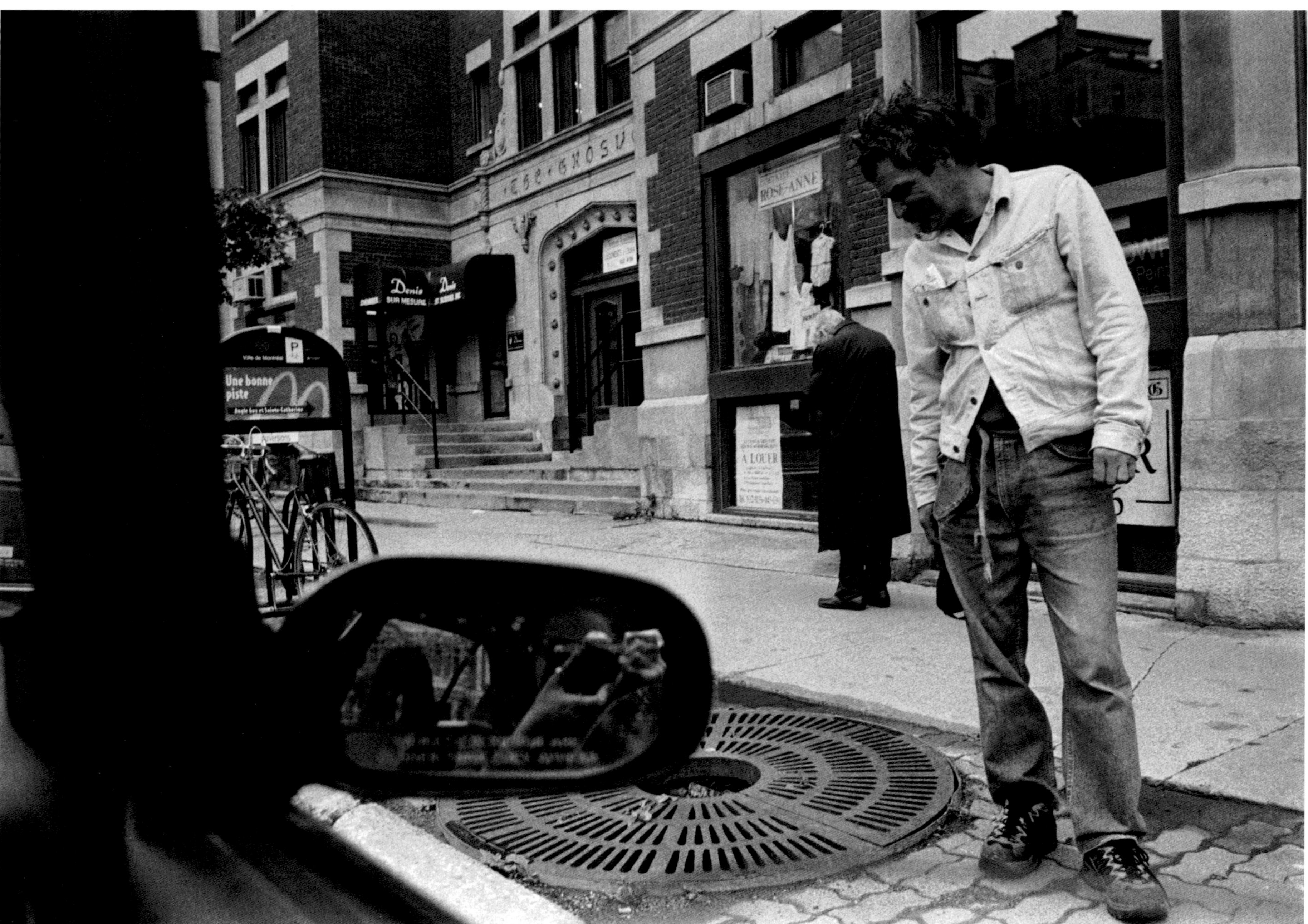

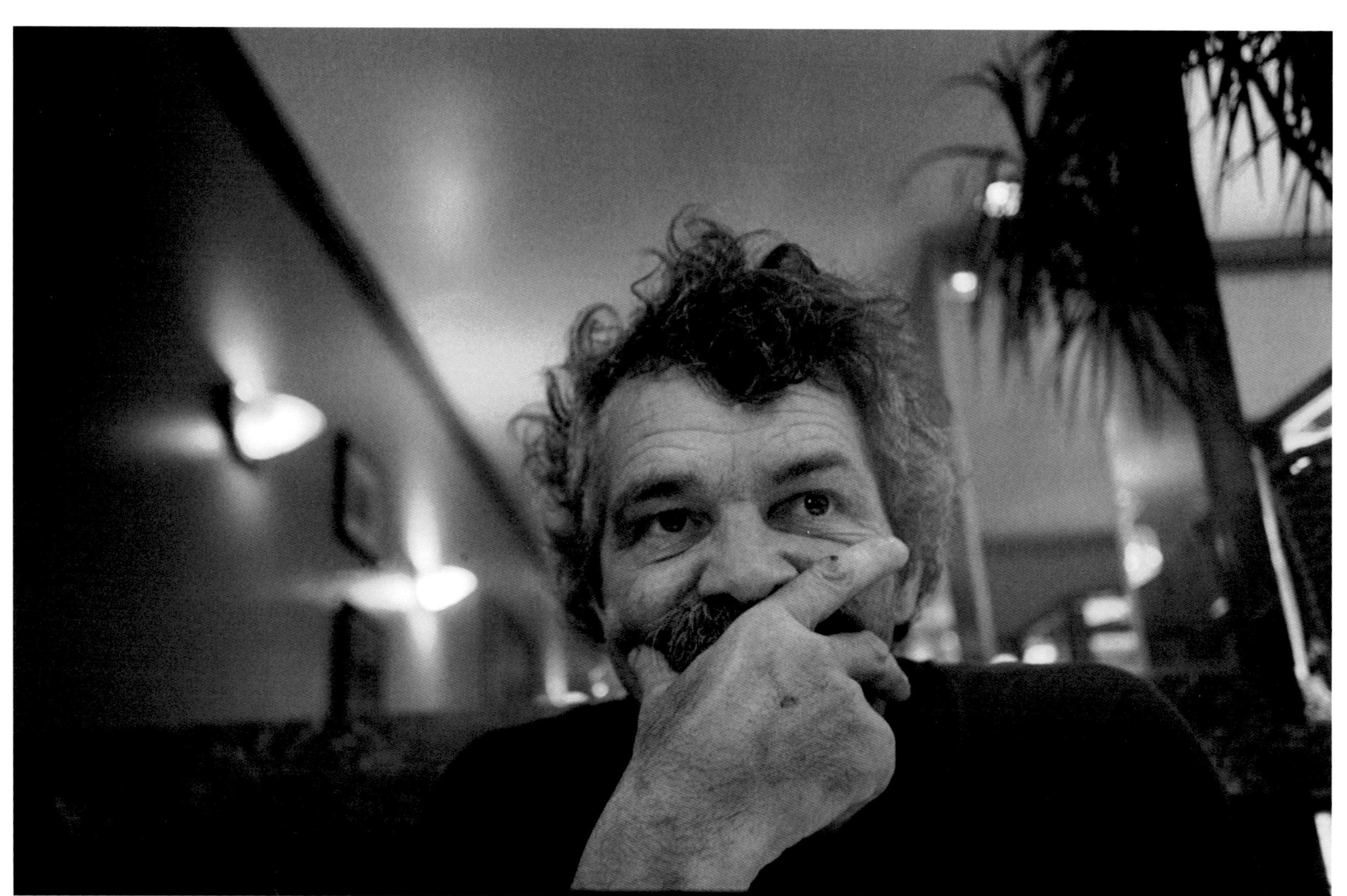

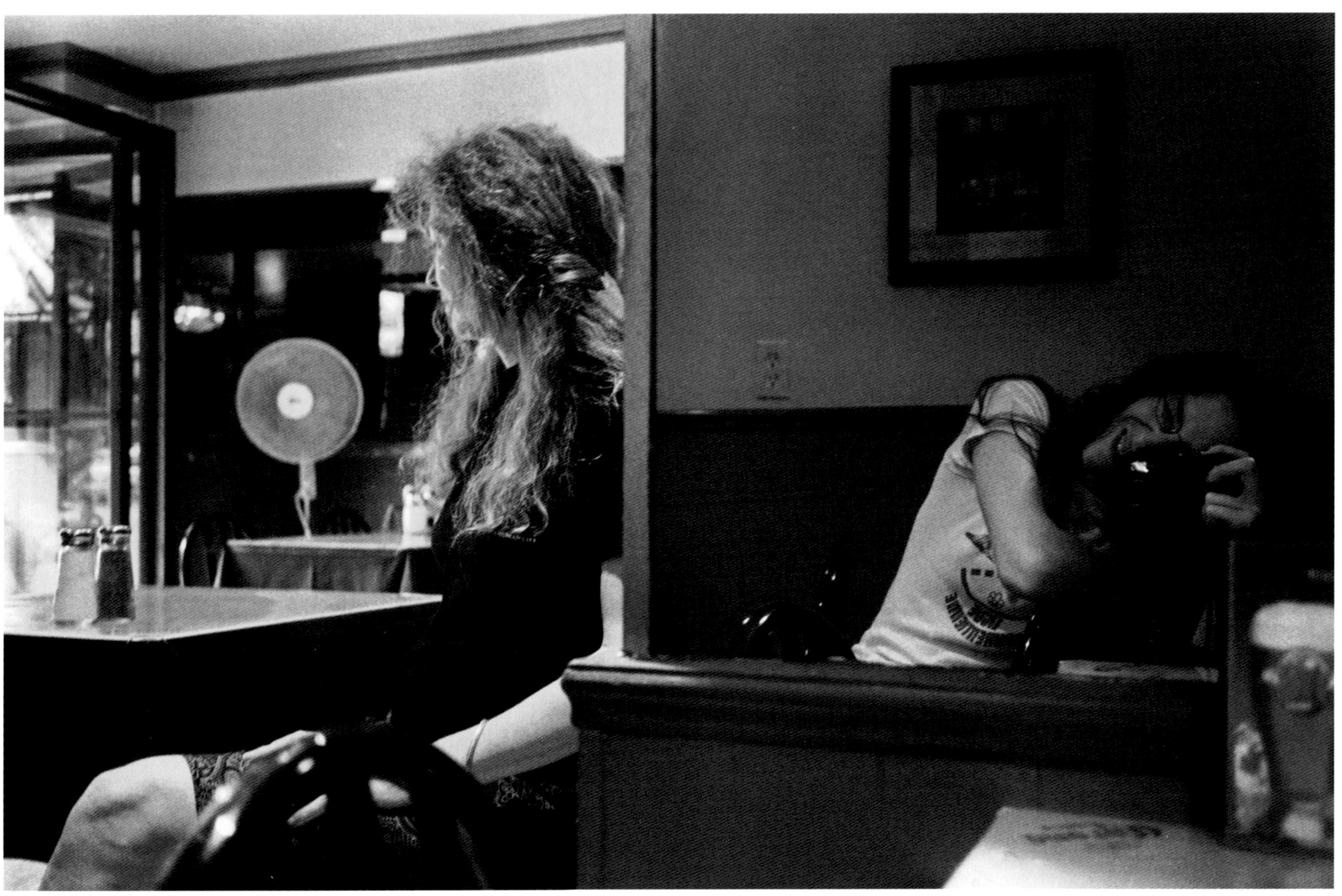

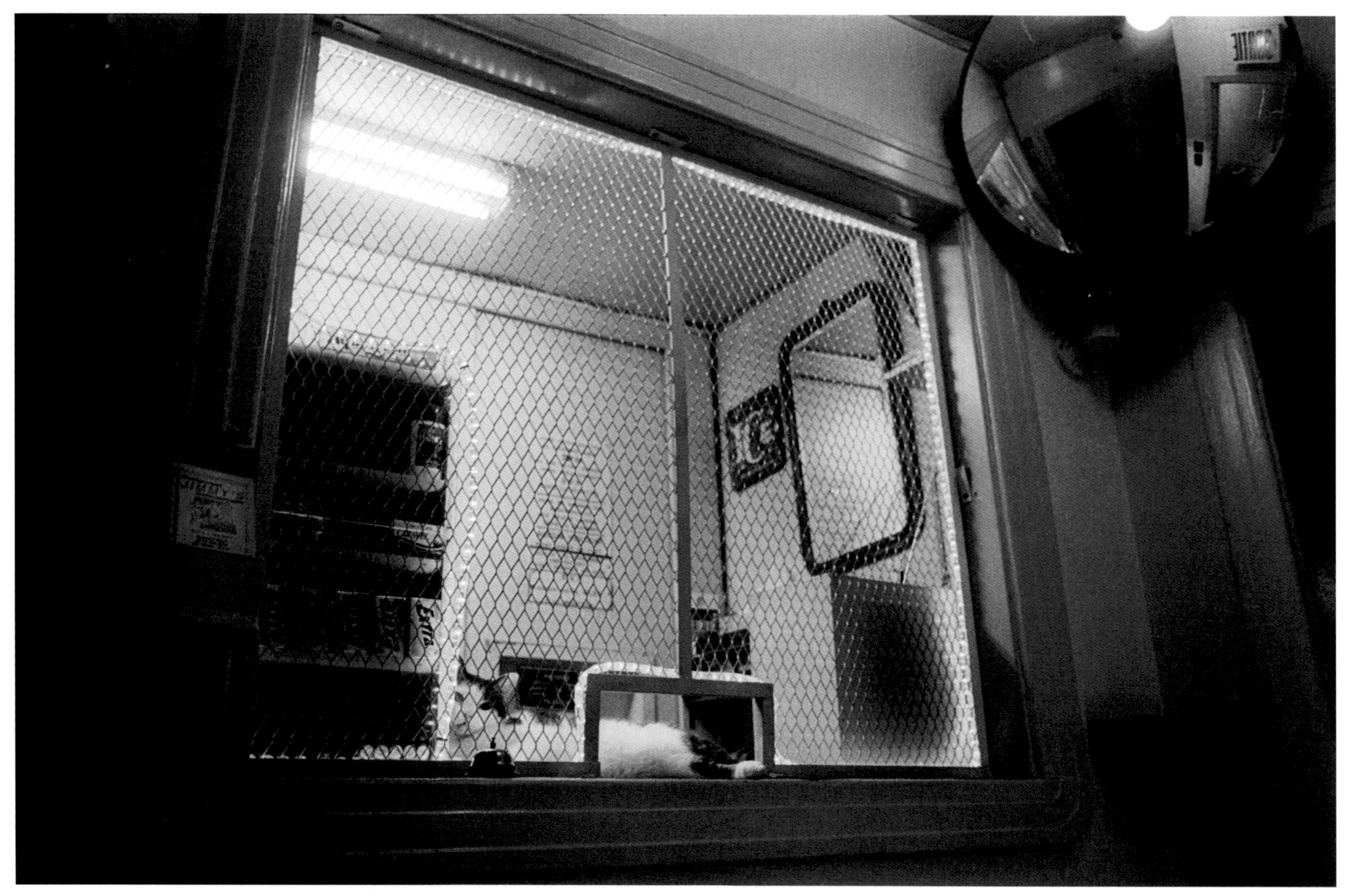

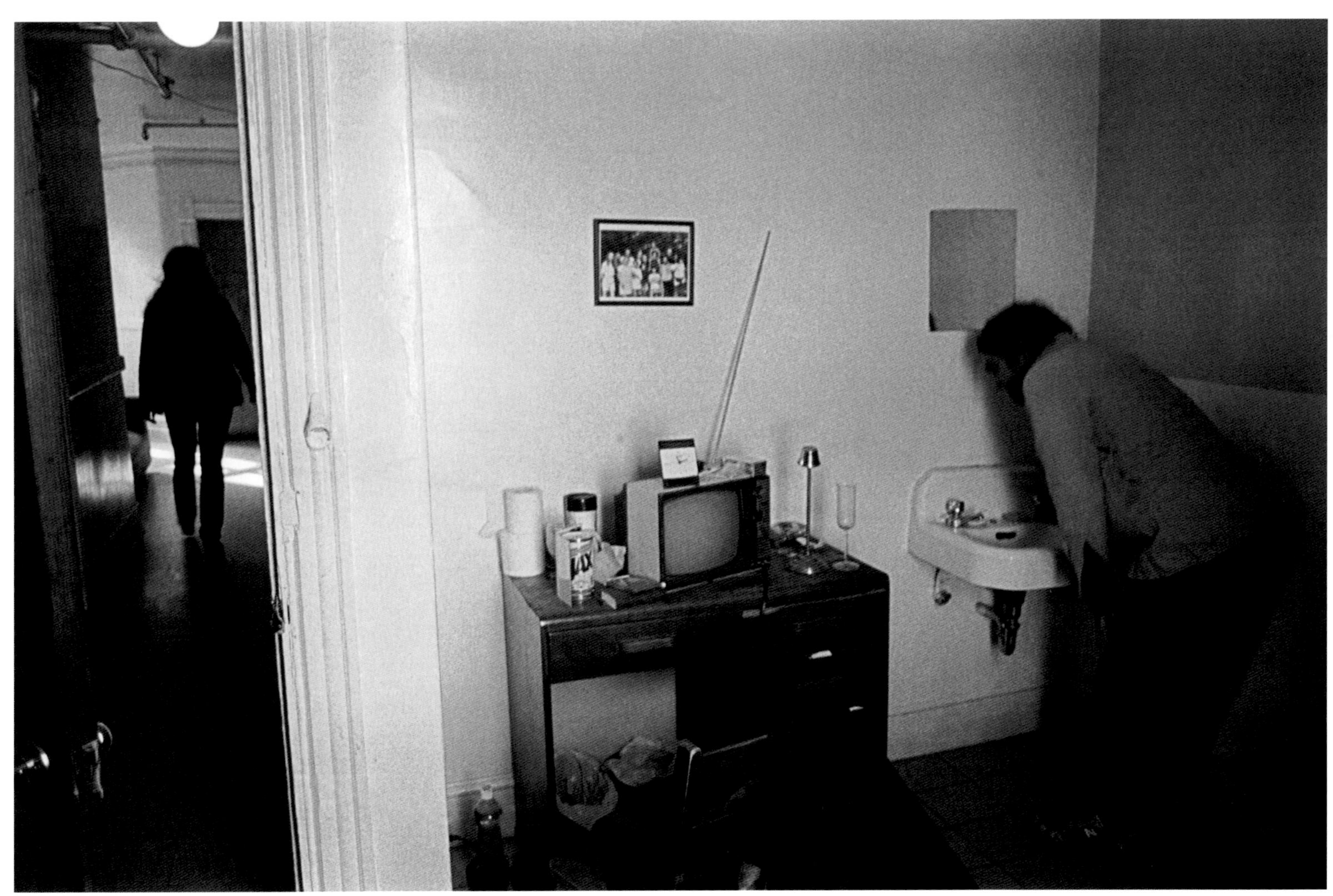

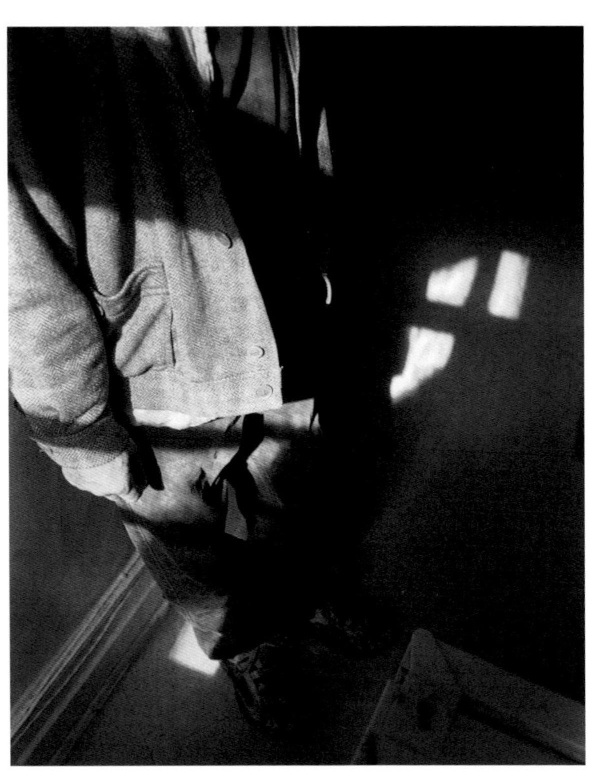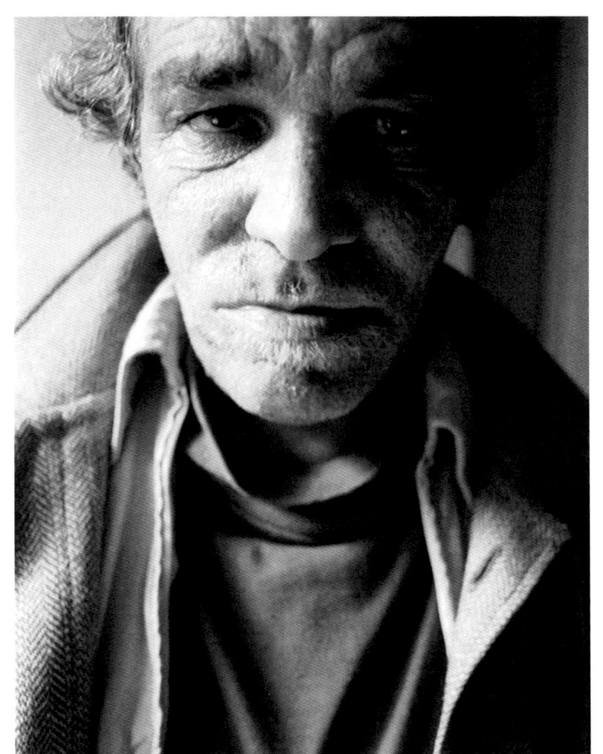

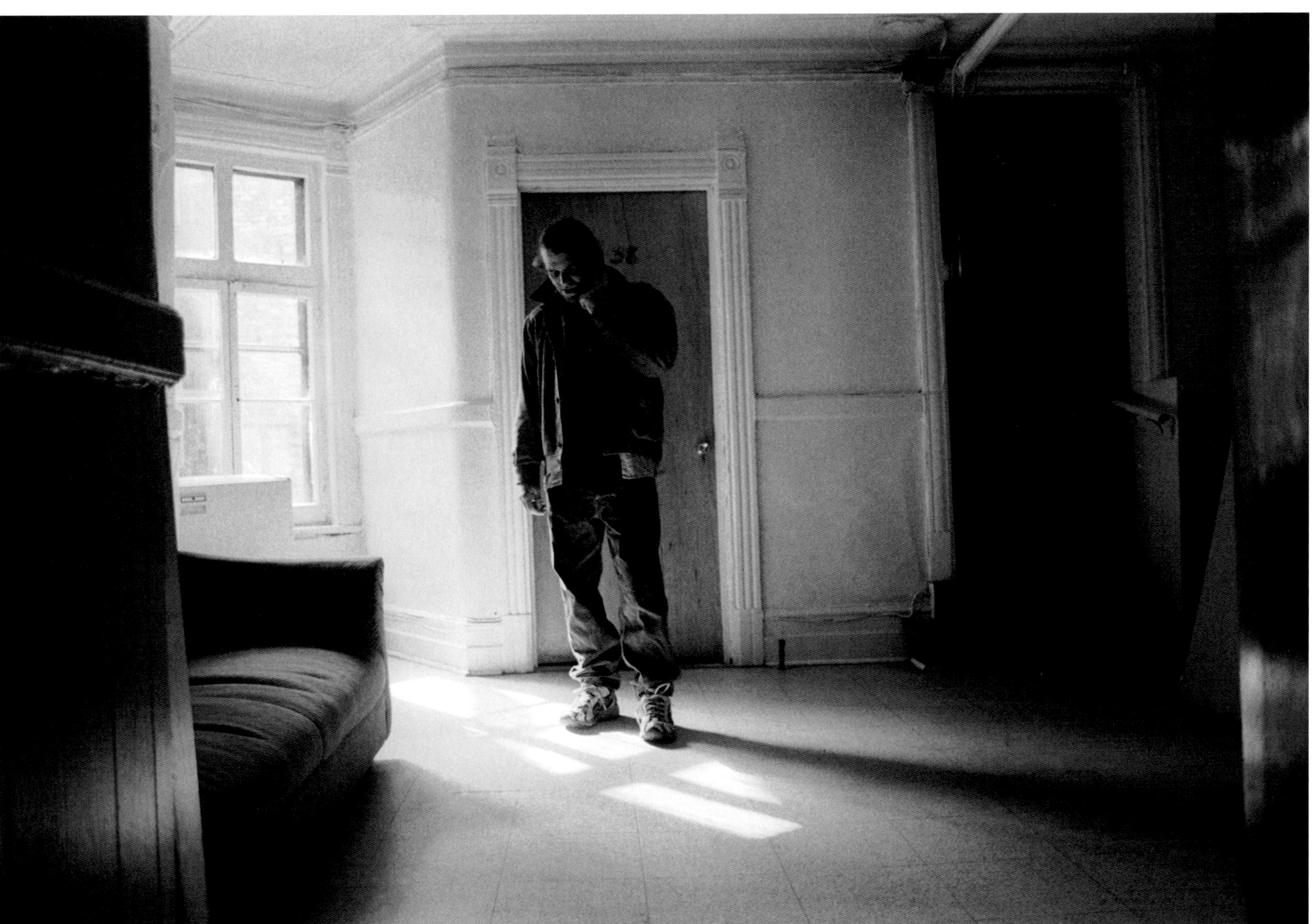

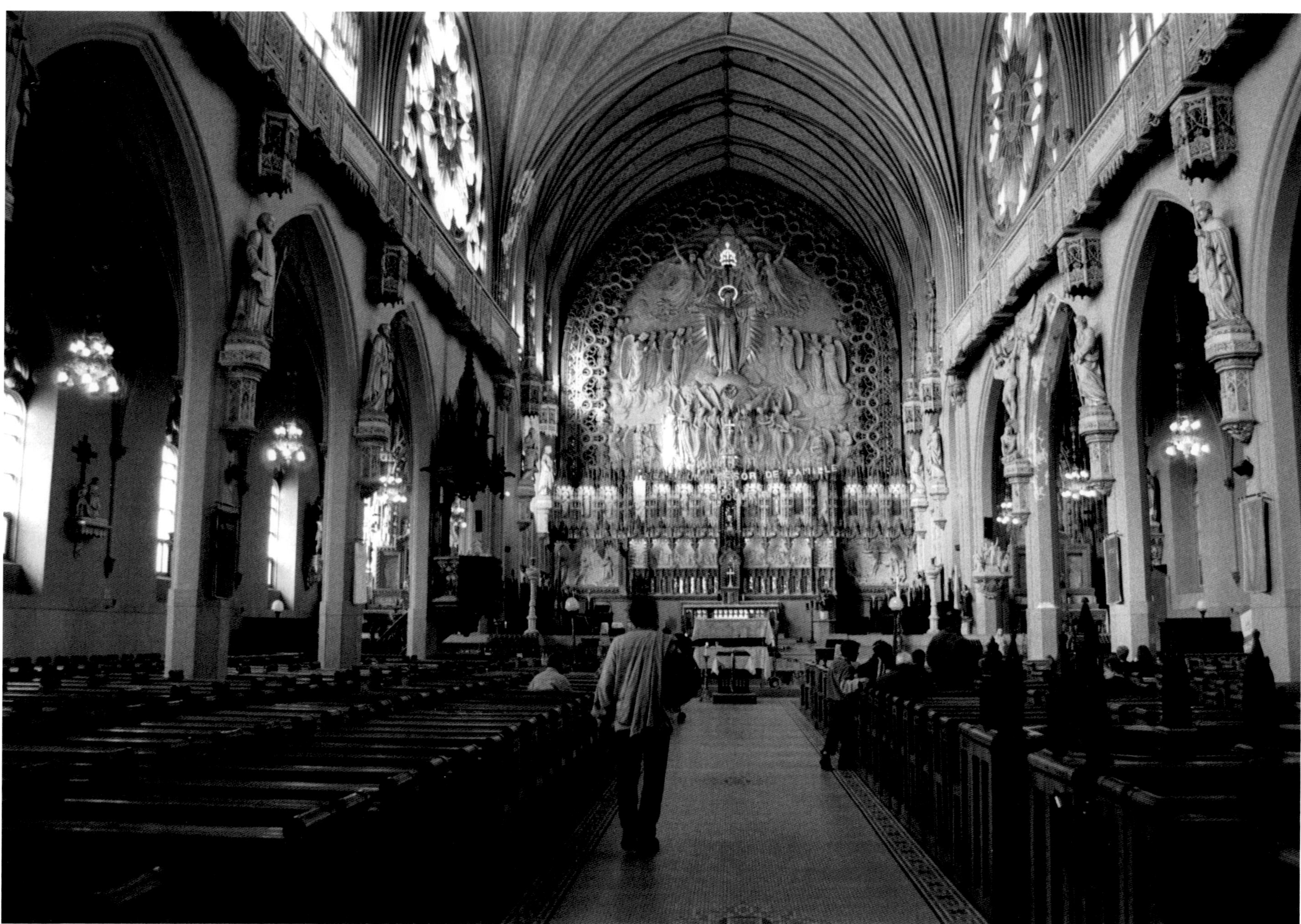

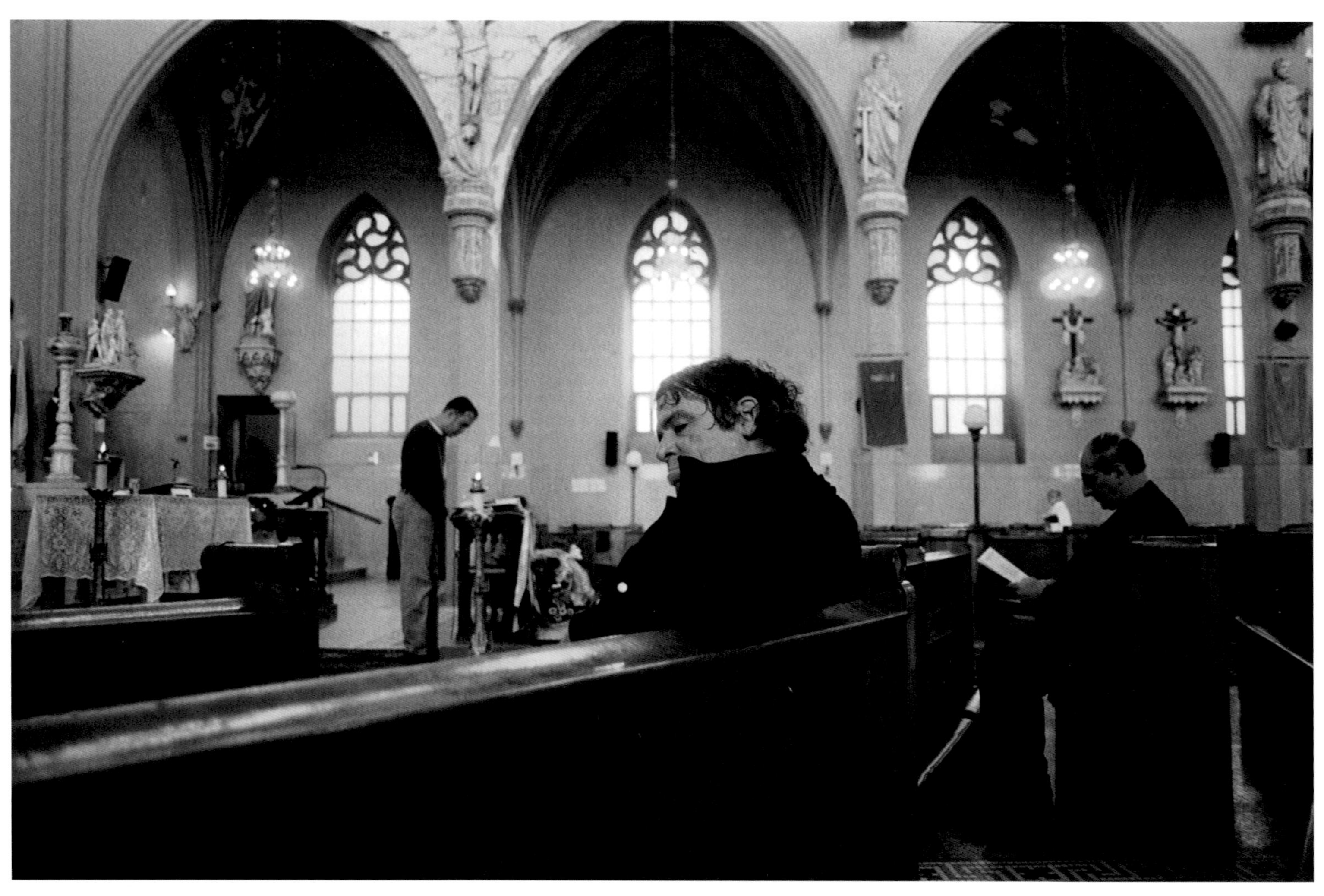

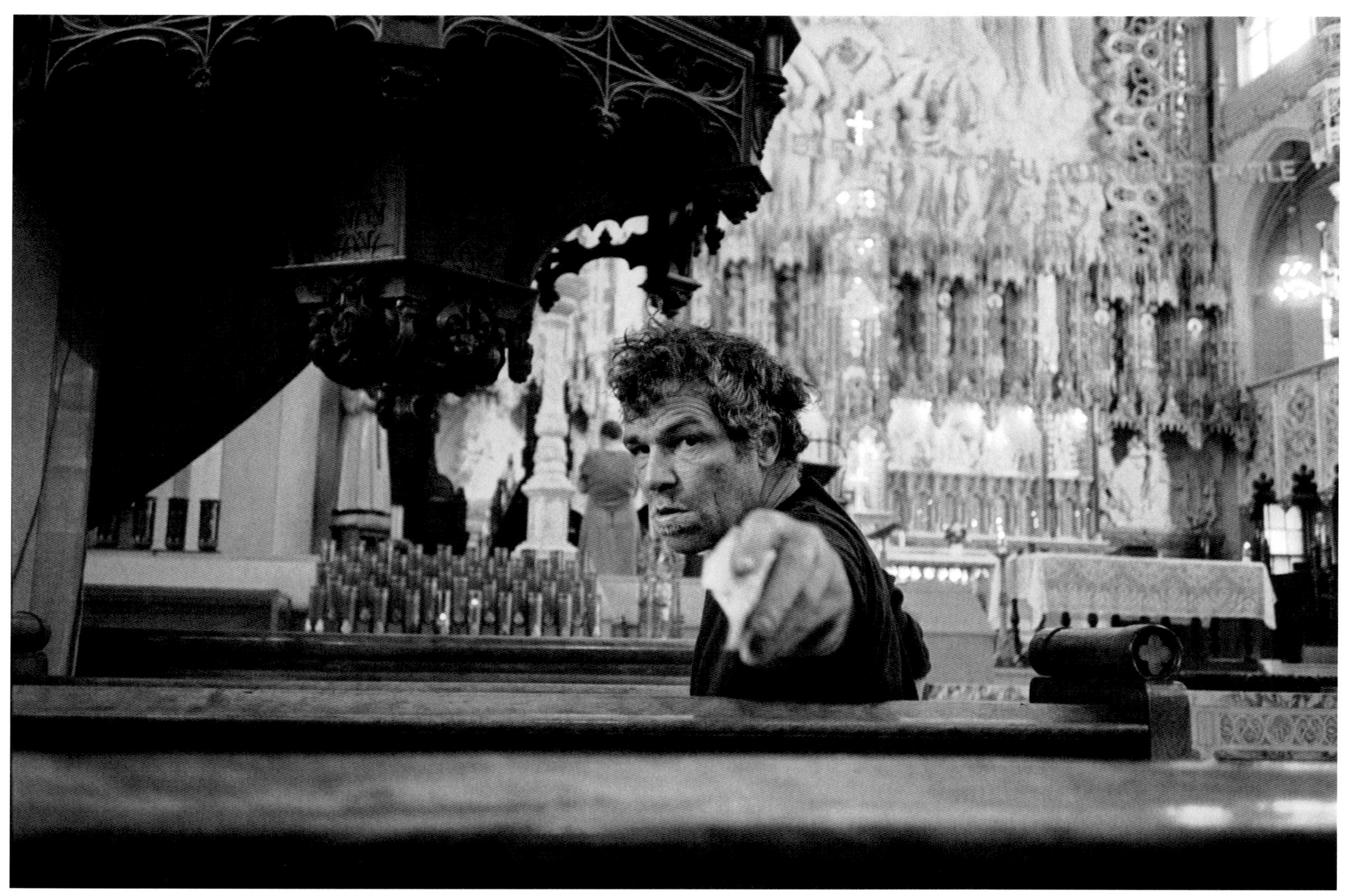

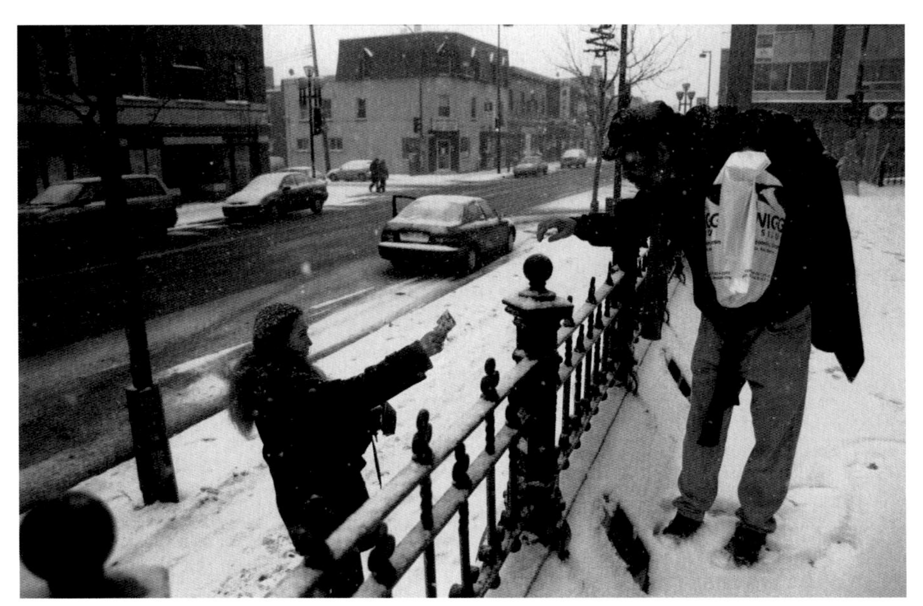

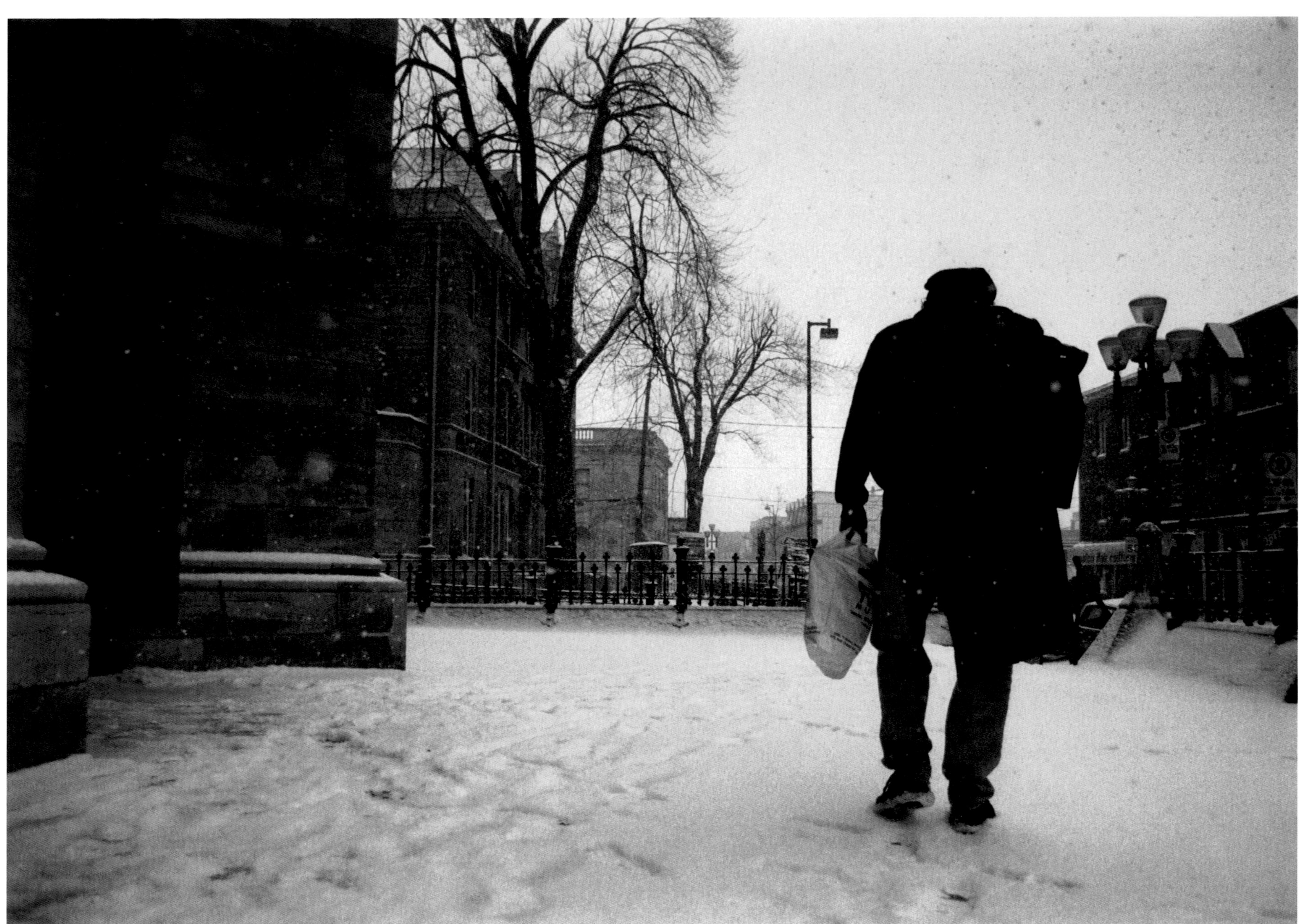

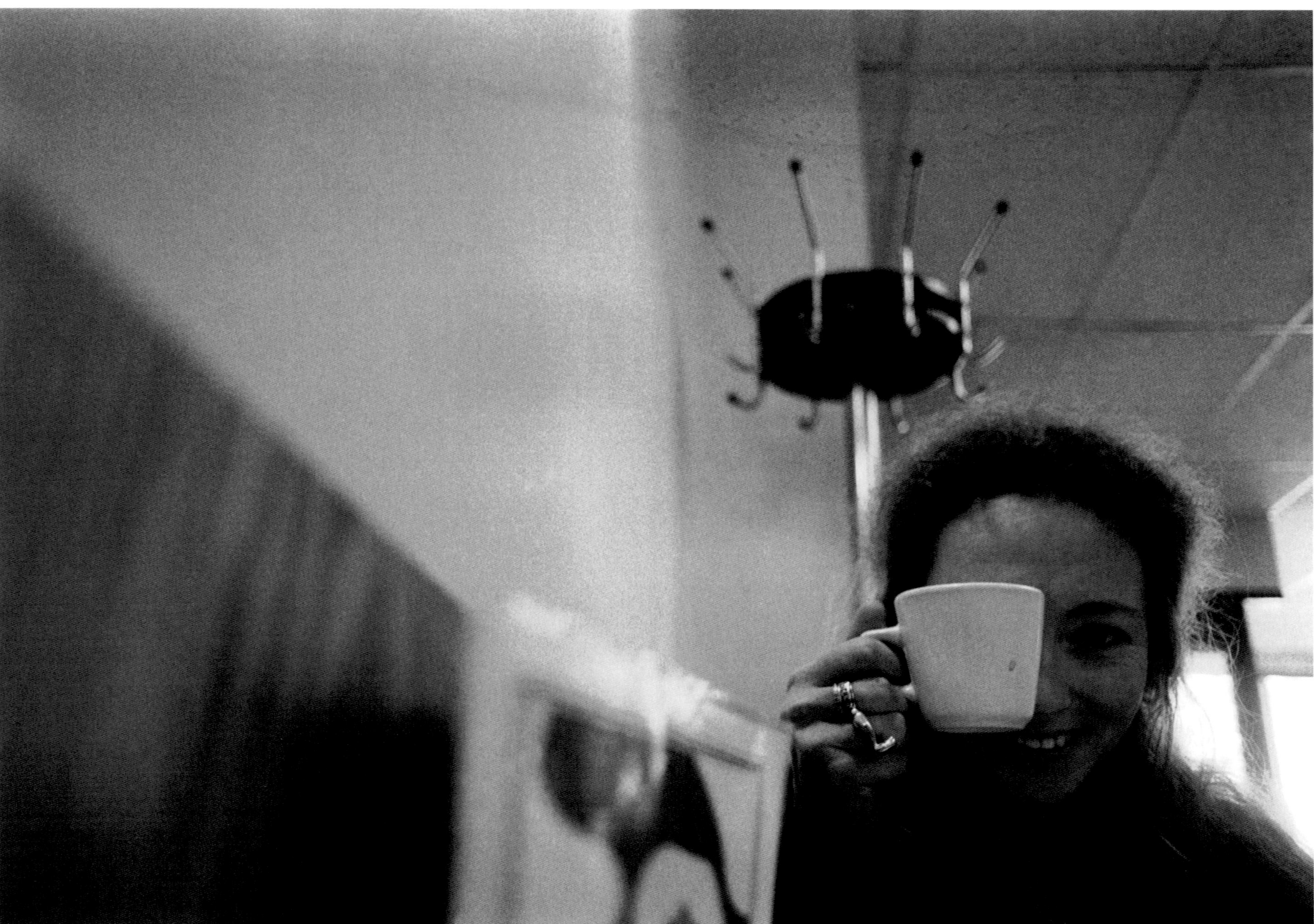

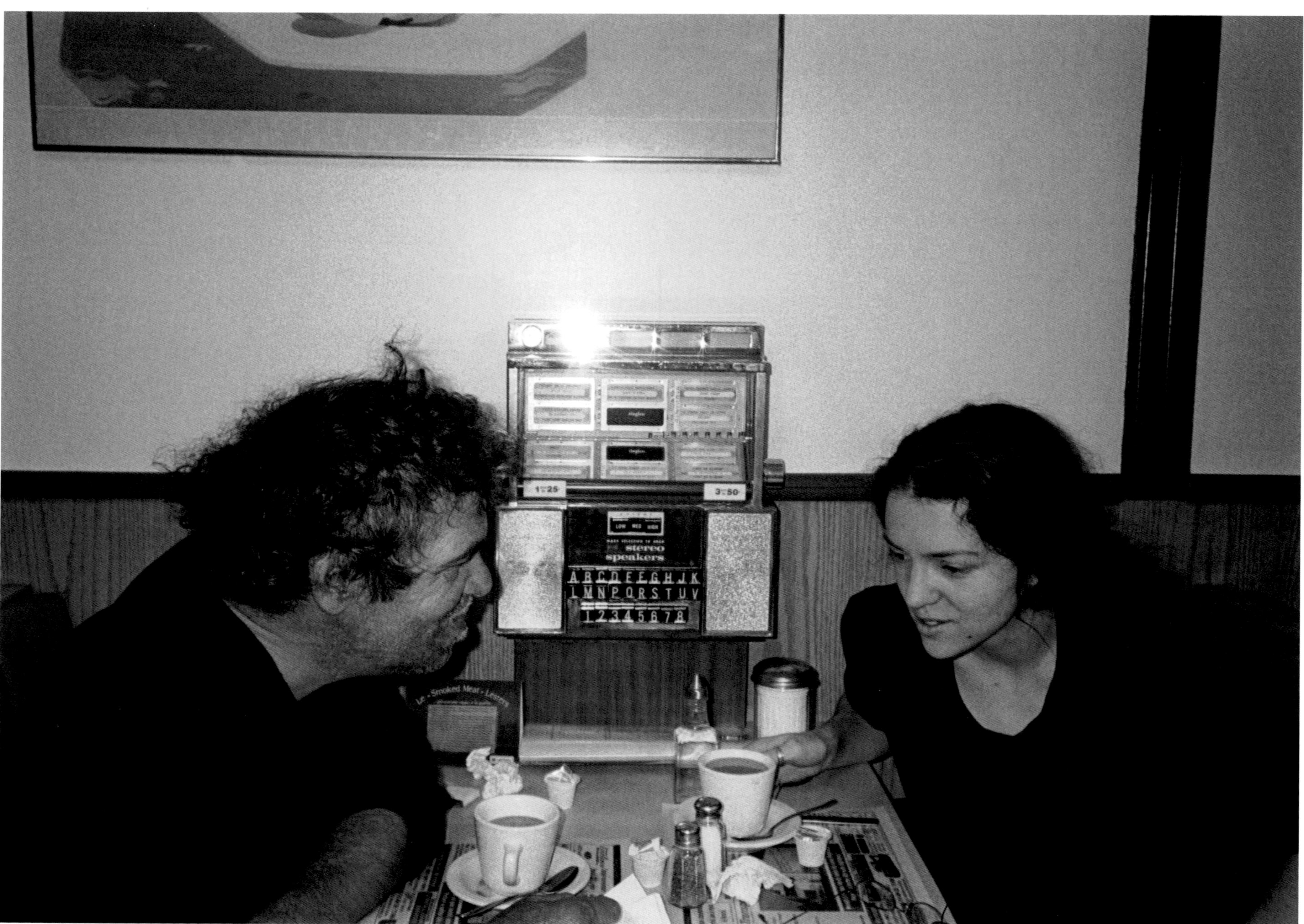

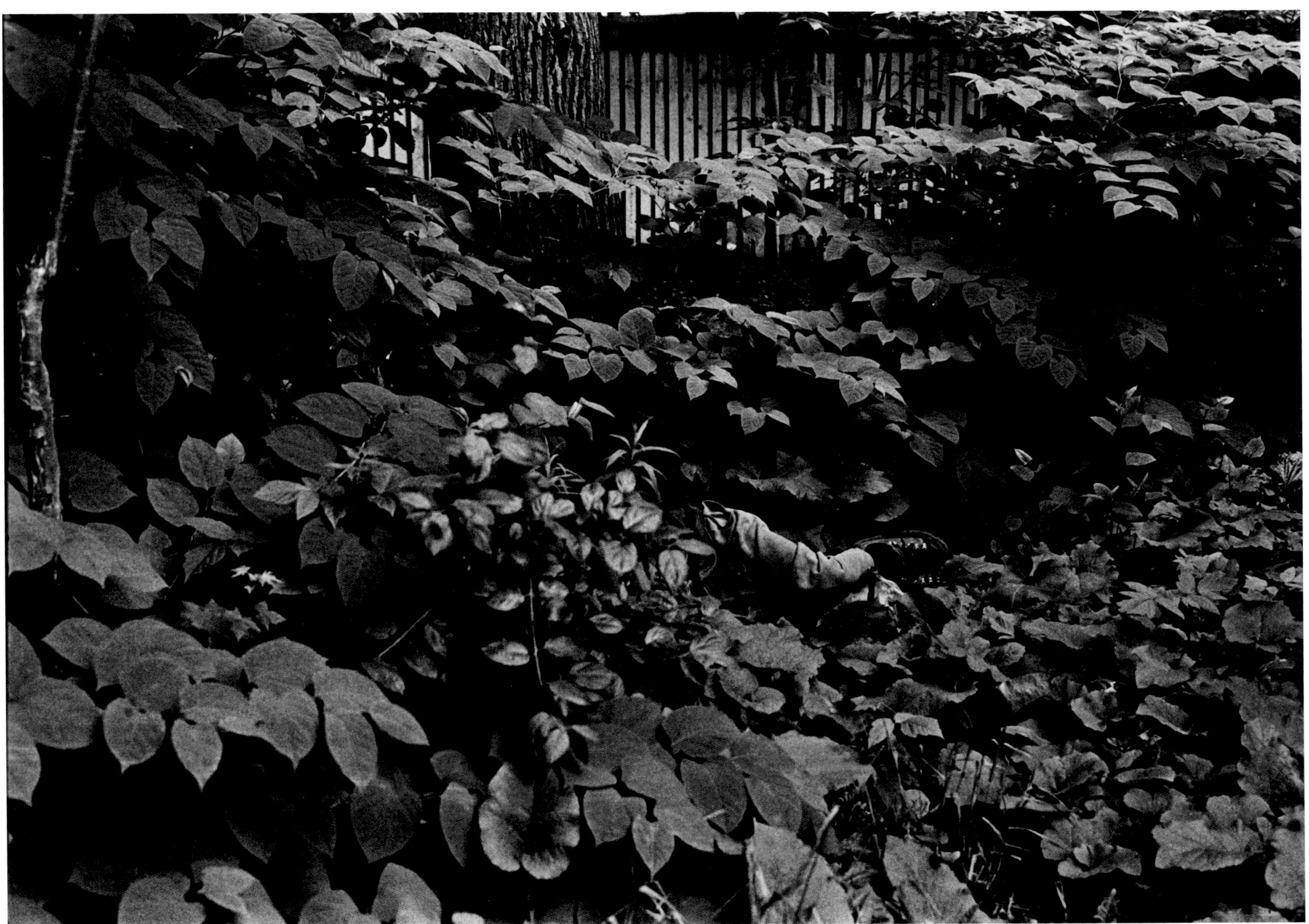

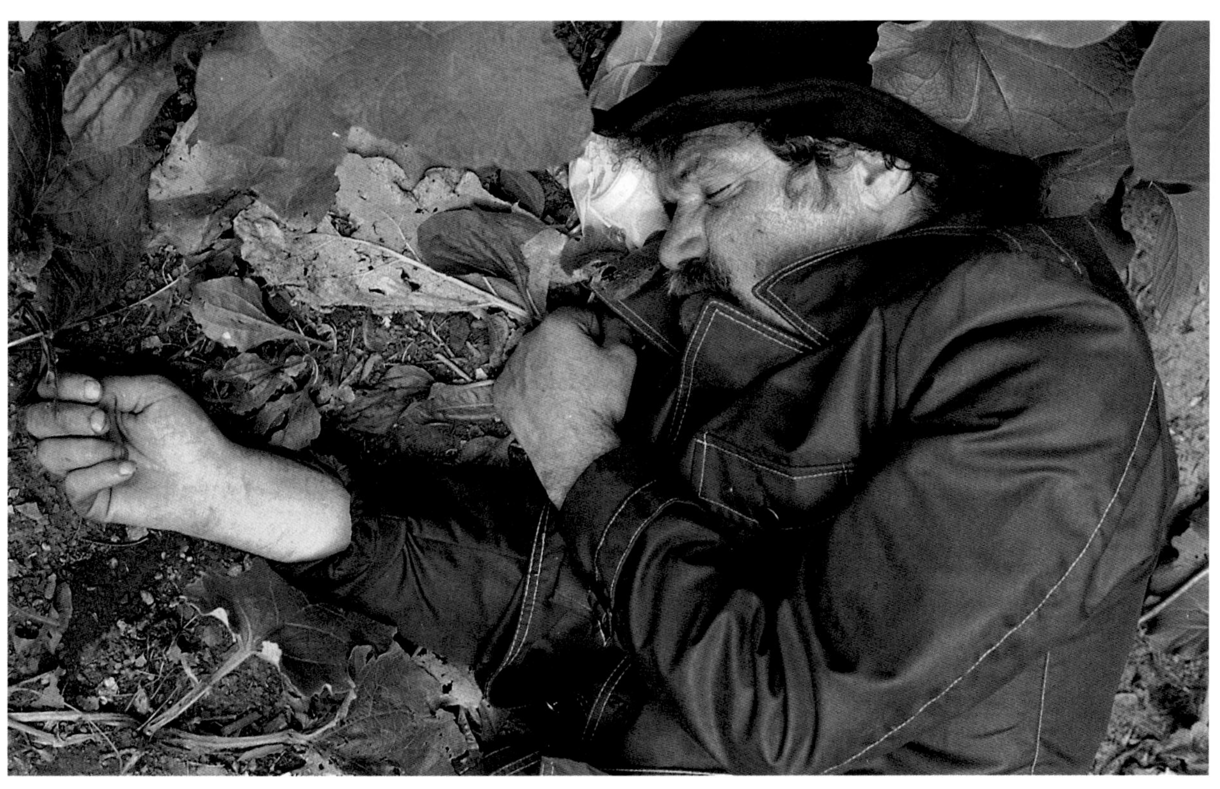

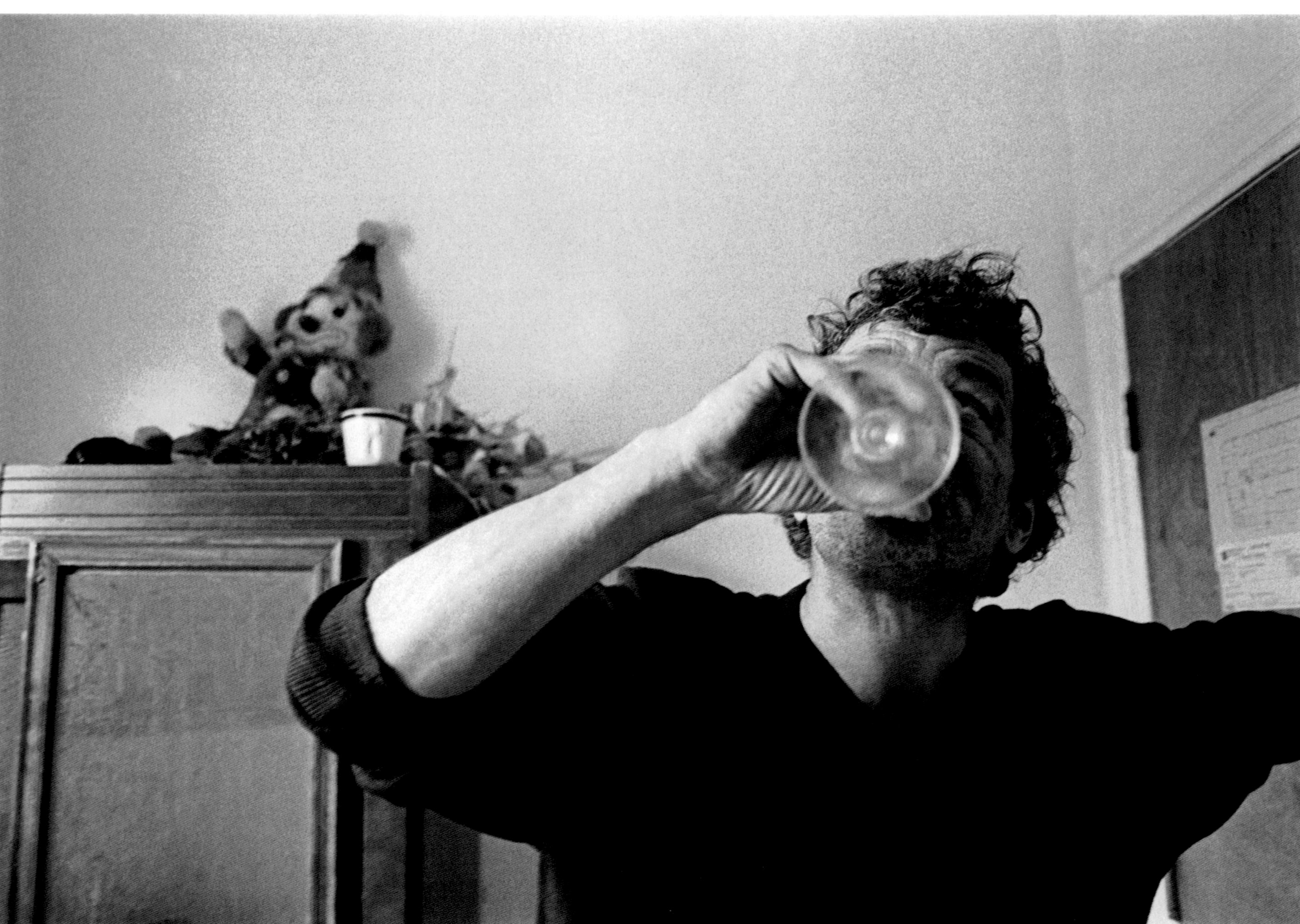

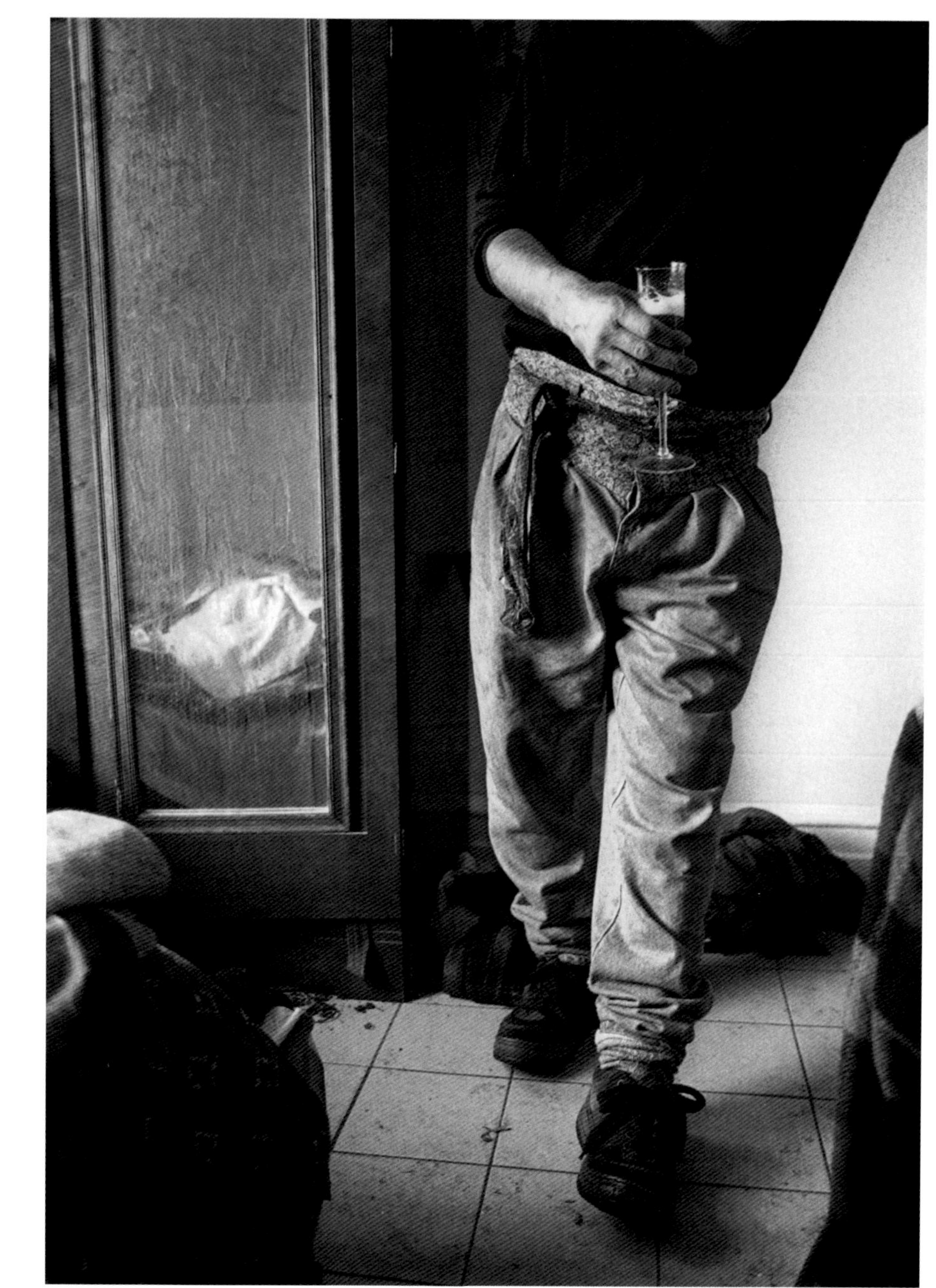

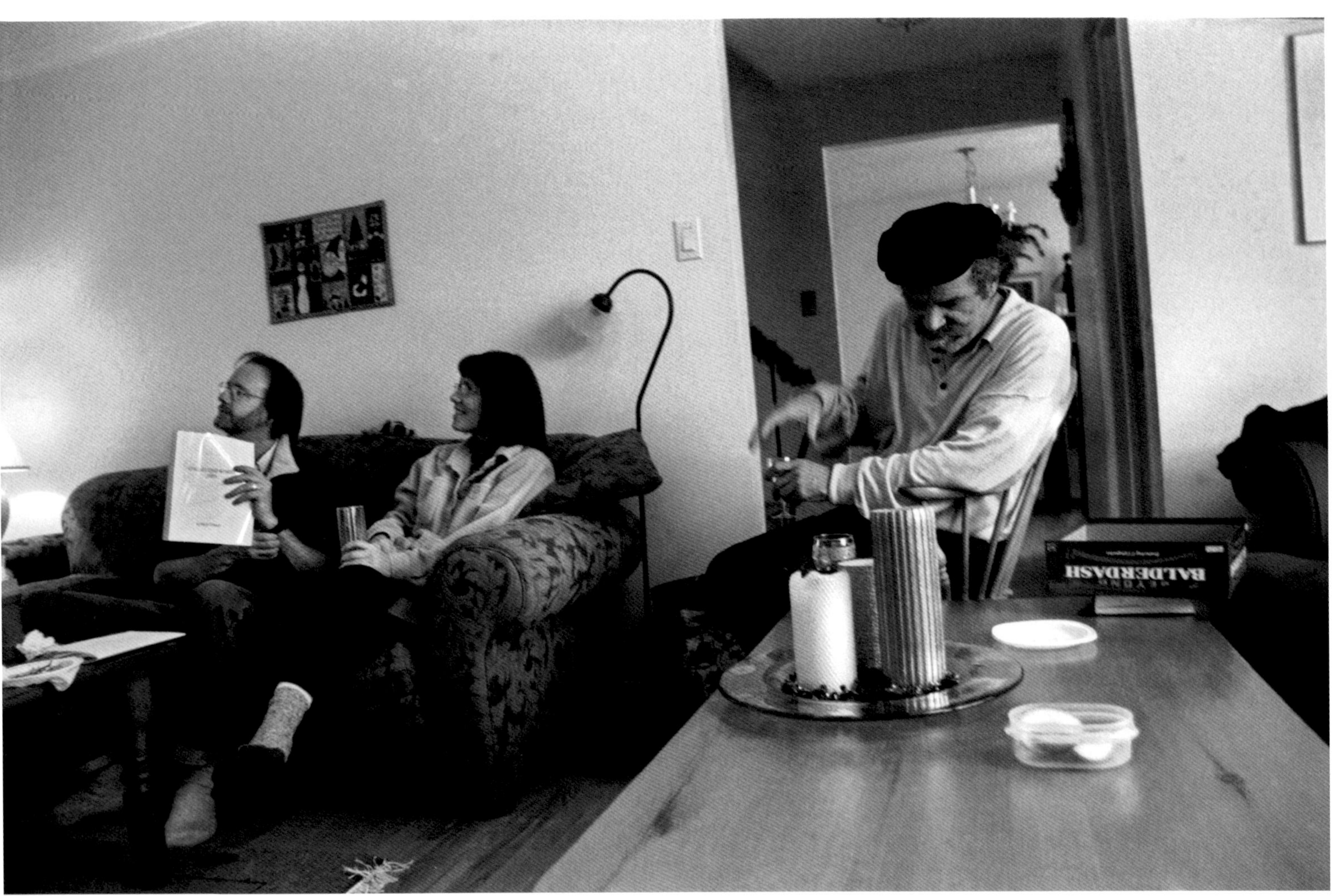

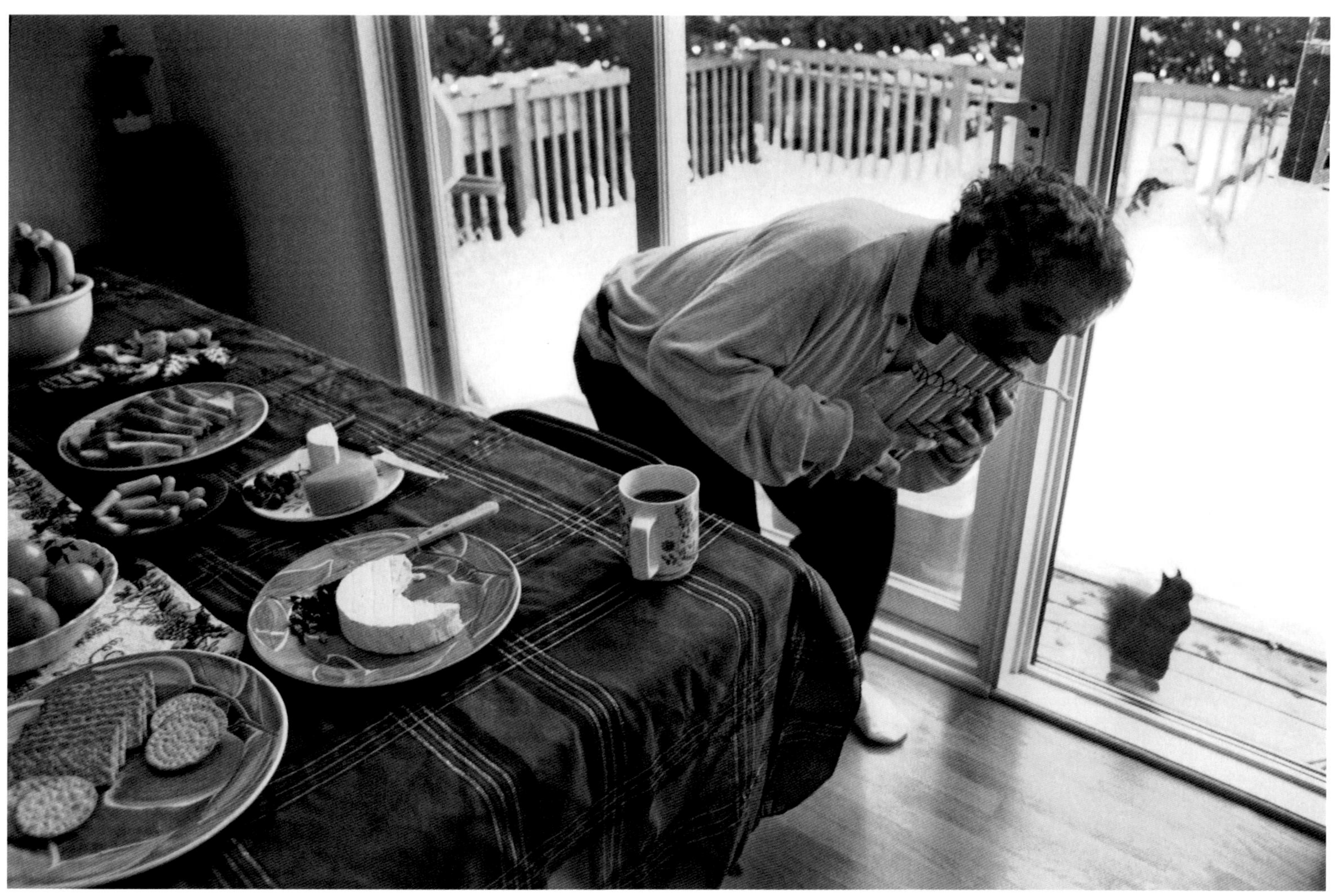

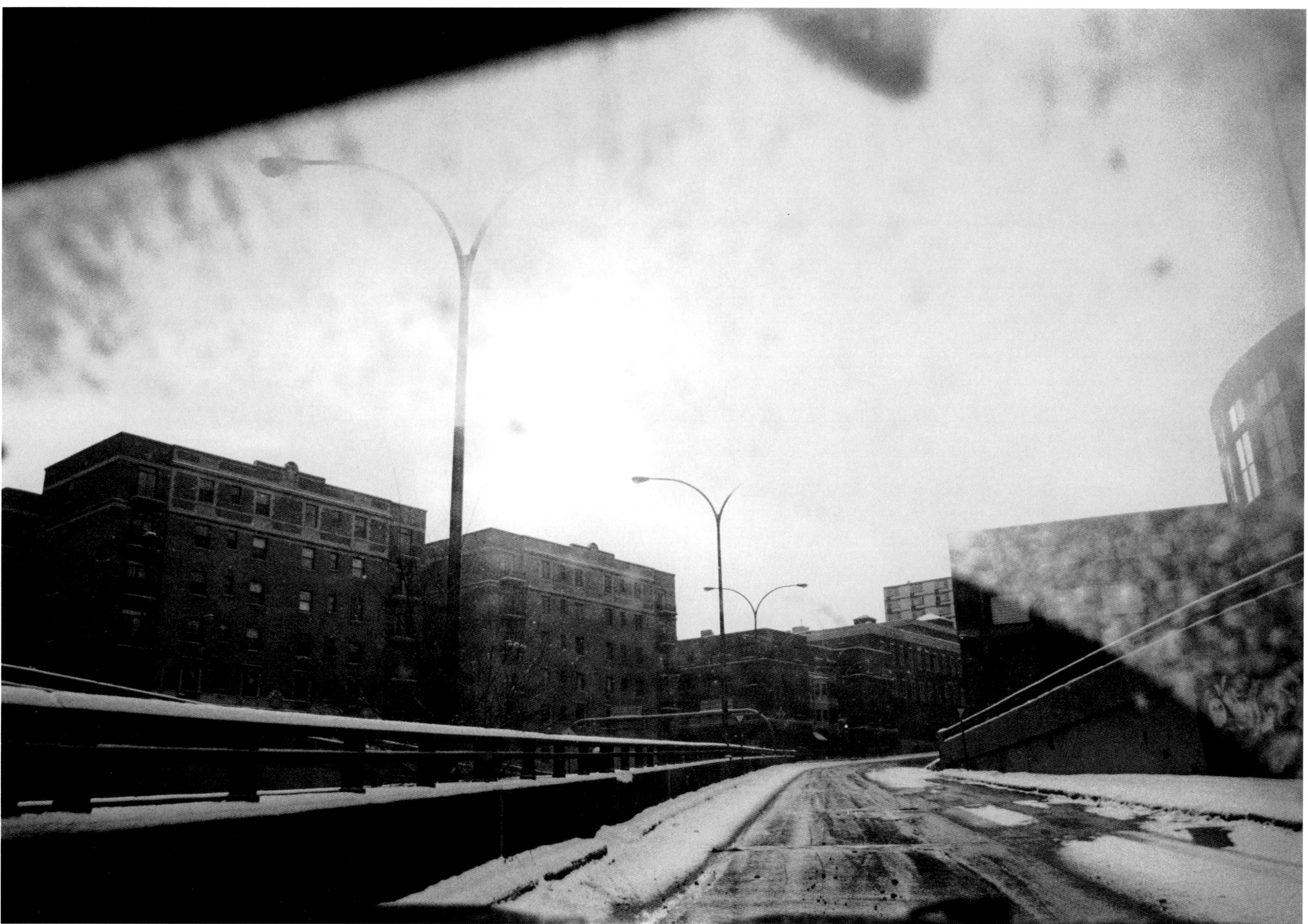

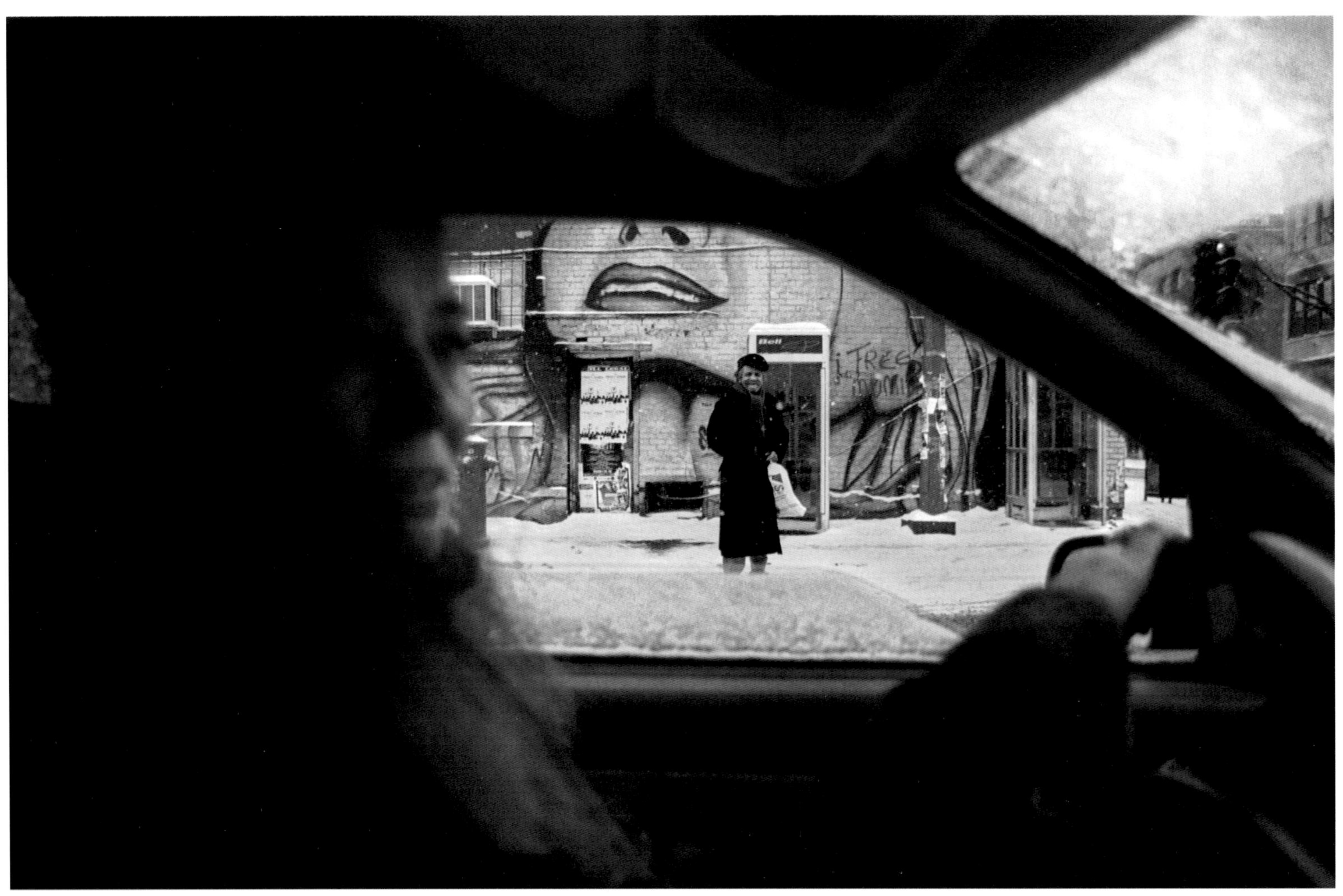

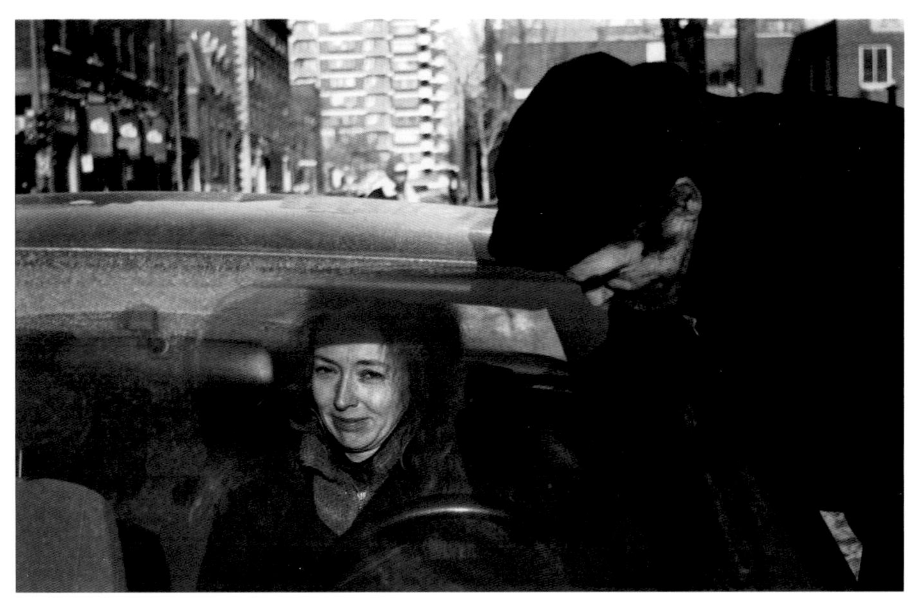

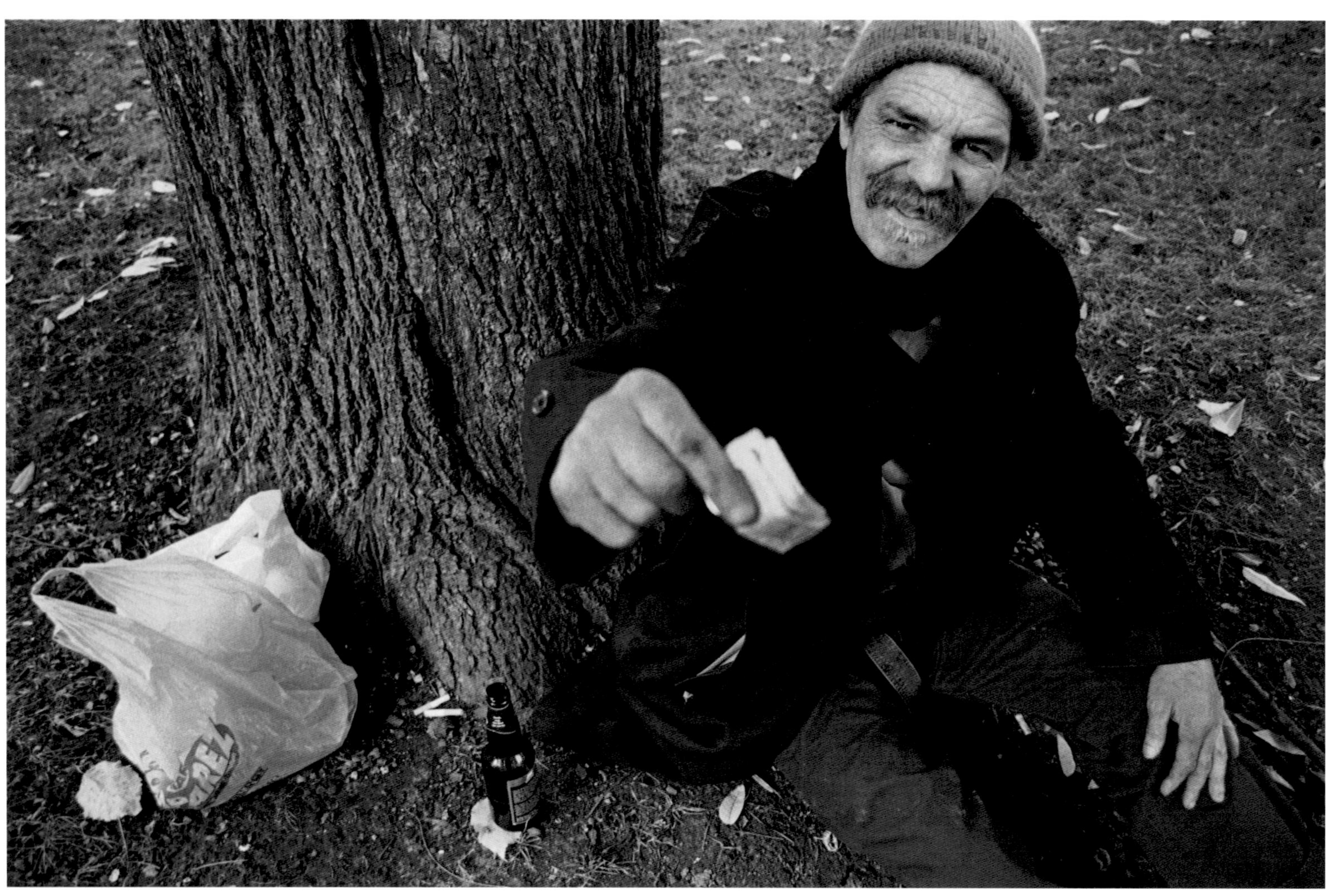

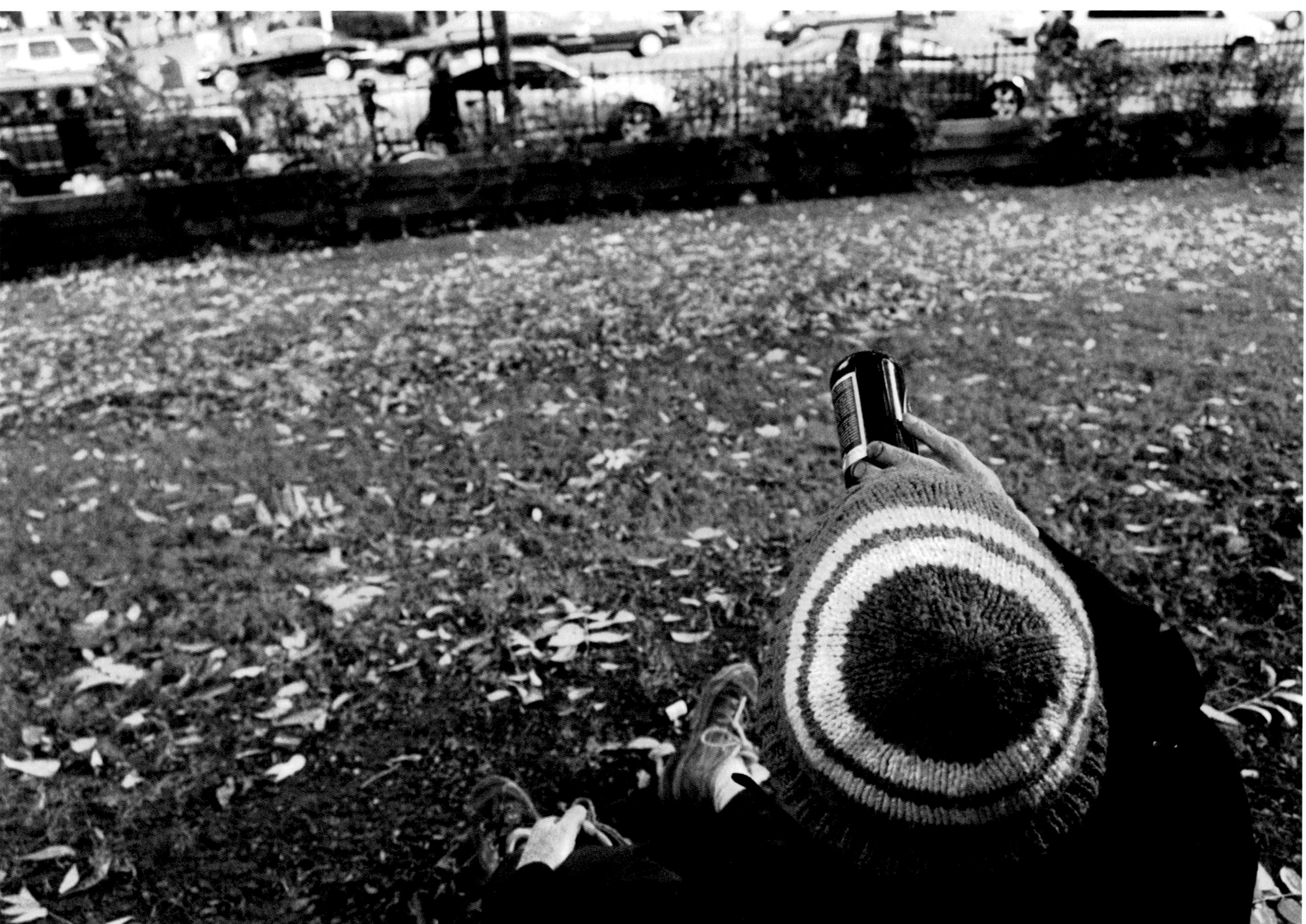

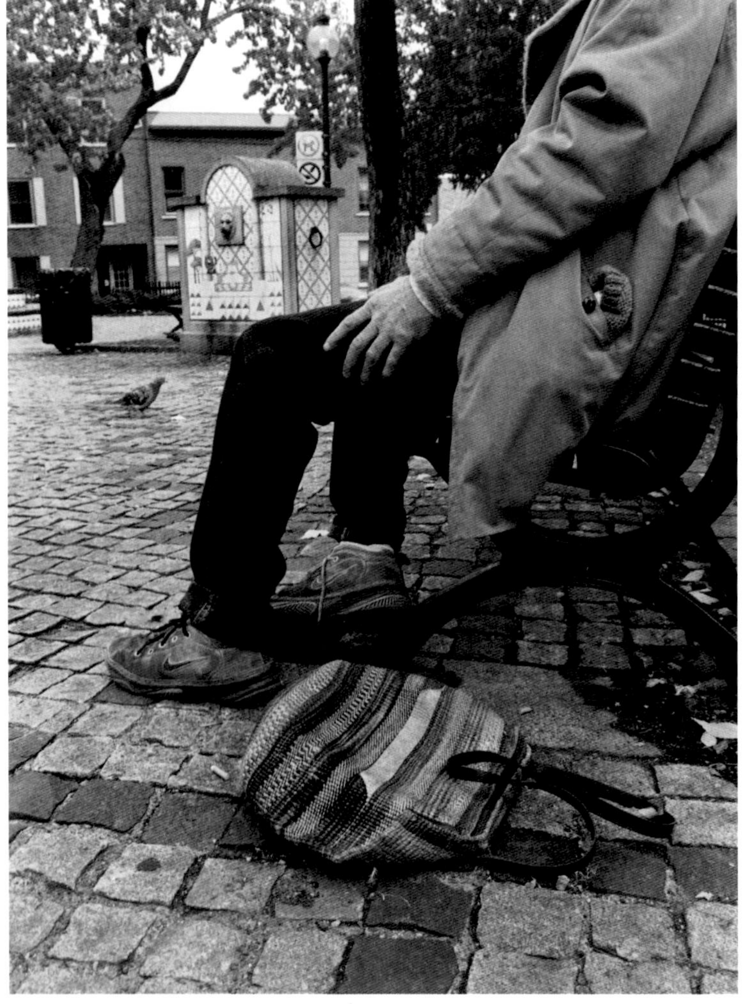

Sing the Song of Squee-gee

I walked the Road
So, as
To pass Time
    passing by;
I catch up to the changing
spheres of peoples' Lives
THere, Living.
And find the squee-gee
    brother-hood
upon car windows,
        Leaning.
Come hee, young girl
    and take this charge
And wash my face with
    your brush;
Then wash my eyes
with tears, that cry
    yours and mine.

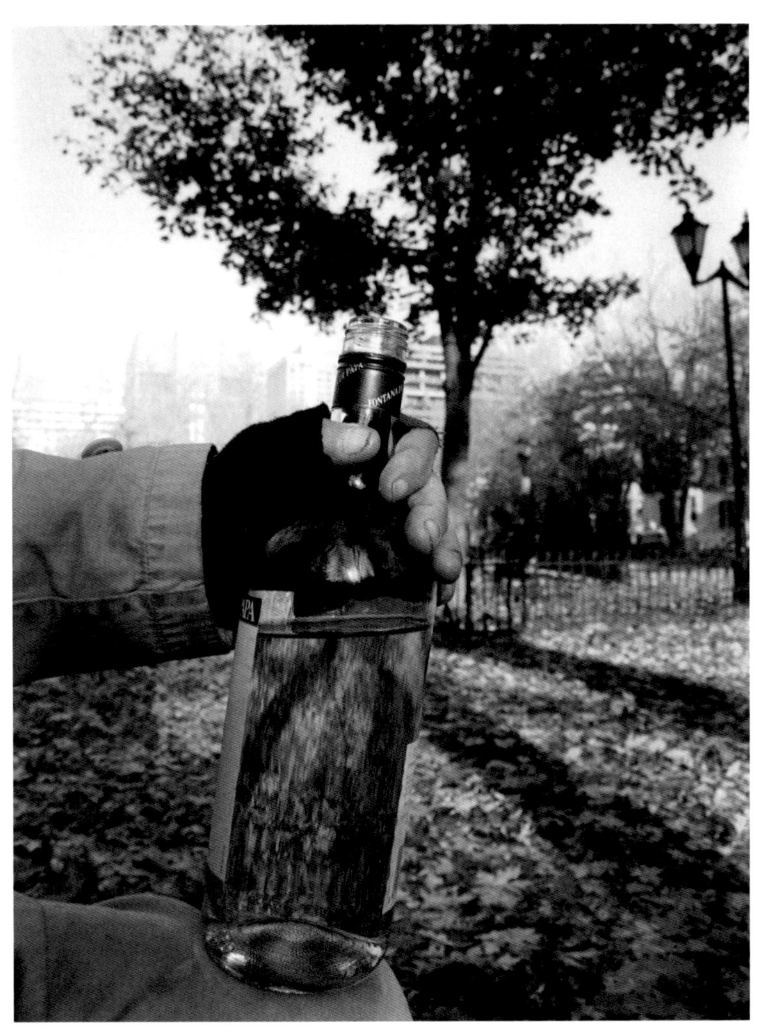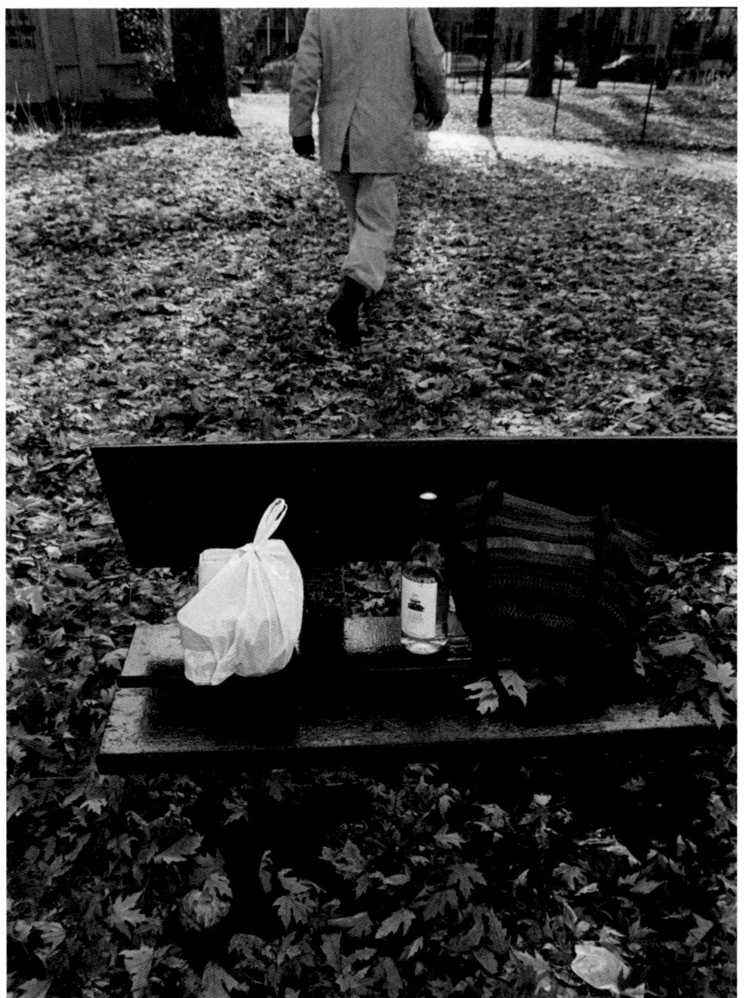

I cannot
    struggle
with the
    sentiment
"that underwrites"
my normal
        state;
I can only
    sustain,
    and sift
the dark
    feeling
through my
    corporeal
    structure,
and watch
emotions dissipate
as tears
surprise your
cheeks,
and cloud your eyes.

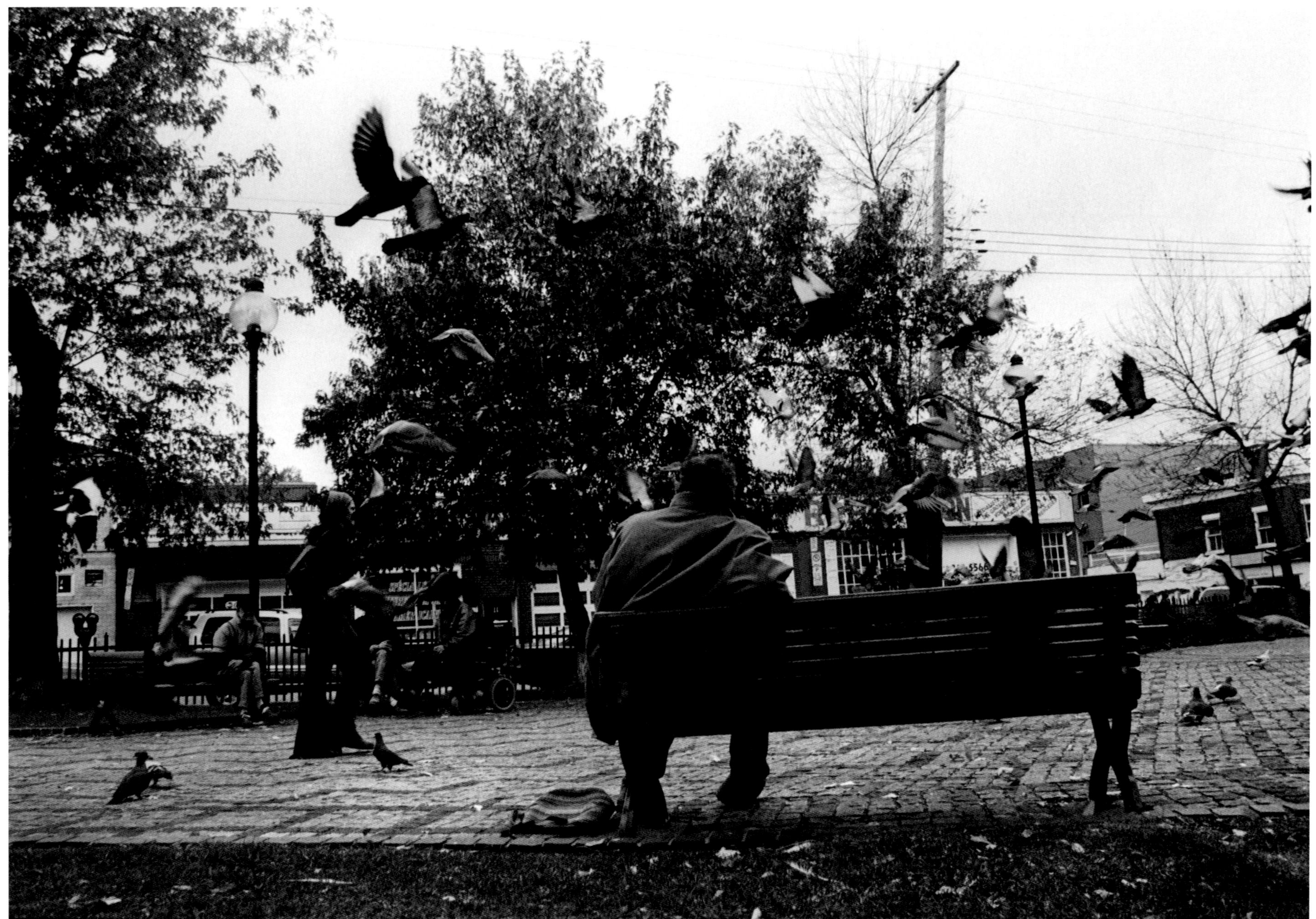

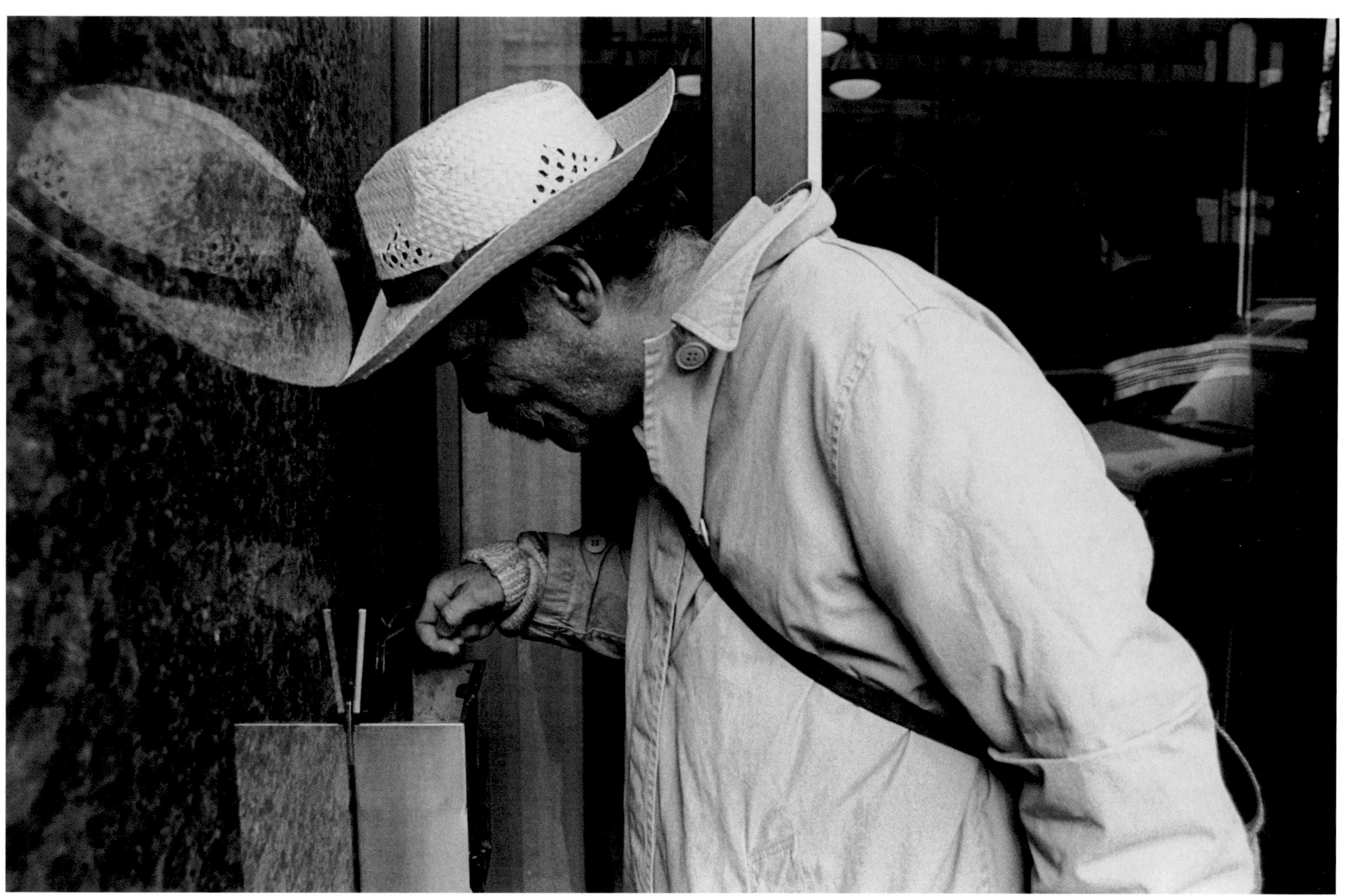

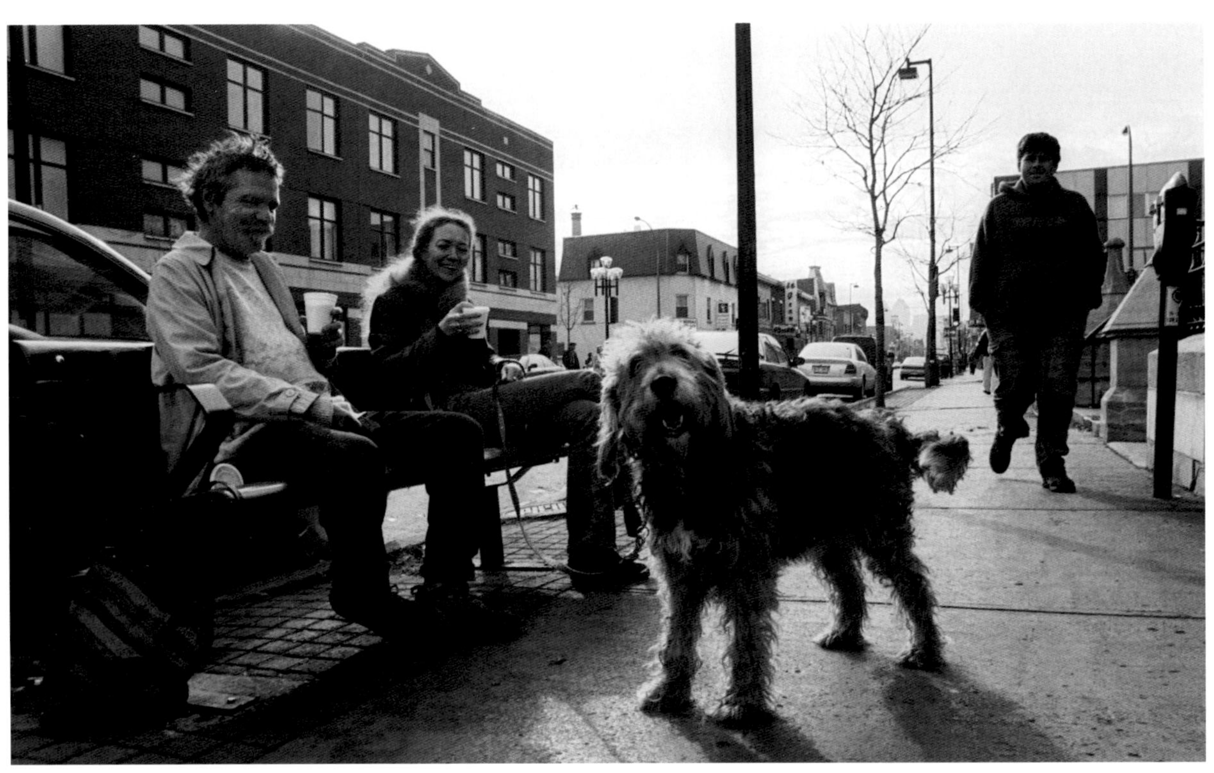

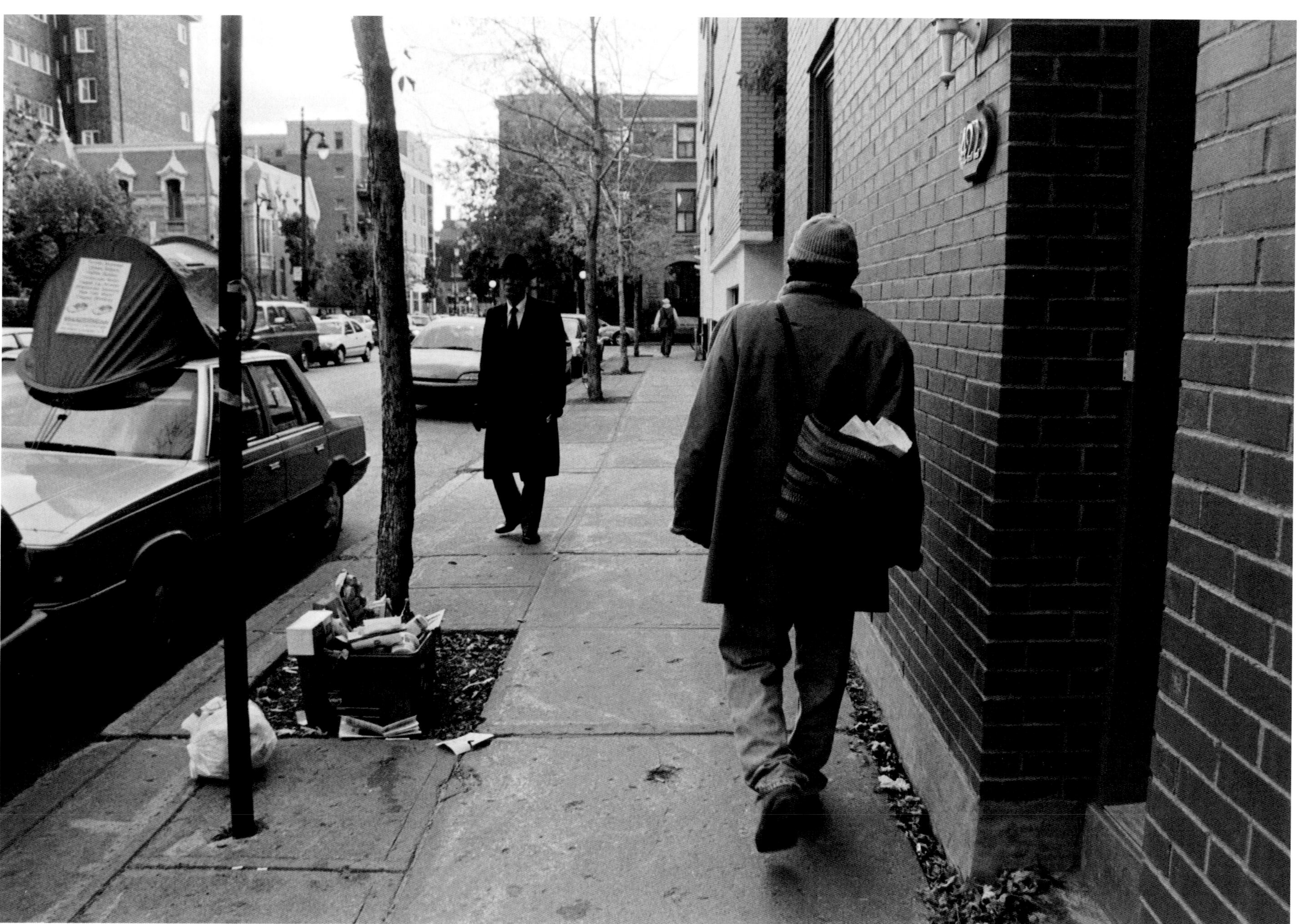

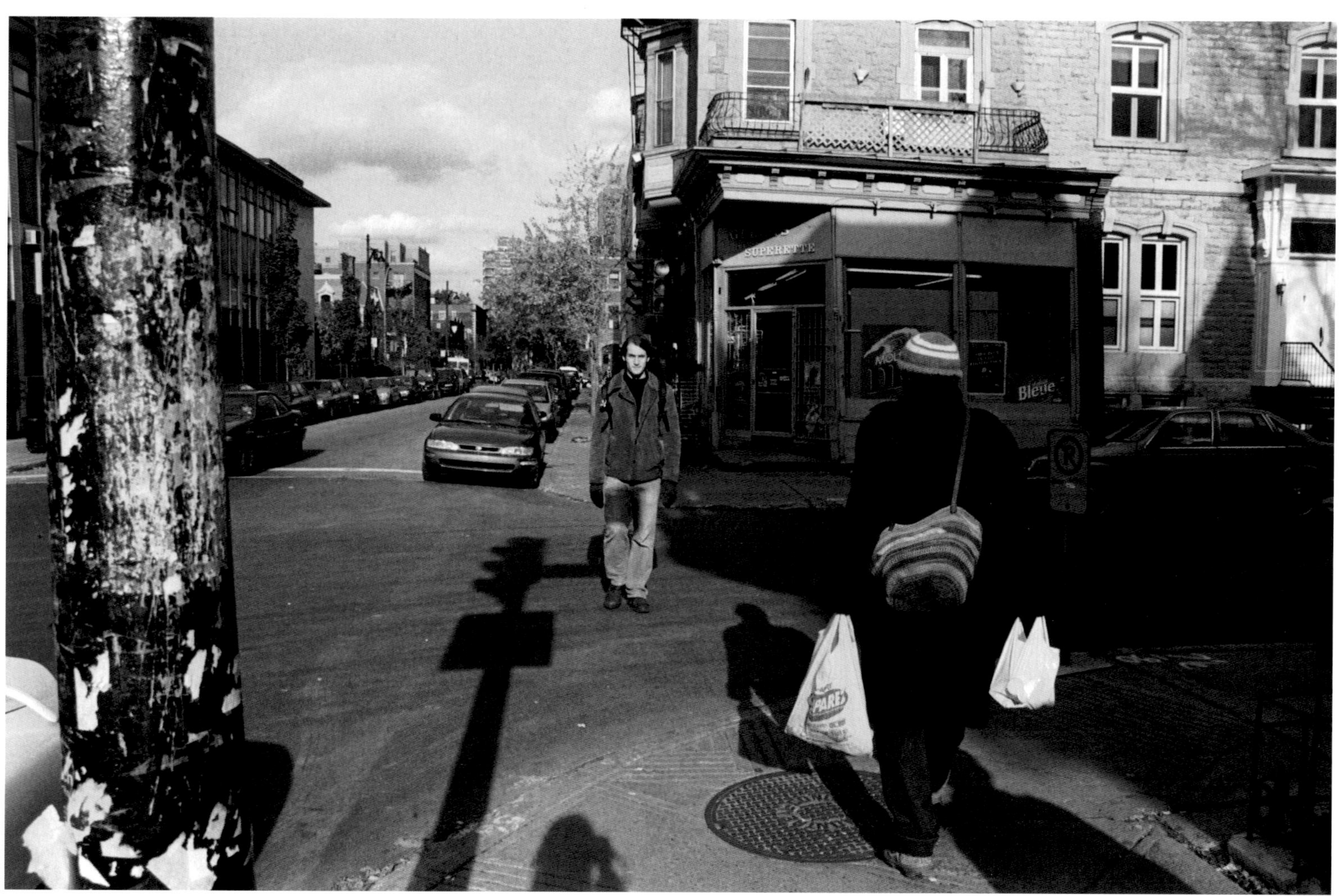

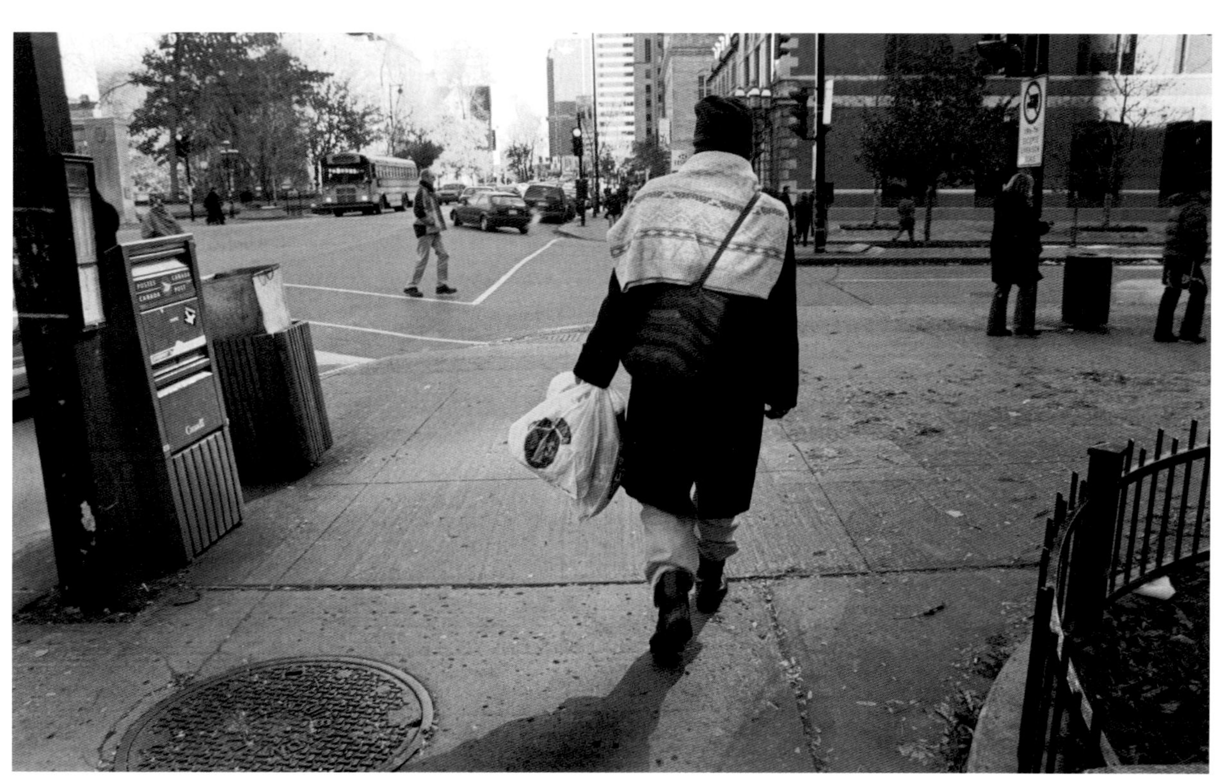

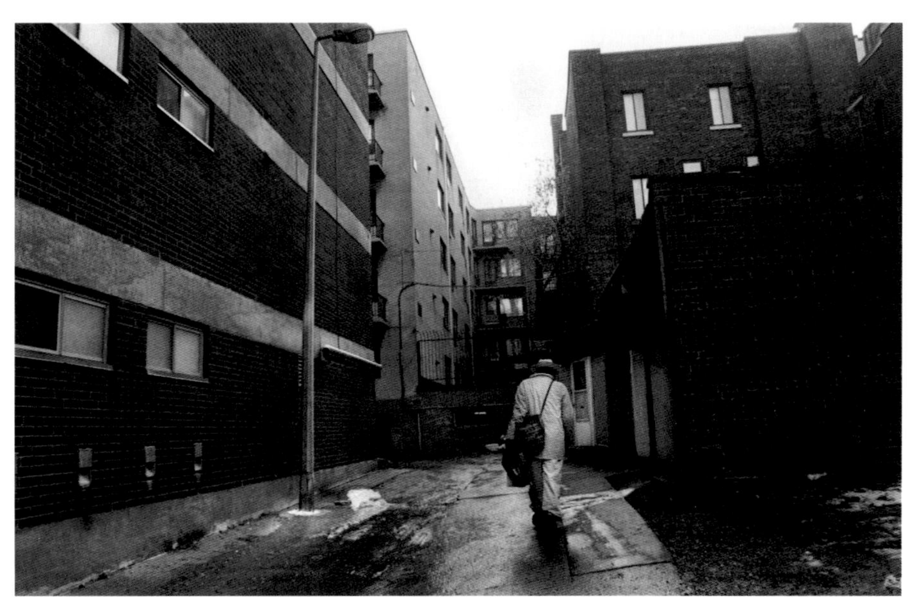

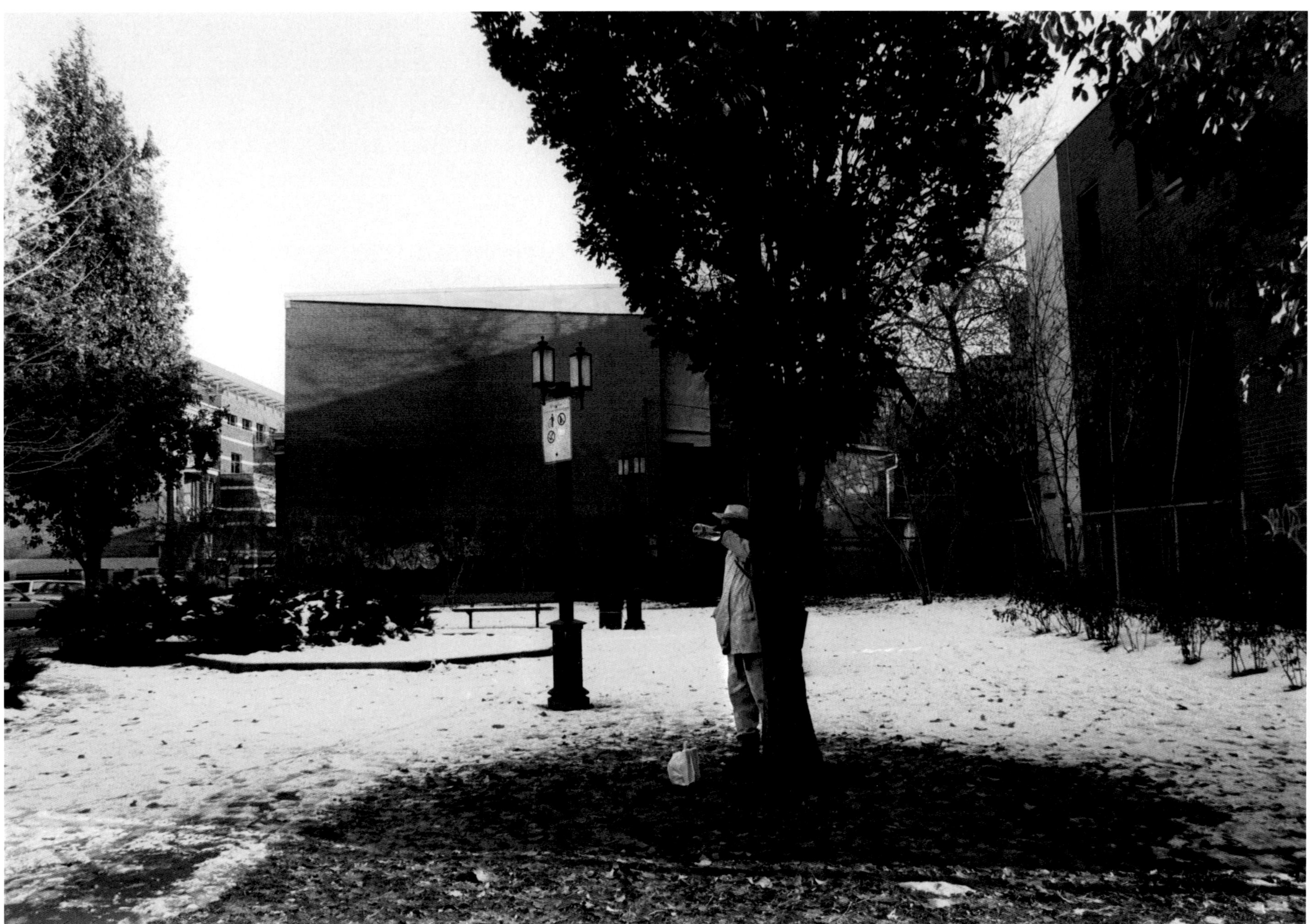

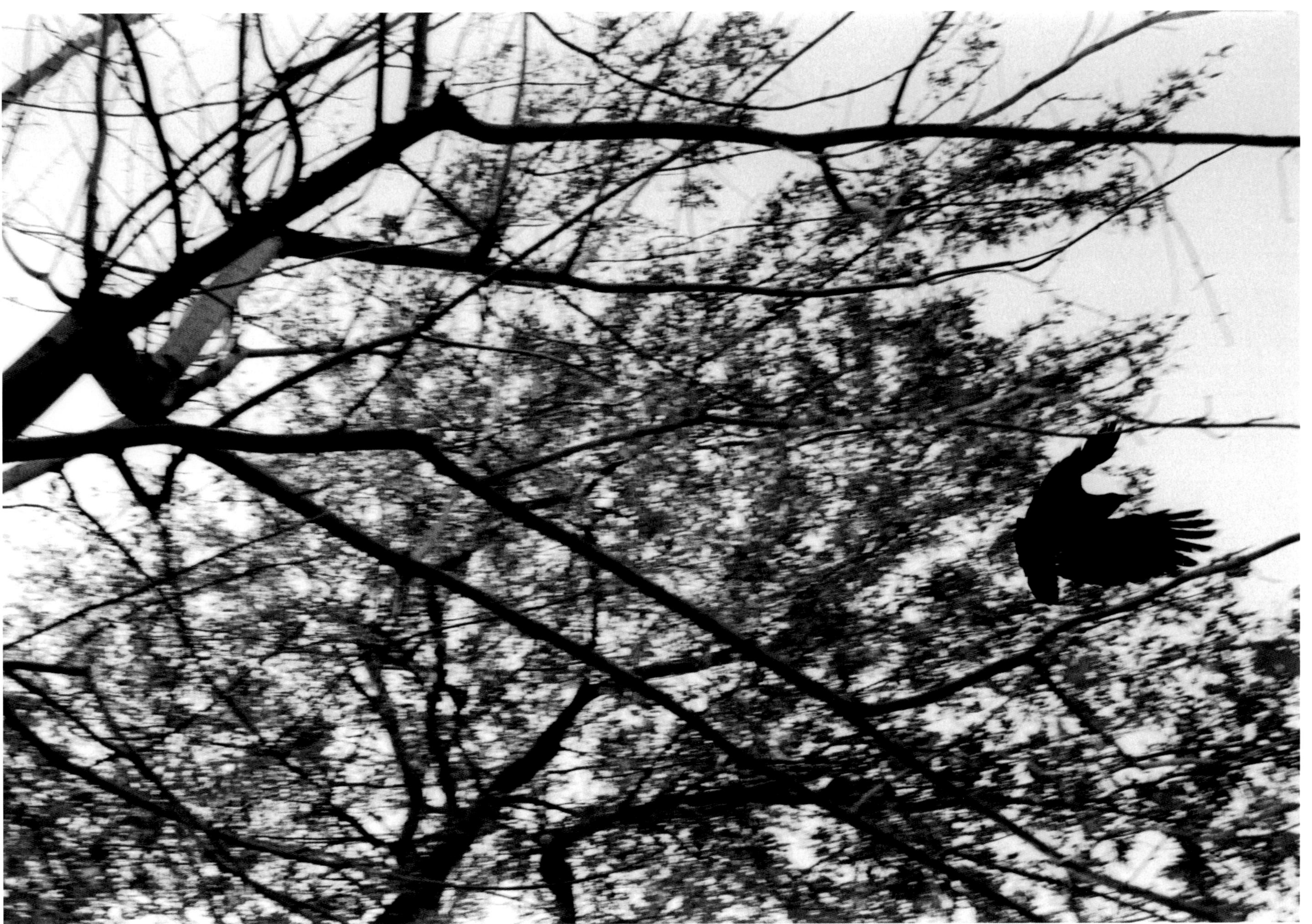

CREDITS

Published in Great Britain in 2004
by Trolley Ltd
www.trolleybooks.com
Photographs, texts © Amanda Tetrault, 2004
Poems © Philip Tetrault, 2004

10 9 8 7 6 5 4 3 2 1

The right of Amanda Tetrault to be identified
as the author of this work has been asserted
by her in accordance with the Copyright,
Designs and Patents Act 1998.
A catalogue record for this book is available
from the British Library

ISBN 1-904563-04-X

All rights reserved. No part of this
publication may be reproduced,
transmitted or stored in a retrieval system,
in any form or by any means, without
permission in writing from Trolley Ltd.,
application for which must be made to
Trolley Ltd.

Design by M+W @ Fruitmachine

Support has been granted by the
Canada Council for the Arts.

Printed in Italy by Soso

A HUGE THANK YOU TO….

MY AMAZING MOTHER NATALIE LORRIMAN, FOR YOUR MAGIC AND UNCONDITIONAL LOVE.

My grandfather Guy Lorriman for giving me my first camera and encouraging me to take pictures. Sudhir and Sandhya Ramchandran for treating me like your 3rd daughter. Sonya Thimmaiah for your limitless friendship and support. Indu and Tim Thimmaiah for embracing me within your family. Cornelia Vanderlinde and Jim Megargee for your friendship and guidance. My grandmothers Peggy Tetrault and Tanya Lorriman for their support. My uncle Johnny Cheesecake for being my Johnny. Lanan Adcock, Sefi Amir, Meadow Laflamme, Julie Verdon for being sisters through the years. Steve McCurry for lending me your camera and Antonin Kratochvil for your inspiration. Gigi Giannuzzi for your spirit and for believing in and making this book. The Trolley team, Ruby Russell, Oliver Wood, Valentina Petrelli, Lorenza Orlando, Martin Bell & Wai Hung Young at Fruitmachine for all of your help in putting this book together. The many friends and teachers who have helped me along the way.

And Phil for travelling this road with me.

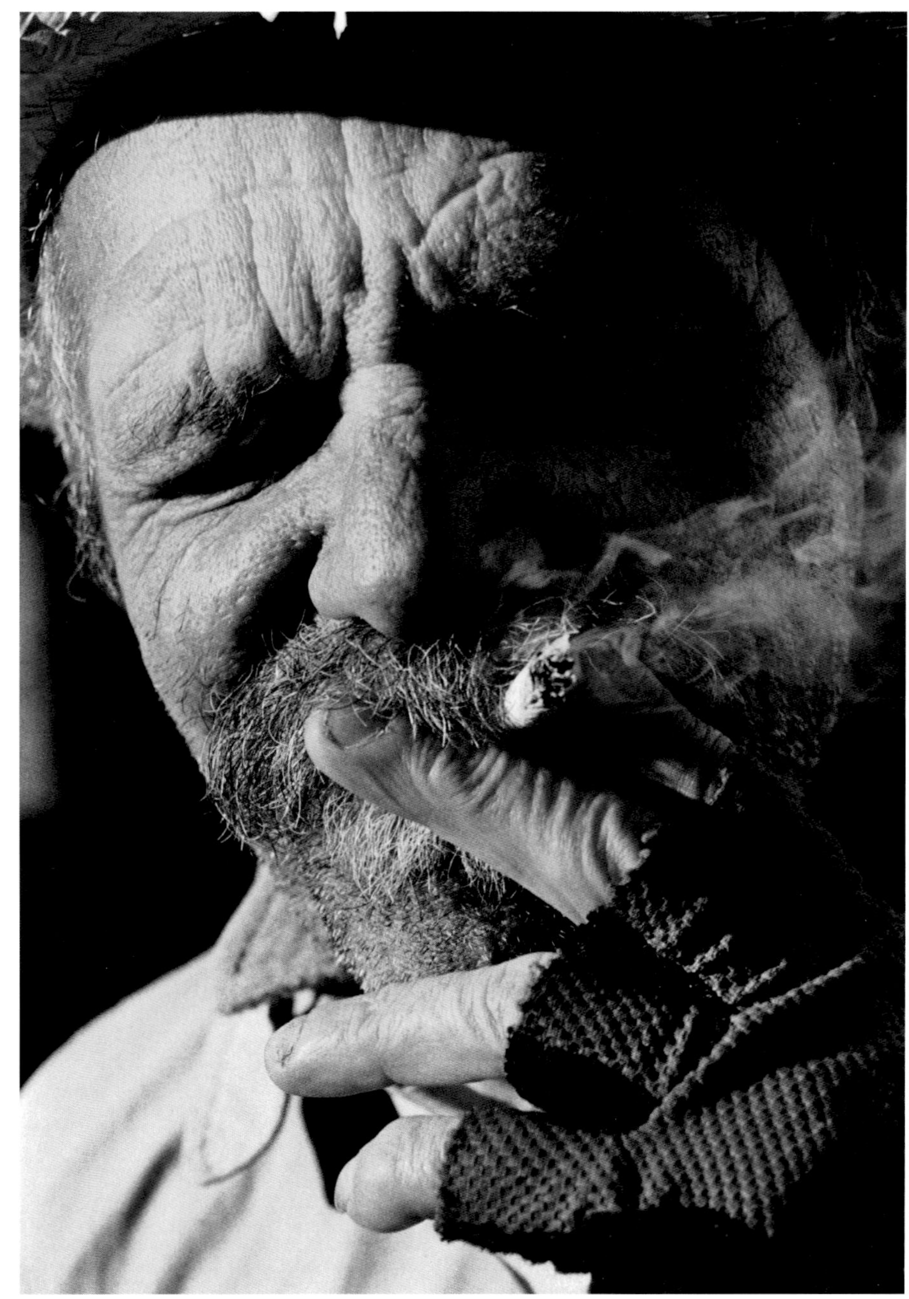

ALL THE PHOTOGRAPHS BY AMANDA TETRAULT WERE TAKEN BETWEEN 1997 AND 2003.

ALL PHOTO-BOOTH PHOTOGRAPHS HAVE BEEN TAKEN SINCE 1975.